Deborah~Pamela~Diana~Priscilla~Valerie~David~Rebecca~Zachary~Paul
WILSON

9 VOICES

THE CHILDHOOD
OF A FAMILY

iUniverse LLC
Bloomington

9 VOICES
THE CHILDHOOD OF A FAMILY

iUniverse books may be ordered through booksellers or by contacting:

iUniverse
1663 Liberty Drive
Bloomington, IN 47403
www.iuniverse.com
1-800-Authors (1-800-288-4677)

Because of the dynamic nature of the Internet, any web addresses or links contained in this book may have changed since publication and may no longer be valid. The views expressed in this work are solely those of the author and do not necessarily reflect the views of the publisher, and the publisher hereby disclaims any responsibility for them.

ISBN: 978-1-4917-2096-7 (sc)
ISBN: 978-1-4917-2097-4 (hc)
ISBN: 978-1-4917-2098-1 (e)

Library of Congress Control Number: 2014900455

Printed in the United States of America.

iUniverse rev. date: 1/31/2014

We dedicate this to our parents, Lee and Jo Wilson.

I give you love
But do not ask it back
Lest it should die with me.
It is for you to give
To spouse, to children,
to friends
That I may see it grow
and know
That it flows endlessly
from me.

—Genevieve Smith Whitford

Contents

INTRODUCTION

It happened more than once. It happened often. In fact, it happened so often I was beginning to develop a complex. I have been a political spouse for over three decades and as a matter of course, I've spent much time attending public functions and fundraising dinners, usually seated next to an unfamiliar face. Also as a matter of course, table talk eventually evolves into inquiries about what I do when I'm not at these dinners.

For a long time, I answered by explaining my role as the mother of five children. As luck would have it, more often than not the inquisitor would smile and then politely turn to the guest on the other side to find a more inspiring conversation, hopefully with someone who actually worked for a living and would be considered more interesting and intelligent.

Then one day, my husband and I were invited to a dinner and as expected, I was asked the dreaded question, "So what do you do?" I sat there momentarily, wracking my brain for a clever response. I simply replied, "Nothing. I don't do anything."

I was seated with then Congressman, Rahm Emanuel, who was apparently listening to our conversation. When he heard me, his head flipped around, and he gave me a delicious piece of advice. "Pam, when people ask you that, just tell them you're writing a book. They'll never know if you're really writing a book, you can make it about anything you want."

So the next time I found myself entrapped in the same conversation, I caught myself just before blurting out that I was writing a book. It occurred to me that this would bring on a whole host of new questions.

Instead, I decided the only solution was to write a book. It would be a memoir co-written by my family, a book we had envisioned for years. Growing up in a family of nine children, we were the center of our own universe, but in addition, our home was the center of our community. Captivated by the commotion and chaos, friends gathered to witness an atmosphere of constant stimulation and inspiration. As adults, when revisiting our youth, we often discussed putting pen to paper and recounting our tales of adventure.

Shortly after my dinner encounter, and several years after we had all fallen out of the nest, the nine of us decided to put our lives on paper. There was no downside. Maybe it would be a bestseller that would be read across oceans. Maybe it would be a sometimes sweet and sometimes savory taste of life that would be shared only with our closest friends and family. Regardless, there was no reason not to tell our story.

Each of us would write a chapter, drawn from our earliest memories until we left home. And, as with all large families, there would be rules. The first was that none of us could dictate what another included in his or her chapter. Each of us had free reign to recount as we saw fit. And the second rule was that no one could read another sibling's writings until his or her own was complete. In addition, just for that little something extra, our book would have a tenth voice. Di's best friend, Audrey, spent such a significant amount of her early years visiting/living/sharing with us that we gave her voice an honorary post before the end of our *novel* novel.

9 Voices is unique. We are quite sure that there has never been a book co-written by nine siblings, all equally sharing in the production and all authored individually without benefit of ghostwriters. We can also attest that all of us are mostly healthy physically and generally healthy mentally and spiritually. Writing our memoir has been cathartic for some of us and exhilarating for others. And now, with this challenge behind us, we look forward to another new adventure.

PROLOGUE

The war had finally ended, and the streets were bustling with young GIs ready to settle down to a new life. Every city and town throughout America felt the impetus to move forward and grow, putting behind the darker decade just past. It was this fever that landed our parents in the unlikely circumstance where they fell into the same town, at the same nightclub, with the same goal: music.

Leland had spent his youth and early twenties as a drummer in jazz bands until the war effort pulled him into new territory. The service of American enlistees was provided without deliberation, a part of the wave of sensibility moving all youth who were ready, willing, and able. Upon enlisting in the army, Leland was marched off to war as a medic to the troops on Guadalcanal. Josephine, trained through high school and college in classical piano and voice, was challenged to join as well. She enlisted in the Red Cross and headed to Guadalcanal too, where she entertained the troops as a back-up singer to the bands and the world-famous headliners who devoted their time to supporting the troops in ways familiar to them—on stage instead of the battlefield.

One might expect that they met during this time, at this location, and the rest was history … but that was not to be. At the war's end, they each packed up their belongings, returned to the United States and, after the appropriate time needed to settle and store the memories and medals and letters from loved ones, headed separately to perform at the Airplane Club in Denver, Colorado. It was there, with Leland on the drums and Josephine handling the vocals, that they met and fell in love. There was, from stories told, more to it than that. First of all, Josephine had to break off two or three previous engagements with gentlemen who didn't meet all her requirements, and she also had to convince Leland that his girlfriend at the time was not the best suited for him. Within a year, they were blissfully married, with a baby on the way, and in transition from Denver to Omaha, Nebraska.

Like many young veterans, the GI Bill allowed Leland to continue his education. He chose to study medicine at the University of Nebraska, an interest sparked by his experience as an army medic. He continued playing drums at night as his source of income while going to classes during the day, and Josephine continued having babies. Upon completing his medical degree, they moved their growing family to California. Over the next ten years, Leland completed an internship in San Francisco, a residency in Eureka, took on his first post as the head physician for the Mendocino State Mental Hospital in Talmage, and finally settled down as a general practitioner and surgeon in Ukiah. Josephine stopped having babies after the ninth. There was nothing in either of their backgrounds to prepare them for this hectic life.

Josephine was the youngest of five children and had a rather privileged life growing up. Her father had already met some measure of success practicing law in Chicago, while at the same time looking after his wife, whose health was somewhat unstable. She suffered from Parkinson's disease and depression, the order of which is unclear. Josephine's father, however, was devoutly Catholic, kneeling in prayer at his bedside twice daily, and the burden of caring for his wife was lightened by his devotion to her. With the assistance of Anna Kay, their German nurse, Aunt Anna, the maiden aunt who lived with them, and Nicholson and his wife, who cooked and managed the house, Josephine was well looked after. She was somewhat detached from her three oldest siblings who had their own lives to worry about. Instead, her constant companions were her brother, Buddy, who was just a year older than her, and her German shepherd, Fritz.

Her father, a mortgage company attorney during the Great

Depression, was sent to various parts of the country to evaluate properties in foreclosure. One such property was a lovely four-thousand-acre farm tucked away in tiny Dublin, Georgia, and he decided to make it his family escape from the brutal winters of the north. During the three months of each year that they spent in Georgia, Josephine was home-schooled with the children of those who lived and worked on the farm. When she wasn't studying or playing piano, she lived for her beautiful chestnut stallion, Thunder. A riding track had been built so she could learn to ride properly in her English saddle, although her later back problems were undoubtedly caused by the numerous falls she had taken from her horse.

Josephine's childhood sounded fantastical, indulged at every turn. Life, however, is never quite so rosy, and conversations only hinted at such imperfections. Whether or not Josephine was aware of problems and conflicts regarding her siblings and her parents, she played all family issues close to the vest. Seldom were the references to her brother-in-law's alcoholism or her sister's infertility discussed in detail. It would be considered a betrayal to family to indulge in such unseemly behavior.

Leland, on the other hand, had quite the opposite experience growing up. Leland's mother, Carrie, was a slight woman with a hawkish nose and a wicked sense of humor. She was born the sixth of seven children on a farm in Iowa, and she spoke with pride of all of her siblings and with great respect for her parents. Living on a farm was the norm and learning to fend for oneself, expected. What was not expected was that she would be unmarried and pregnant at the age of eighteen. Her father was appalled and ceased speaking to Carrie for an entire year, though they shared the same house. He shunned little Lyle when he was born, but as babies tend to do, Lyle softened his grandfather's heart by the time he was walking. Carrie was a good mother; she worked hard and was diligent in all she did. She was religious, too, a God-fearing churchgoer, and she played the piano and sang in the Methodist church choir.

By the time she was twenty-five, she was pregnant for the second time, but Lyle and his new brother, Leland, did not share the same paternity. This time, Carrie's father took a liking to his second grandson right off the bat, and Leland benefited from the undue attention paid him. By Carrie's third pregnancy eight years later, no one was surprised, and no one asked any impolite questions. Instead, she continued working, this time as a store clerk, to support her growing family.

In looking at Carrie's three sons, no one would ever know that their upbringing was uncommon. They were hard working, industrious, intelligent, and responsible in all they undertook. Their lives were simple, not asking for much but giving whatever was asked of them. All in all, it could be said that Carrie did a great job raising her boys. The fact that they never had a father—or fathers— was not extraordinary at that time; many fathers died by the time they were forty, not seeing their children grow into adulthood.

What was extraordinary was the openness with which the subject of Leland's upbringing was broached within Josephine and Leland's new family. While she had been raised to steer clear of all conversations regarding finances and the family's "dirty laundry," Josephine found that her journey into marriage with Leland brought with it a certain amount of freedom of expression—a liberating concept for someone with her innate straightforwardness and candor. Determined to be open and honest with her children, they learned of their father's background in candid discussion with Josephine, without judgment and without regard for any impropriety. Her pronouncements of Leland's childhood may have been issued to point out the vast difference between her experience and his and what was considered proper and acceptable, or it could have been that she was equally mesmerized by his family history as was anyone listening to the story for the first time. It also cemented their purpose together—their pursuit of a family based on honesty and integrity and intelligence. As Jo and Lee raised their nine children, these tenets continued to be an integral part of their resolve to produce imaginative and interesting and inspired children.

PRIMA VOCE ~ DEBORAH ANNE

I WAS BORN WITH MY EYES WIDE OPEN. THAT'S WHAT MY MOTHER told me, and I have chosen to believe it. She watched my birth in a mirror, which was attached to the ceiling at the foot of the delivery table, so she should know. For many years, from about the age of nine or ten through my teens, I had a recurring dream, except that it would happen as I was falling asleep. I don't dream it anymore, but the images have always remained the same. I am lying down, and the ceiling is very high above me. Everything seems white around me, and there are sounds—voices?—all around me. Suddenly, three people come into the room: first, a man with glasses and a mustache, wearing a white coat, then a woman in a white coat, and then another man. Everything is in black-and-white, which is odd because I have always dreamed in color. The only thing I can compare the place to is a hospital, but until very recently I have never been in a hospital, except for my birth. Now in this dream-memory there are more sounds—the voices of these three people. They come toward me, and I wish they would all be quiet and go away.

Also in black-and-white, but apparently some months later, I am seated on a counter. A man—my father, I think—is propping me up, and another man—Uncle Buddy?—is tickling me or cooing at me. The men are happy and laughing. I wish they would go away and leave me alone.

In Omaha, where I was born and where the events above occurred, I fall in a hole in the snow. I'm walking with my mother who is pushing a baby carriage—the big old-fashioned kind. My new sister, Pam, is in it, and she is tiny. We are eighteen months apart and

I was born in May, so I can't be more than two years old. The hole is probably very shallow but to me, it is a shock, hidden under the snow, and I am suddenly frightened when there is no more solid ground.

Now I am being held up at the window in a door by someone other than my mother. I am crying and the lady is telling me not to worry, that my mother will be coming back. I believe they are on the way to the hospital to take Pam there after I closed the edge of a door on her fingers while we were playing. I wish my parents would come back and not leave me alone in this strange house with this strange woman.

When I was two we moved to San Francisco. My father, who had been a professional drummer for fifteen years and had put himself through medical school partly by studying during set breaks in clubs, had an internship at a hospital in the city. There is a newspaper photograph of my mother sitting on a sofa, with me on one side, my sister Pam on the other, and the new baby, Diana, just a few weeks old, in my mother's arms. When my parents got to San Francisco, my mother was eight and a half months' pregnant, and they couldn't find a place to live. In desperation, my mother took out an ad in the newspaper saying that if someone didn't come up with a house for them to rent, she would be forced to give birth in Golden Gate Park. Within a day or two, they had a house out in the Avenues, in the Sunset District.

San Francisco: feeding ducks by a lake in the park; my mother reading *The Ugly Duckling* to me as I am supposed to be taking a nap. She has fallen asleep on the bed beside me before she has finished, and I am pondering the sadness of the story. Now, standing by an easel at the de Young Museum, where I am enrolled in a children's art class, I have just mixed blue and yellow paint together and discovered *green*. I feel certain no one has ever done that before, that I have just discovered something unheard of in human existence. It is very, *very* exciting. There are other vague pictures in my head of a lot of children on our street, and young parents, and baby food cans being blown up on the street on the Fourth of July, but most of those are stories I was told; they are not my pictures.

Two years later, we moved a few hours north to Eureka, California. Eureka is on the coast, and my strongest impression of it is a kind of constant grayness. There must have been a lot of fog, but more than that, the sky was always gray; one woke up to grayness. To this day, I cannot stand more than a few days of waking to that kind of weather. Living in Paris is out. I believe that part of that grayness—that dull, depressing feeling that I had in Eureka—was due to my parents' unhappiness. I don't know what their life was like, but during that time, another sister, Priscilla, came along; I saw the only fight I remember seeing my parents have; there was a terrible earthquake; and my first two years of school were filled with feelings of isolation and depression.

On the other hand, there were interesting things there. We lived in a little house on a broad, busy street, and logging trucks would rumble past with long tree trunks chained in across the back of their flatbeds. My mother was always afraid when driving behind them, certain that the chains would break and the logs would come rolling into our car, killing not only her but all four of her daughters.

One time I was walking home from kindergarten with Jimmy Wilson, a boy my age who lived next door. For some reason, he pushed me out into the street as a truck came roaring by. From a block away, our mother saw it, and she tore down the street like a beast gone mad, screaming at Jimmy. When she reached him, she grabbed his arm and yelled in his face. He started crying and ran to his mother, who pulled him into their house without saying a word to my mother.

In our backyard, rhubarb and potatoes grew wild. The lady who had lived there before us had thrown potato peelings out into the yard and they had taken root. I hated the texture of cooked rhubarb, although I loved the red stems fading into green. But I loved the potatoes. Behind our property was a little alley, and beyond that, a big field. With a couple of neighbor kids, we would take potatoes into the field and dig a hole. Someone almost always had matches, and we would try to cook the potatoes in the ground. I'm not sure we managed very well, because I only remember learning to eat the potatoes raw with salt, and liking them at the time.

There were girls on our block who would dress up and come over to play with Pammie and me. Pam was very small, and these girls would dress her up in their dolls' clothes and push her around in a toy baby carriage. I must have dressed up as well, because I remember wearing an old-fashioned bonnet and walking with these older girls around the neighborhood. There was a Great Dane that would occasionally scare the bejeesuz out of me when its enormous head suddenly appeared over our back fence. My mother would roller skate with us or try to teach us, and one year, while she was eight months' pregnant, she fell off the step from our yard to the sidewalk and cracked her tailbone. Usually, she roller-skated in our basement. She had some trouble after the cracked-tailbone incident and spent some months in pain as a result. I learned to ride a bicycle there, with my mother holding the back of the seat as I tried to balance. I hated it and felt that I would never learn, and it felt like a full year later that a friend came over and wanted to ride bikes and finally, wanting to save face, I got on and just rode.

Three things stand out from that time. One is the only fight I ever saw my parents have. I don't know what the argument had been but in the middle of the night, we three girls, who slept crosswise in a double bed, were wakened by something, and when we came to the door of our bedroom, we saw our parents in the hall between the two bedrooms of the house. Daddy was standing in the doorway of their room, and Mama was in the hall with blood running down her face. They had had some kind of fight and he had pushed her, and she fell onto the heating grate in the floor, which cut her forehead. When he tried to look at it, she said, "Don't you touch me," very dramatically. I don't remember the outcome other than to hear my mother laugh about it later, mainly for refusing medical help from the doctor close at hand. I never saw them fight or argue again.

During the time that we lived in the little house, and while Mama was pregnant with Priscilla, there was a very strong earthquake. There had been a stronger tremor in the night, but I only remember the second quake the next day. Pam and I were on the floor of the dining room, playing near the table, and little Diana was on the

4

children's potty in toilet training. Mama was on the back porch doing laundry. Suddenly, everything was shaking, and a leaf for the dining table fell across the room and caught by about an inch on the edge of the table. Pam was sitting directly under it and missed being smashed by that tiny margin. I ran to the back porch, noticing that Diana was sitting contentedly on the potty, but when I reached the door to the porch, Mama was trying frantically to get to us and couldn't. There was an enormous, heavy, full-length ornate mirror that had fallen from its place behind the door, and Mama couldn't lift it up to get past. I was scared, and I could see she was scared as well. She finally managed to heave the mirror back up and gathered up the three of us. Pam had been a near miss, and it turned out that Daddy had been in a records room at the hospital and had felt the entire building shivering and slightly twisting around him. He said he had wondered if the building was going to collapse and kill him; that it was one of the only times he had thought he might actually die right then.

School is the final significant image from that time, and it is not pleasant. In kindergarten, there was a girl who would be my friend one day and not the next; I developed an understanding of cliques at an early age. For first grade, I was sent to the Catholic school and taught by some order of nuns. I remember being pushed down outside, and cutting my knees on gravel, and sitting on someone's desk while a nun tried to pick the gravel out of my freshly grated flesh. One lunchtime, after the afternoon classes had started, I was kept in the cafeteria by a nun who tried to force me to eat all of my fruit-laden Jell-O, which only made me gag. Didn't she realize that if I *could* have eaten it, I would have? Why would I want to be kept there and be late for class, where I would feel humiliated going in late and alone? And to this day, I cannot figure out why someone would force a child to eat something that kept making her gag!

I also remember waiting one stormy afternoon for Mama to pick me up in the car. When she didn't come and she didn't come, I decided to walk home by myself. I was scared, but I thought something had happened, so I set out on the busy broad street that I thought led to home. There was thunder and lightning and cars whizzing by and I

5

remember being very afraid, but having only the thought that now I had to keep going. Somewhere along this boulevard, my mother drove up in the car. She had gone to pick up my grandfather, her dad, at the airport, and she had my sisters with her. She was angry and gave me a fierce scolding. I realize now that it was because she had been so scared at not finding me waiting at school, and I learned once and for all to stay put if I was expecting someone to meet up with me.

We called our grandfather Papapa, with the emphasis on the first syllable. Mama's mother, Grandmama (emphasis on the first *and* final syllable) had died when Pam and I were very small, and I barely remembered her. Papapa was fun, and he had false teeth, which he would always pop out at us to scare us. He had a gregarious personality and always dressed rather formally in tweed suits, but he could be incredibly intimidating. Grandma would come to visit from Denver. She was Daddy's mother and always fun, and she had the most fabulous box of cheesy costume jewelry, which she let us comb through and wear. Once during a party at our house, my parents were doing the wheelbarrow, where one person would walk on his hands while someone else held up his feet. Grandma was the wheelbarrow, and she laughed so hard that she wet her pants right in the midst of the guests. She always smelled good and had a soft feathery powder puff and very soft skin, and she was witty and laughed easily. Sometimes at naptime I would sit on her lap in the rocking chair, cuddled against her pillowy bosom, and she would sing in her quivery voice, "Put on your old grey bonnet, with the blue ribbons on it, while I hitch old Dobbin to the sleighhhhhh. Through the fields of clover, we will ride to Dover for our golden wedding day."

Then we moved a few hours south to Mendocino County, and life began in earnest.

Two Years in Paradise

The house was big and surrounded by a cornfield in front and alfalfa behind. To the west and across the road that ran along the east side of the house, there was a pear orchard. In our yard were fourteen black walnut trees, and there was a big drive that swept in from the road and divided into one driveway that led to our house and another to the only other house visible, where there lived an older couple who kept chickens. Behind the house was a row of hollyhocks and beyond that, my alfalfa field. Just into the alfalfa was a small, lightly cleared circle, and with my two just-younger sisters, we set up our secret space. There was a small piece of rug, toy dishes, and a doll or two, and a section of log that had been cut so that we could sit on it and use it as a rocking chair. It felt as if no one could see us, that we could live a special life in this little place hidden in the alfalfa, behind the fence and the hollyhocks.

My father had taken a job as at the local mental hospital, and our house belonged to the state. We would go to the hospital and hear Daddy play drums in a band there and later, we would go there as a group, my three sisters and me, and sing for the patients.

The women were always more overtly crazy than the men. The men would sit quietly during the entertainment but the women would dance around. One woman, sitting in a chair, conducted us with her legs. Another time our family was sitting on the lawn, listening to the swing band with the other staff and the patients, and a woman came up and tried to take the baby from my mother's arms. Mama patiently explained that the baby needed to stay with her, so the woman went dancing off across the lawn, her old, sagging breasts flapping with her arm movements.

The hospital grounds were beautiful and vast. They had their own dairy, and they grew vegetables. Some of the men who lived there were called terminal alcoholics but were not considered insane. These men had jobs and as a result, we had a gardener from the hospital who came to take care of our yard once a week. Other men were the garbage collectors, and sometimes when they came driving into the yard, we could hear the truck from inside the barn where we were playing. We would sneak up onto the corrugated metal roof and throw walnuts down on them, but they never seemed to figure out that we were the culprits.

Some distance to the west of us, maybe a quarter of a mile, was the Russian River and the Talmage Bridge, which connected us to the main town of Ukiah, the county seat. There were stories of homeless men who lived under the bridge, and often, men would come to the back door of our house, and Mama would give them food. She found a mark on the wall of the barn one day, and she asked the next homeless man if he knew what the mark meant. She knew that a half-moon on a shed meant it was a toilet. He said it indicated that a "soft touch" lived in the house and that people would always be fed. Mama removed the mark from the barn, perhaps because by now, there were five little mouths to feed, but she continued to give handouts nonetheless.

We played outside a lot, although there was a beautiful glassed-in porch that held most of our toys on one side of the house. On the other side was a wrap-around open porch where we would roller skate endlessly. We had started our family with a cat named Muffy, which Mama had once deliberately spun round in the dryer, because the cat kept sleeping on the freshly laundered diapers. Muffy never did it again. But soon there were cats everywhere. At one point there were twenty-two cats living at, in, or around the house, and some of them were feral. Daddy sat up all night once with a gun balanced on the bathroom window and pointed out toward the barn and shot a cat that had been tearing up the others. Another time he tried to limit the population by taking the cats, one at a time, and driving them farther out into the country to let them out, hoping they would find another home. Once he put a relatively feral cat into the car and was driving out of the yard, but the cat went crazy inside the car. It kept running all around the car and getting under the gas and brake pedals. When the cat started running back and forth on the dashboard as Daddy tried to drive, Daddy gave up and let the cat back out into the yard.

We also had milk delivered in glass bottles by the local dairy, and the man who dropped off milk, butter, eggs, and cottage cheese would let us ride through our yard, standing up in the cab space or on the running boards of the truck.

The two years we lived out in the countryside were my favorite years of childhood. There was always freedom and beauty and sometimes, the sadness of nature but mostly there was security, openness, and a particular kind of creativity in inventing play within the quiet stillness of the country.

UKIAH

By the fourth grade, we were living in town, on Oak Park Avenue, in one of the oldest residential areas. It was a tree-lined street with beautiful houses on it, big for the time and place, probably what would be called craftsman houses. Our house had a huge living room—about thirty-six feet long, with a fifteen-foot ceiling. One end of the living room and the dining room were enclosed with narrow French doors. The living room had plenty of room for Mama's Steinway grand piano, Daddy's drum set and, eventually, Jazzberry Jam, Daddy's jazz group that often played there at night while we fell asleep on the stairs listening to live Dixieland and '40s swing music.

Just as the country had open, free space in it, the town, which at the time had a population of about twenty thousand at most, was made up of pieces of life and geography. These corresponded to the compartments of home and family, school, Daddy's office, and the hospital. My memories are so numerous and detailed that I have decided to present the rest of my childhood in these relative fragments of life.

SEX

To begin at the beginning, I don't remember ever *not* knowing where babies came from. Mama was very open about the science of sex, and she would draw pictures of fallopian tubes and eggs and sperm and then, when we had misinterpreted what she was explaining, one of us would overhear the error and she would call us back down to clarify. Somehow, the physical basics were never a mystery. When I was about three, still living in San Francisco, a neighbor boy came over to play. I was in Mama's bedroom, talking to her while she nursed Diana. The little boy was my age, and he was disgusted by Mama's breast-feeding. She said it was natural and took her breast and squirted milk at him to show him how it worked. This same kid also became upset when Mama cut my long hair into a bob. I think he eventually became a priest.

My first erotic image was a painting of a young man and young woman in flight from something not seen. They were pale against the dark, forested Renaissance background, and while he had a cloth draped around his hips, she was naked, although draped in a transparent curtain of fabric, which the boy was holding over her head as protection from a coming storm. Something about their closeness and nakedness and perhaps their seemingly illicit flight, awakened my sense of the erotic. There was also, when we lived on Oak Park Avenue, a man who visited the neighbors on our left. I don't remember this man's name, but he was an African- American doctor who drove a racy Jaguar convertible, played the bagpipes, and best of all, he wore an eye patch. He was the sexiest person I could imagine, and he was the model of everything romantic that I wanted in a man.

I first remember the heat and difficulty of "sex" when I was in third grade, and a group of boys from my class pinned me against a chain-link fence in part of the schoolyard, so that Frank could kiss me. I didn't mind the kiss, but I did mind the force, and I was mad and somehow embarrassed. I never felt attractive, even from my earliest memories, and I could never understand why boys liked me or why little, skinny Larry in third and fourth grade always wanted me on his softball team, especially because I sucked at baseball. I also knew that he liked me in a special way that I found aesthetically incomprehensible.

The great love of my childhood years was a boy named Jerry Druliner. He had black hair, and big blue eyes, and long, long black eyelashes, and a big wide smile. I told Mama at one point that we were going to get married when we grew up, and she bluntly said no, we wouldn't. I wasn't fazed. I knew he was my guy and that we were meant for each other. Of course, we didn't get married, and things changed radically later in childhood, but throughout grammar school, he was *it* for me. We alternated being president and vice president of our class, and he was my first kiss—outside in the front yard under the big, pink-blossom-laden crabapple tree that looked like an old lady's party dress.

In fifth grade, suddenly all the boys began telling dirty jokes and making sexual references to the girls. Seventh grade brought the beginning of dating, although it was surreptitious for many of us. Mama had told me that I couldn't date until I was sixteen, and I said that was too far away and I might not even live that long. By the time I was sixteen, I was fat and shy, and dating became moot. As Auntie Mame said, "My puberty in Buffalo was drab." But back in seventh grade, my best friend, Kathy Johnson, and I would go to the movies on Saturday afternoon, she with her boyfriend and me with someone I barely remember, who was nice but who didn't really interest me. Oh, the awkwardness of trying just to hold hands for the first time! My great love interest had moved on to other girls, and my shyness made it hard to initiate any contact that might lead to boyfriend/ girlfriend status. I was always surprised by how forward the girls could be with the boys and wished that I could be as bold and free as they were. But they were tan and skinny with blonde streaks in their hair, while I was white and freckled and redheaded, with a lopsided smile and pale eyelashes. What would the boys see in me?

Throughout high school, I was single—one of the art crowd, I think, not part of the jock and cheerleader group, who seemed so successful in their domination of the teenage social structure. I had had seven years of ballet, during which I was thin and, to my eyes, somewhat androgynous physically, as I was late in developing breasts. In seventh or eighth grade, I went to a sleepover party and was the only girl still wearing an undershirt as opposed to even a training bra. It made me feel shy. During eighth grade, our ballet teacher moved away, and puberty struck just as dance classes ended. My body exploded into traumatic teenage fat, and I took refuge in food, art, and masturbation for about four years.

SIBLINGS

Imagine yourself as the eldest of nine children. What kinds of things might you be doing? How about changing diapers, rocking the baby to sleep, singing toddlers to sleep, and always having to play the teacher when you play "school"? All of those were actually easy. Mama used cloth diapers and before putting the soiled diaper in the laundry, you would rinse it out in the toilet. Occasionally I cheated and flushed the entire diaper down the toilet, hoping all the while that it wouldn't cause a disgusting backup and overflow, for which I would have to answer. Usually, it worked. I was twelve years older than the youngest, my brother Paul, and I remember spending more time walking hand in hand with him than with any of the others. For a time, I had a wart on an index finger and when we would walk for a while I would casually say "Wart hand," and Paul would squeal and yank his hand away. Then we would laugh.

A new baby was always an exciting event at our house. When Mama came home from the hospital (where she would always try to squeeze in an extra day or so of rest and relative quiet), we would all sit on the sofa in chronological order, and the new baby would be passed from child to child, so that we all had the opportunity to meet him or her, and so that, I imagined, the youngest would be comfortable with touching and holding such a tiny, floppy creature.

Mama had wanted twelve children—God only knows why. I think it had to do with a movie she had seen or maybe because as the youngest of five and having never been allowed into her family's kitchen, she wanted to play house herself. I know that we were all wanted and loved and though there were certainly personality differences among us—and between all of us and Mama—we all knew, deep down inside, that we were loved. Family was probably the most important thing to my mother, and we were often reminded of that. She was a strong, dominating force in the family, and in having all of us, she also put herself in the position of being the one against many. There were times when we would gang up on her, although I'm not sure we knew exactly what we were doing. Two obvious examples of this involved religion.

While Mama was very, very Catholic, Daddy was completely uninvolved in any kind of organized religion, although his mother was Methodist, and he himself was probably the kindest person I have ever known. I have always felt fortunate that Mama's relatively extreme beliefs were counterbalanced by Daddy's apparent absence of religion, though he had a quiet but emphatic morality. At some point midway through my childhood, Mama decided that we would pray the family rosary every evening, sans my father, of course. He was either working at his office or the hospital or enjoying himself playing drums after hours at a local dinner club, or if it was the weekend, he might be found down at the fire department, watching football with the firemen, since we didn't have a television at home. So this family rosary event consisted of all nine of us kneeling on the hard wood floor of the living room, rosaries in hand, while Mama led the prayers and we followed along with the Hail Mary's and all the rest. I even seem to recall a statue of the Virgin that was placed on one of the bookshelves or the mantel, as a point of focus. It was a disaster. I don't think we ever got through the entire rosary even once, and this family spiritual gathering didn't last a week. We were fidgeting, laughing, saying the prayers in loud, overtly bored voices, or fighting with each other—anything to get out of doing this for what seemed like an eternity.

The second family event that backfired on Mama also involved religion. One year she decided that we would go to early Mass every single morning of Lent. That is six days a week, in addition to regular Sunday Mass, for six weeks—again, an eternity for a child. We lived a five-minute walk away from a convent, which was attached to a kind of orphanage. The Dominican order of nuns ran this home and school for children who were orphaned, unwanted, or unable to live with their parents. The convent and school were old by California standards, but the chapel was new and minimalist in design. Weekday Mass was at six-thirty in the morning, and Mama would wake us up and rush us to get dressed and around the corner in time. When we arrived, we would usually be the only people in the congregation. The chapel was quiet and simple, the only sound the voices of unseen women singing matins. It was beautiful and unearthly and I loved it. Unfortunately, it was six-thirty in the morning, and I hated that part. Among ourselves, we decided to take turns picking a fight so that we could prove to Mama that going to church every morning was not benefiting our souls and that sleeping later might make us nicer children. I'm not sure we made it all the way through Lent, but I do know we only had to do it that one year.

At dinner, we were divided into two eating stations. Daddy and Mama and the little kids sat at the table in the breakfast room (the dining room was reserved for birthdays and holidays), and the three or four oldest of us sat at the counter in the kitchen. We were verbal and witty and caustic, and often, when Mama would try to start a conversation over dinner, her earnest determination sent us into waves of smart-mouthed wit that either would get one of us sent up to our room or send her in tears to my parents' bedroom. Sometimes we would go upstairs, mad, usually because someone else had caused the problem or had been the "mouth," and the person sent up was merely a scapegoat. More often, however, we went up laughing behind our hands, knowing that another of us would sneak food up to us later, or because we had managed to discard the hated part of the meal that had provoked our dismissal into a napkin or onto someone else's plate.

We stuck together, and it wasn't until our teenage years that we began to break off from each other in a more conscious way. The beauty of the big family, for me, was that I always had someone to play with. The problem with the big family, for me, was that I was not good at making friends. Although I always had one best friend at a time throughout my childhood, my five sisters and three brothers were a built-in playground. The only real difficulty with my siblings was when I began to have to babysit them. It is impossible to babysit people, especially your own family, who are only eighteen months to four years younger than you are. There were many times when I was left in charge and the next two siblings, Pam and Diana, refused to help or obey what I felt had to be done. They would threaten to run away and leave the house, and when they did go outside, I would retaliate by locking the doors, at which point they took revenge by running around the house and ringing all the doorbells endlessly, usually just at the point when I was trying to put the little kids to bed. Twice, they actually ran away, and one of those times they got as far as the road out of town, where a semitruck driver saw them hitchhiking and told them to go home.

Pam was younger than me by only eighteen months. She was smaller and much fiercer than I, and when I was left in charge, I would use her to help get the little kids to stay in bed and go to sleep. She was my sergeant-at-arms, and the threat of sending Pam in to take care of things was often enough to make the kids quiet down and at least stay in the bedroom, if not in bed.

When we first moved into the house in town, there were only two bedrooms upstairs for the six—eventually nine—of us. Initially, Pam, Diana, and I shared a bedroom, and Mama had three desks built along one wall to accommodate our studying. The other bedroom was big and held two sets of bunk beds and, eventually, a daybed as well. By the time there were nine kids, the two littlest were sleeping in a bottom bunk bed feet to feet.

Soon after that arrangement, my parents renovated the house and added a family room, guest bath, and expanded laundry room downstairs and two additional bedrooms and a massive bathroom for the six girls upstairs. The girls' bathroom was fabulous. It had an enormous two-sink counter across one wall where one could comfortably sit and shave one's legs into the sink, and with two toilets behind swinging doors, as well as separate tub and shower partitions, we could hang out there for hours. If we turned on the fans, we could deny that we heard Mama calling us from the bottom of the stairs.

Pam was social and outgoing, and my memory of her can be summed up by Shakespeare's line about Hermia in *A Midsummer Night's Dream*: "though she is little she is fierce." In high school, Pam was everything I wanted to be: popular. She had curlers in her hair any time she was not in school or going out with friends. She and I ended up sharing a bedroom; she was neat, and I was messy and smoked. One day she took a piece of chalk and drew a line on the carpet, dividing our sections of the room, and told me that nothing of mine could cross that line.

Something happens when you grow up sharing a room with a sibling. A particular relationship develops that is different from your relationship with the rest of the kids. Because of the number of us, we sort of naturally divided into two groups—the big kids and the little kids, with Valerie, the middle child, relegated to the little kids. For years, she struggled to be included with the big kids and eventually, we accepted her into our lofty group. Our family was dominated by women. In addition to my mother, who had a dynamic personality, there were five girls born before the first boy came along.

We were so excited about finally having a boy in the family that I always felt that both he and Valerie—just above him and the fifth girl—got the short end of the deal: he, because he got too much attention from all us women, and Valerie, because she didn't get enough. When David was born, the rumor was that his eyelashes were so long they were stuck to the end of his nose. When our housekeeper—a big, raw-boned, redheaded Texan—saw him, she burst out, "Jesus Christ, what a goddamned good-lookin' kid." He was a beautiful and sensitive child and exceptionally brainy (he was fascinated with Sputnik when he was four, and since we didn't have a television, no one could figure out where he got any of that information). At the end of the first day of kindergarten, he announced to my mother that he couldn't stand it and was not going back to school. Finally, she was able to pull out of him that the teacher wore her lipstick painted on in a garish manner, and he couldn't stand to look at her.

Valerie, the middle child, looked like a pixie and was a terror when doing after-dinner dishes. We all had chores that rotated weekly, and when it was her turn to do dishes, it invariably led to a screaming and crying match between her and Mama, who, of course, always won.

Priscilla, just older than Valerie, was the only blonde in the family and was beautiful, with big, innocent blue eyes. She looked like an angel, but she had a wicked and subversive sense of humor. She always seemed quiet to me, but she would do outrageous things without saying a word. Once, Daddy was going away on a trip, and he was kissing us all good-bye. When he got to Priscilla, who must have been three or four at the time, he bent down to kiss her, and then she promptly blew her nose all over his tie and just looked up at him with those big, innocent eyes. Later on, as a teenager, she would listen to a piece of music once and then sit down at the piano—she didn't have the piano lessons that the three oldest of us did—and pick out an accompaniment to what she had just heard.

Diana, who came between Pam and Priscilla, became the teenage rebel. She had more boyfriends than any of us, and once, when we were driving through town in the early evening, she talked me into picking up a young guy hitchhiking in town. He was headed out to the campground at Lake Mendocino, north of town. By the time we found his campsite, it was dark. An older man there invited us to stay for a cup of coffee, but there was something about the man that made me anxious, so I said no, that we were expected back at home. I noticed firelight from camps in the area, but no one was close by this camp. I don't know how it started, but the man began saying things that had a dangerous tone to them, although he wasn't saying anything explicit. But then he said something like, "Why don't we keep them here with us?" The words weren't quite that clear, but there were a number of sentences like that, and I said that if we weren't home at a certain time, our family would search for us. Finally, I just firmly said "thank you" and walked toward the car. On the entire short walk to the car I kept expecting to be grabbed, but we got in safely, and I drove away as fast as I could. I was furious and told Diana never to ask me to pick up anyone again; that even if I seemed chicken or conservative (as she had implied when I initially hesitated about picking up the hitchhiker), I would never do that again. She never seemed to feel the danger that I did.

Becky, the youngest girl, was sandwiched between David and the last two kids, Zack and Paul. I don't know much about the personal lives of my youngest siblings, as I was just changing their diapers or babysitting them, but I always had a suspicion that they terrorized her a bit. When she was around nine, the boys and some friends dared her to jump off the second-story roof with an open umbrella in her hand, and she did it. When I got out to the side yard, she was lying on her side in the grass. Nothing was broken, but she must have bruised her ribs, and she had trouble catching her breath for a few minutes.

David, Zack, and Paul, along with a kid from down the block, were known as the Oak Park Commandos, named by A. C. Swan, the mother of their cohort. Across the street from us was Mrs. Golden, who lived in a beautiful, old, dark house on a tree-filled acre. She had a pond in her front yard with what we called big goldfish, which were probably koi. The Commandos would sneak into her yard and go fishing in her pond and she would always catch them, and they would run away and hide in someone's yard.

There were always accidents with my brothers and sisters, and they seemed to happen frequently when I was left in charge. My parents traveled occasionally to medical conventions, and I remember once that they had barely been gone twenty minutes when Valerie cut the palm of her hand, deep enough that the fatty tissue was visible. The bathroom sink was running with pink water as I tried to stop the bleeding by alternating a fresh cloth diaper with pressing the sides of the wound together, while holding it under cold water and ignoring her screaming.

Another time, some of the kids and a friend or two were playing baseball in the living room with a ball and a board. I told them to stop because there were windows everywhere, and they were bound to break one. They went on playing, and then I heard yelling. When I went back into the living room, one of the kids, I think it was David, was bleeding from the back of his head. Valerie had decided that he had been the pitcher long enough and when he wouldn't give up the position, she hit him with the board they were using as a bat. Unfortunately, the board had a nail in it and had cut the back of his head. It wasn't a bad cut but since the head bleeds so much, it looked like a disaster. I sent him next door where the exotic doctor was visiting – I think I was too shy to go and ask him myself, *and* I had a terrible crush on him – and David came home with a butterfly bandage on a newly shaved patch of scalp.

We fought a lot as teenagers. I don't envy my mother's having had five girls all in their teenage or prepubescent years at the same time. Pam once threw a radio at me and another time threw a hairbrush through the back-door window. While Pam, Diana, and I were all in high school, Pam and I had an altercation over a tube of mascara. We were in the girls' bathroom upstairs and I had the mascara that Pam claimed was hers. She was backing me into the shower stall, which meant I was going to be in big trouble—no one messed with Pam, and if I got cornered, there was no way out without a fight. Just as I backed into the tiled stall, Diana came into the bathroom and I said, "Di, didn't I buy this mascara at the drugstore?" Diana answered something noncommittal but positive—like "Yes. Why?"—and Pam turned around and punched her. Diana punched her right back, and the next thing I remember, I was downstairs in the kitchen, consoling Mama, who was crying and saying, "I'm raising you girls to hate each other."

I told her not to worry. Pam and Di were upstairs in the girls' bathroom comparing the size of the black eyes they had just given each other and having a wonderful time. They were very free in explaining to everyone in high school how each had gotten her shiner.

Although we fought, we also played together a lot. Mama wouldn't allow television in the house—she said the commercials were bad for our mental development—and so we invented games endlessly. We made a circus in the backyard and tried to put our cats and dog into it as the wild animals. The swing set became the trapeze, and we were always trying to make our friends agree to become aerial artists or clowns.

We also made a performing space out of the family-room fireplace. There was a light that we could move and focus on the hearth, and when friends came over to play, we would have them stand in the light and perform songs or jokes for us. When we got our first portable cassette tape player, I would take it in the living room and make up stories, influenced by the radio dramas that still existed then, with sound effects that we invented partly from the piano and drum set. By stroking the strings of the piano, we could make eerie background music, and the drums could make everything from a knock on a door to sudden thunder. I made up one story about a killer cat that terrorized a neighborhood. There would be a knock on a door and the creaky sound of the door opening, followed by an old lady's voice saying, "Who's there?" Then there would be a meow, and the lady would say, "Oh, hello, little kitty. You're so pretty." The cat would meow again, and then the meow would turn into a snarl, and suddenly the sound of the cat shrieking, and the old lady screaming, and the thumps of furniture all came together. Then there was silence, except for the delicate sound of some toy being dragged over the upper register of the piano strings. Then it would all start again.

RELIGION

I loved church. I loved the ritual, the lights, the colors, the music, and the costumes, and I loved our dressing up for church. There was a niche in the hallway outside of Mama and Daddy's bedroom, where our missals were kept, and I loved the old leather-bound missals, whose covers had become soft and limp from use. Every Sunday morning, before we all became teenagers and things began to change, we would dress in hats and gloves and our Mary Janes. We would take our missals and sometimes our rosaries, pile into the station wagon, and head off to St. Mary of the Angels Church. Mama always made us sit close to the altar and because there were so many of us, we must have been quite the parade as we marched up to take over a whole pew. Daddy only went to Mass with us on the big religious holidays and one Easter, when Mama was the choir mistress, she wore an outrageous hat. She had a wardrobe of expensive hats and some were lovely, but the one she wore this Easter was pretty extreme—deep royal blue wool felt, with pansies on it, interspersed with rhinestone dots and although she had worn hats that might have been appropriate for upper-class Chicago or New York in the 1940s, this hat really was an eyesore. Daddy wouldn't ride in the same car with her, and we fought among ourselves to see who would get to ride in his plush, leather-seat car. When we got to the church, Mama went up to the choir loft, and Daddy sat in a little section on the side near the front of the church. When Mama came down his aisle after Communion on her way back up to the choir, Daddy turned his face to the wall so he wouldn't have to look at her hat.

Although Sunday mornings were hectic with kids who wanted to sleep in and avoid having to go to Mass, once we were there, I loved the quiet. For a long time in my childhood, the Mass was still in Latin, and my missal had the words in Latin on one side and in English on the other. I always followed along in Latin, and I can still remember many of the words of the songs that were sung, such as "Tantum Ergo."

At school, the first Friday of every month was celebrated by a walk from school to the church for Mass. This was some distance, perhaps half a mile, and shortly into my years at St. Mary's, this long procession ended. But while it lasted, our monthly Mass was topped off by hot chocolate and doughnuts when we got back to school. This was an incredible treat, as doughnuts were not something we got at home. They were frowned on as not nutritional, which was ironic since Mama always had some kind of sweet for dessert.

Over the years I retained my love of being in the quiet, with the choir singing, but when the Mass was changed to be heard in English, and the choir was transformed into mostly badly sung, vapid lyrics, struggling to fit a preexisting tune and played by guitarists who had only learned to strum their instrument, I lost interest. I realized that I was in love with the theatrical side of my religious experience but not with the dogma. I could never understand my mother's firm belief that Christ's body actually existed in the host she received at Communion. To me, it was always the literal flat, pasty circle that stuck against the roof of my mouth. Confession was a bit of a lie to me, and I would make up sins to tell the priest until, after years of this, I was afraid the priest would recognize my voice, as well as the monotonous list that I recycled once a month in the confessional. The most difficult part of the Catholic ritual was the long Good Friday Stations of the Cross. Kneeling for three hours was hard on the knees and was much harder than the fasting that we still did and that Mama adhered to long after the church fathers changed the rules and allowed us some little breakfast between midnight and Sunday Mass.

In high school or just before I entered high school, I went on a religious retreat for a weekend. The retreat house was near Sacramento and I fought Mama about going. As usual she won, and with a few friends from school I spent the weekend in a beautiful convent with extensive lawns and beautiful gardens. We were supposed to be silent the entire time and were encouraged to spend time alone in contemplation. Of course, we managed to find time to get together at night and whisper and laugh. We'd hold our breath if we thought we heard someone coming, perhaps attracted by the late-night light in a room, as well as by our voices. My memory holds nothing of the religion of that weekend, but I do remember the lovely green peace and quiet of walking alone around the grounds. That may have been the first time in my life that I had stillness and time to myself.

SCHOOL

All through grammar school, with the exception of a hellish kindergarten and first grade in Eureka, I felt creative. Second grade is unmemorable, but in third grade, I had a wonderful nun who had red hair—at least her skin coloring suggested it, as her habit concealed her hair. She was young and kind to us and had a wonderful sense of humor. When a couple of boys put a frog in her desk, she just laughed when it jumped out. The nun in sixth grade was the opposite of the young, red-haired nun. Sister Geraldine also had the complexion of a redhead, but with it, she had a red mustache and looked like a frog. She was mean and made music class particularly frustrating, unhappy, and uncreative. The grades of all the boys plummeted in sixth grade. Fortunately, their grades all reversed themselves and soared in seventh grade when we had Sister Benedict Marie, another young nun, this time beautiful, dark, and exotic-looking. All the boys had a crush on her. In addition to her beauty and kindness, she was a good teacher. With the exception of fourth and fifth grade, all my grammar-school teachers were Dominican nuns. In the fourth grade, we had a lay teacher, a woman who every year showed us slides of the places she had visited during her summer vacation. Her slides of Egypt—of the pyramids and of her riding camels—were vivid and adventurous, and she gave me a love of travel and of learning about other cultures and other peoples. She was also the only teacher who ever humiliated me in class. I do not remember the circumstances, but I do remember a sudden and overwhelming feeling of shame, of my face getting hot, and of vowing inside never to let that feeling happen to me again, especially so publicly.

In the eighth grade, my teacher, Sister Evangeline, was also the principal. She was fair but tough, and all the boys were afraid of her, because she looked as if she could physically take apart anyone who crossed her. At some point in the seventh grade, my best friend, Kathy, and I got into a fight, the only one we ever had. It was physical, with us pulling hair and slapping, and a crowd of other girls circled us. We were pulled apart and sent to the principal's office, where we had to stand while Sister Evangeline scolded us. By this time we were so scared that we had rebonded and were trying not to laugh. When Kathy let out a gurgle, Sister slapped her in the face, which sobered me up immediately. We had to write letters to our parents and set up a meeting with them and the principal to ensure our future good behavior.

On the other hand, this same principal heard about us kids in the band loading some instruments onto a pallet wagon (used for moving stacks of chairs in the auditorium) and then rolling the music and musician-laden wagon down Dora Street toward the public school. Rumor had it that she just laughed when she heard what we had done, and we never got in trouble for it. We also never made it all the way to the other school; the wagon was too heavy to push with all of us on it.

From the beginning of my time at St. Mary of the Angels Catholic Grammar School, I had fun overall. In the early grades, we had religious holidays that were celebrated by processions and creative projects. In May, for the feast of the Virgin Mary, we made crèches out of shoeboxes, which we decorated in various ways to make a symbolic home for her statue. In each grade, someone was selected as having the best or most creative shrine, and then someone was picked out of the whole school to lead the entire student body procession as we marched with a large statue of the Virgin at the head. Where we went with this procession I don't remember, but I longed to be the one chosen to crown the statue with a little wreath of flowers, and one year my wish came true. I was thrilled, elated, proud—everything one could be ... except that when I had to step out of line and walk in front of everyone to carry out this little honor, I was terribly anxious and shy. This same anxiety recurred any time I was singled out and had to stand or walk in front of the other students, whether it was to march to the front of the class to pick up my report card or to step forward to receive a holy medal or some other award. I much preferred a private creative task, which, in the middle school years, included sitting at the back of the class with my desktop slightly opened so the teacher couldn't see that I was making paper dolls for my friends around me. But the religious processions were beautiful and special and filled with color and music and they lifted us out of our ordinary daily existence.

We had an art class one year in which, for one hour a week, the radio in the back of the classroom was tuned to a classical music station, and while we listened to the music, we drew or painted on large sheets of butcher paper. I learned to grid a picture and reproduce it, as well as to draw freehand and copy something just by looking at it and letting my hand move my eyes into a new reproduction on paper. I was good at drawing and painting, and with the music playing in the background, I loved the focused, quiet attention while making something come alive in front of me.

I also played drums in the band. I wanted to play trumpet, but Mama said no, it wasn't ladylike, and she couldn't stand seeing female trumpeters, which I found ironic since she was always saying to us, "You girls can do anything you put your mind to." Instead of trumpet, I moved to the ladylike flute, but I couldn't control my breathing enough to make it work, and I got so frustrated that I quit. That talent was left to Diana, who was and is an extraordinarily talented flautist and musician. Instead, I got Daddy to back me up in my desire to learn to play drums. I loved it from the moment I started and became good enough to be asked to be the drummer at school for the swing band. As I was the only girl in the percussion section, I got teased a lot, and the boys were always trying to lift up the hem of my uniform skirt with their drumsticks. They were very irritated when I got the job as drummer with the swing music, but I didn't care. Even though there were times when their teasing felt deliberate, I was having too much fun, feeling the cohesion, the leading, and integration of playing drums with a small band. I would imagine my father sitting at the drums in the living room, his head tilted so that his left ear seemed to be listening harder as he held the center of Jazzberry Jam together via his beat.

Throughout grammar school, my grades were good. It wasn't until high school, when life became an unconscious struggle, that my grades began to steadily drop, except for art class. In younger grades, I was anxious about tests and grades, but I loved learning in general. I read constantly and had a book for bedtime, a book for reading in the bathroom, and a book for downstairs or to take with me in the car. I was good at English and bad at math; good at geography and social studies; and mediocre in history. In high school, I studied Latin for a year, followed by three years of French, with two simultaneous years of Spanish. I had a wonderful French teacher, Mr. Sherman, who always had an early Bastille Day celebration with us. We would dress up as famous French characters and eat French food. My English teachers were not so creative. In fact, they tended to be boring and their teaching felt general. There was one English teacher who was very popular but I was never able to get into his class. His class read Shakespeare and performed *Macbeth* in the classroom, with the teacher's chair set on top of his desk for a throne. The other English classes were invited in to see the reading, and I was even more disappointed that I had missed the opportunity to study with him. Instead, in my class, we had a substitute teacher named Jim Jones. He was popular with a lot of the students, but I thought he was an idiot. I could not see that he was actually teaching us anything. It seemed to me that he talked generally about a lot of subjects and was good at injecting his own personal stories into his lectures. Later on, he died with his cult in the infamous Jonestown massacre.

High school overall was emotional hell. I've always said I'd commit suicide before I'd repeat my teenage years. There is a photo of me, taken when I was about twelve, that shows me as a lanky tomboy. The next photo I see is me in my freshman year of high school, and I have turned into a butterball, the semi-invisible wallflower girl of all the Disney movies of the time—short, curly red hair, turquoise dress, and all. The end of ballet and the onset of hormones combined to create a nightmare that only enhanced my shyness, and that self-image stayed with me for many years. No boyfriends, no proms for this girl, and dances were an exercise in balancing one's pride with the constant anxiety that one would—or would not—be asked to dance. Either option induced panic.

PLAY

It always seemed to me that essentially, I was raised to vacation very well. While we always had chores, and Daddy worked long hours seven days a week, and Mama imbued us with the respectability and value of honest work, it seemed we were best at playing. Perhaps because we didn't have television and had to make up our own entertainment; perhaps because there were so many of us, always together—whatever the reason, we were good at all kinds of games, from cards to inventing plays to street baseball at the end of our block.

Play started in Omaha, riding tricycles around the cement yard in the apartment complex where we lived. From there it evolved to collaborating with the older kids in the neighborhood in Eureka, who would dress up my sister Pam and drive her around in a doll carriage, and to trying to dress up the cat in a bonnet. When we moved into the town of Ukiah, our play became more sophisticated. For the first year or two that we lived there, Mrs. Cash, the elderly woman in the dark house in the forested acre across the street, would come to our house to judge a costuming contest. We would take small dolls and make clothes for them, cutting out pieces of satin or faille ribbon or cotton chintz and trying to force our unskilled fingers to cut and sew by hand the tiny pieces of skirts and jackets. It was obvious that we had little ability and somehow the jackets never needed to button, and as long as they wrapped around the little dolls they counted as clothing. Sometimes we invented hats with the occasional sequin or even a tiny feather we had found in the yard. Mrs. Cash, whose wealth confirmed her name, was very democratic with her awards. We would gather around a card table set up on the front porch, and Mama would serve drinks to all of us—tea for Mrs. Cash and lemonade or milk and cookies for us. While we ate, we would wait for our individual commendations, an award for best design or maybe an award for most improved in sewing. In any case, it never felt competitive but rather a collective endeavor in which each of us had equal fun and equal reward.

As we grew up, we had music and dance lessons. I studied piano as well as drums and studied ballet for seven years and tap for three. Our dance classes consisted of my sisters and me, and I loved them. For some years, we would arrive for ballet just after some older girls had finished their ballet and pointe class, and I envied them. They seemed so grown up *and* they were toe dancers. I could not wait to reach that level of skill. Our dance teacher wore her hair in two braids wrapped around her head. She was older and very strict. We were never allowed to say "I can't" in class, and she often carried a long yardstick that she used to tap our knees at the barre if they weren't straight enough. Once she sharply reprimanded Diana for saying "I can't," and I went to Diana's defense, saying that if she could, she would.

We also had singing lessons for years and sang publicly. At first, there were the four eldest girls, and later, Valerie was added to the group. Pam, Diana, and I started singing lessons with a woman who had been an opera teacher and who had a daughter who sang opera. These lessons were classical in training and to this day, I can remember many of the sequences we moved through. Later, we had an accompanist, Mrs. Orsi, who epitomized patience and diplomacy, for we were not always attentive to our practice, even when we had a recital lined up somewhere. Mama played piano once or twice for our rehearsals, but we were badly behaved with her, and one time she stormed out of the living room, saying she would call the people hosting the event and cancel, since our raucous behavior was preventing our being prepared to perform. When she left the room, I grabbed the music and said, "Come on. Let's show her we can do it ourselves. We don't need her." We continued to rehearse, Mama came back, and we played the gig.

We sang at school events, local church and civic groups, and resorts around the county. Mama made our costumes, which we sometimes hated; there was only so long one could remain attached to kelly-green felt circle skirts. As we got older, we didn't want to be the cute "Wilson Sisters." For me, appearing in public was more fraught with anxiety as I got older. My sisters didn't seem to care, but I would get very tense just before going onstage, wanting everything to be perfect. I'm not sure what eventually ended our singing career, but by the time I entered high school, that part of our life was over.

Our family always had a vacation in the summer. For a number of years we went to a dude ranch near Willits, north of Ukiah. It was a family vacation spot with a central lodge, cabins for families, horseback riding, swimming, and outdoor games. We had one or two cabins, and every night we would eat at the lodge. Never, in all the times we stayed there, was there a dinner at which someone did *not* spill a glass of milk all over the table. The waitresses never seemed to mind. Perhaps they were used to it, but over time, I became very embarrassed by it. After dinner, we would go into the bar, where there were always old men who looked to me like cowboys. They would sing and teach us to dance, usually the box step or the two-step.

Other vacations were spent in a house at the end of a lane on the Mendocino coast. The house belonged to someone Daddy knew, and it was the only time that no one from the hospital could reach him, so we loved being there. The ocean was far below us and to get to the beach we had to hike down the cliff behind the house. Once, at the ocean, Daddy hiked over the rocks with us, out toward the line where the tide had gone out. We played in the tidal pools and clambered over rocks and into caves all afternoon until we realized the tide was coming in, and we had to get back to the beach. I can still feel my stomach tighten as I watched my father, the last one in from the incoming ocean, struggle to maintain his footing on the slippery rocks as he scrambled after us. It was the first time I ever thought of my father as vulnerable.

One summer, Daddy was not with us at this house, but the rest of us were all together, along with our surrogate sister, Audrey. In the late afternoon, Audrey and I and one of my sisters, maybe Diana, had driven into Fort Bragg to get some food for dinner. By the time we returned, it was dark. We drove into the yard, and there were no lights on in the house. Assuming that everyone had gone down to have a bonfire at the beach, we entered the house with our groceries. As I went into the living room, I stumbled over a piece of furniture, which was overturned on the floor. Someone turned on the light and sure enough, there was a chair upside down in front of me. Over on the sofa lay my mother, face down, with her hands tied behind her. My first thought was for myself, that I should run … but where? Out the front door? Out the back door, to a cliff and a long fall in the darkness? Then I heard voices—laughing—coming from the bedroom to my right. Pam and the other kids had convinced Mama to join in this so-called joke on us. I was furious and for years, Mama would apologize and say she didn't know what had gotten into her to agree to something like that.

The best vacation, however, was the summer we took a houseboat cruise up the San Joaquin River, from Stockton toward the Sacramento River. We had a boat that slept eight, but there were all nine of us kids, plus Audrey, my parents, and our dog. The first day out, Daddy learned how long it took for a boat to respond to turning the wheel and a few of us had scratches down the sides of our bodies from where we had come too close to the shore and been scraped by the blackberry bushes that grew along the banks. Every evening we would play cards and laugh at Mama as she weaved and bumped against the galley counter while her sleeping pill took hold. On that trip, we were awakened one morning by a river patrol, who told us we had to get the boat back into the river. During the night, the tide had gone out, and we were stranded twelve feet up onto the sand. All of us dug for what seemed like hours before we could rock and push the boat enough to move it back into the water. One day, Daddy took a turn up a little estuary and guided the boat in to the bank, but when he jumped off to anchor the boat, the rope slipped out of his hands, and the boat drifted back into the current. The area we were in looked like something from *The African Queen*, and when all of us had to jump overboard and kick to push the boat back in to shore, all I could think about was the potential for leeches to adhere to my feet and legs. Another day, we pulled up to a bank that was glittering gold in the late afternoon sun. It was pyrite in the sand, and it looked like a golden beach out of a fairy tale. We swam and washed our hair in the river and stood on top of the boat to see what the land looked like from inside, on the river. At the end of the week, Daddy's feet were swollen from sunburn because he had been sitting while trying to fish off the back of the boat. Priscilla got very, very sick suddenly and Daddy thought she might have appendicitis, so we returned a day early. I can still see Daddy carrying Prissy into the emergency room of the hospital, and the people treating him oddly, because his shoes were open and flapping around his feet. He had taken the laces out because he couldn't tie them over the swollen redness. No one at the hospital realized at first, of course, that he was a doctor himself.

There are many more details I could add, such as my best friend in fifth grade, who slept with her eyes wide open, or watching stampeding cows at her father's farm. Or all the dressing up at Susie Gulyas's house in the beautiful kimonos her parents had. Or the *amazing* cross-country trip we took when I was eighteen, the nine of us, and our dog crammed into a station wagon without air-conditioning, and piloted most of the way by Mama. But that last would make a small novella.

I was born with my eyes wide open and I often wonder if my recurring, falling-asleep vision of the people in white and the intrusive murmur of voices was an actual event, and if I am having an accurate memory. I don't dream it any more, but the images have always remained the same. If it is, as I believe, true, I find it ironic that I am surrounded by other children and that there is so much noise and that I wish they would all go away. Because, of course, I have been surrounded by other children, and they do make a lot of noise, but I am glad they have not gone away.

The 2ⁿᵈ Voice ～ Pamela Jane

Our parents had settled in the northern California community of Ukiah following our father's decision to practice medicine in this pristine town surrounded by majestic redwoods and nestled in the foothills of the Cascade Range. During the 1950s, the two points of interest geographically were the Masonite plant, which employed a majority of the townspeople, and the Ukiah International Latitude Observatory, one of only six in the United States. Although the world had not yet discovered the many redeeming qualities of wine, as we grew so did the advent of viticulture, the grapes at first harvested just for a few random wineries, but in the fifty years since, Mendocino County holds its own as one of the premier wine regions in the world.

I was the second-born. My voice was meant to reiterate the intent and purpose of my older sister. She was definitely in charge, and all of us knew it. It wasn't that Debbie was bossy or dictatorial, but she knew what she wanted and was confident in all she pursued. She was artistic, intelligent, extremely well read, and had an entrepreneurial streak that led her to open a shop of gift items in our neighbor's basement at the ripe old age of fifteen. Everything for sale was handmade—from painted rocks, to ties gloriously colored à la Peter Max, to personal stationery printed with whatever the purchaser desired. As the second born and as one who cherished order, I became the perfect sergeant at arms. When our mother gave Debbie a task—after all, she was the oldest and her position demanded that all directives should flow through her first—the appointed order was often one that didn't interest Debbie in the slightest. The thought of

33

sitting on the couch for fifteen minutes to give one of our siblings a baby bottle was the farthest thing from her mind. So it was reasoned that the job should be passed on to me. It was fortunate for Debbie that one of the things I enjoyed most was attending to the "little kids." I thought they were adorable in nearly every way. And there were a lot of them.

In twelve years our parents had nine children. We were born in 1949, 1950, 1952, 1954, 1955, 1956, 1957, 1959, and 1961; five girls, then the first boy, then another girl, and then the final two boys. It was a lot of work, but it was a lot of fun. The most fabulous part of being from a large family is the camaraderie; the sense that there is always someone around to indulge in games, listen to music, share clothes or stories, commiserate, and on occasion, just have a good fight.

Our family was different in many ways; one being that instead of living on a farm or ranch like the majority of families with multiple children, we lived in the center of town. We grew up on Oak Park Avenue and, like many American children in the '50s and '60s, we walked or rode bikes to school. We spent every day of the summer playing outside from the minute the breakfast dishes were washed until the street lights were lit in the evening, and if we chose to play sports, we found our own way to practice knowing it was unlikely that our parents would turn out on game day. We also knew everyone in our town by name—or at least, they knew us. We were special, and we knew it. No one ever spoke of it overtly, but we just knew. We were special for several reasons.

As the epitome of a country doctor, our father was adored in our community. Everyone in town knew him. He was their doctor and he delivered many of them, and then he delivered their children, and then their grandchildren. He never spoke to anyone without a warm smile and a gentle hand resting on their shoulder, and he made house calls, sometimes taking one or more of us along to keep him company when the visit was a good distance from our home. We kept him company on all sorts of outings, ranging from a visit to the roadside Black Cat Café, some fifty miles away, where a barfly had collapsed and fallen off a barstool in the middle of the day, to the

Red Cross blood drives at the county fairgrounds. Our photographs appeared in the local newspaper with an assortment of us hanging all over our dad for a snapshot with volunteers and donors during these special events.

Sometimes patients would show up on our doorstep unexpectedly. Those were the days when the easiest way to get in to see a doctor in case of an emergency was to stop by his home. One particular day our neighbor, Mr. Turney, appeared, looking desperately gray. He raised horses, and he looked like he raised horses. He was enormous, and he drove an enormous truck and rode an enormous stallion. Unfortunately for him, his enormous stallion was in a testy mood and instead of eating the carrots that were offered to him, he decided to eat Mr. Turney's face. Mr. Turney showed up in our front yard holding a towel on his cheek that was soaked in blood. As our father took the towel away to check the bite mark, we noticed a gaping hole the size of a fist where his cheek was missing.

Our small-town celebrity status was apparently reason enough for strangers to approach us as if they knew us. When we went out for a family dinner, we could expect an assortment of patients to grace our table. They would ask for our dad's advice or diagnosis about a bad knee or a ringing in the ear, and they always called him "Doc," which sounded to me more like a cartoon character than a real doctor. He had tremendous respect for everyone he met, never judging or treating one different from another, which is probably the single reason everyone loved him. And he had our mother to act as a buffer when needed. She was not prone to small talk and had little tolerance for idle chitchat. She would noticeably squirm when our dinner was interrupted, and she made it abundantly clear that it was time for the medical evaluation to be finished.

Life in our tiny town could be brutally boring if you let it. So our mother, morally obligated to providing us with a life rich with experiences, determined that the best way to accomplish this was to promote trips to San Francisco, a three-hour drive away. Traveling with eleven people in a station wagon was no small effort, and ensuring that our father could take the time to go with us added just one more element to the planning. In an attempt to make the best use of our father's time, we would leave home late at night, all packed into our car. At least four of us could lie down in the back and sleep. We would arrive at our hotel around midnight and be tucked in, three or four to a bed. I would lie awake listening to the strangest noises—garbage trucks, street cleaners, fire engines, and police sirens. The city lights and the flashing neon signs kept me on edge, anticipating the days ahead. The faint glow of yellow that permeated the city sky was a lifetime away from our pitch-black night back home. I knew after each adventure to San Francisco that my future would not be a life in a rural community. I loved nothing more than the noise and the excitement and the commotion.

It was decided that to make such adventures worthwhile, they should be centered on more than just the fun of the excursion, so shopping in Union Square for our seasonal wardrobe met the practical component of our venture. Our mother had developed a relationship with Mrs. Milan, a sales clerk (probably the first personal shopper) at I. Magnin's department store. Prior to the spree, Mom would touch base with Mrs. Milan and arrange the date that our family would be going to San Francisco, and Mrs. Milan would have ample time to set aside clothes on sale for our arrival. Our shopping excursions were simply abnormal—the appropriate attire was mandatory, no questions asked. The girls all wore dress coats with matching hats, black patent leather Mary Janes, and white gloves. The boys had suits, and if they were young enough, the suit pants could be shorts. But everything matched. Everything.

With a tone signaling immediate action, she would utter, "We're going to the city for two days, and the first day we'll be downtown shopping in Union Square. I don't want any arguments about what anyone will be wearing; you know where your clothes are, so bring your play clothes and underwear down for me to pack. I'll get all the good clothes together, with the coats and hats, just remember to bring me your dress shoes, as well. I don't want to hear anyone tell me on our way out of the hotel that they forgot to give me their good shoes or clean socks. Now go and get your things together. *Now!*"

It was absolutely fabulous, and it was orderly. We walked in three rows of three, hand in hand. The three oldest girls were in charge of two little kids each. Debbie was in charge of Paul and Valli, I was flanked by Prissy and Zack, and Di held onto Becky and David. Our mother walked behind us to ensure that no one fought or got lost. We were always met with stares as passersby gawked at the remarkable vision. We shopped all day, with only a short lunch break at the basement cafeteria in Macy's on Geary, and we always shared a meal. There was nothing more aggravating to our mother than to see food left over on the plate.

"Pam, why don't you see who wants to share that club sandwich with you?" And then she would add, "Your eyes are *always* too big for your stomach. You'll *never* be able to finish that sandwich by yourself. Besides, if you can't finish what's on your plate, you won't have room for *dessert*."

The word "dessert" was uttered in almost a singsong fashion, her voice rising in the middle, spoken so sweetly that she tempted us to resist. I don't think she ever made us share dessert.

We covered as much territory as we could in the first day, leaving the second day to visit the sites. Mom looked forward to the Japanese Tea Garden, but I was fascinated with the aquarium in Golden Gate Park. Stretching over the guardrail as far as we could without becoming the bait, we watched as hundreds of alligators writhed in the pit below. The smallest of the babies could trick us into believing they were adorable and harmless, but our instincts screamed that these prehistoric leftovers with teeth the size of nightmares rested only fifty feet below.

Instead of accompanying us in our shopping quest, Dad searched the city for record shops and audio equipment; his goal was to build a state-of-the-art sound studio in our living room. If our trip was in December, his pursuit included the purchase of a single, extraordinary family Christmas gift for all of us to enjoy. One year it was a "surrey with the fringe on top" that seated six and could be pedaled. Other years, he bought us a unicycle, a bicycle built for two, and a trampoline. The December dinner in the city was often a birthday celebration for our father, our youngest sister, Becky, and me. The Powell Street cable car delivered us to the top of Nob Hill where we commemorated our birthdays at the Tonga Room in the Fairmont Hotel. We devoured the flaming Baked Alaska as the band played on a rotating island under a rain forest. The evening would be perfect until an admiring older couple, trying to compliment our parents on such a well-behaved family, would unwittingly mention the lovely "grandchildren." It seemed unlikely that a bald man and his completely white-haired wife could actually be the mother and father of such a large and young brood.

It probably was the perfect match. When they married, Dad was thirty-six and Mom was thirty. They weren't quite young enough to have had as many children as they did, but they knew what they wanted—or at least Mom did. Our mother understood her role as matriarch, and she ruled with a vengeance. Her ability to adapt was remarkable. In her youth, she wanted for nothing, and in her married life, she was willing to sacrifice greatly to preserve her dream of family. Daily, she marched through the routine of managing babies to toddlers, youngsters to preteens, and finally teenagers to young adults. While our father dedicated his time to his patients, moments with our mother were filled to brimming. There was not one card game we couldn't play; there was not one board game missing from our den; and when life was boring, we made up our own games. Our jigsaw puzzles, always made of wood, were illuminated by at least three lamps, and upon completion, they were glued for framing. And we drank coffee—lots and lots of coffee. With so many puzzles and games to finish, coffee was mandatory for all ages. If we were too young to really enjoy the taste of coffee, we just added a few more spoonfuls of sugar, and then it was on into the night—nights that never ended before one in the morning.

The late nights also afforded us the opportunity to see our dad who usually made it home around eleven at night after evening rounds at the hospital. He never sat down to play cards with us but instead read the newspaper, cover to cover, in an adjoining room. He much preferred his drums and his record collection over the noisy crowd gathered around the kitchen table. Aside from Dad, we all played, no matter what the game, no matter what the age, no matter who was visiting. We all played.

Our clan was also distinctly different because we were entertainers. Our parents lived for their music. We were the only family who had a thirty-six by forty foot living room with fifteen-foot ceilings, a Steinway grand piano, and a complete drum set; and we were the only family who had jam sessions in our home. The furniture in the living room was moved to the periphery so visitors could dance while the dining room table was loaded with cold cuts and casseroles and cakes. The musicians brought with them an assortment of food and family and guests, and our mother welcomed them all. Barbara Curtis was on piano, Ben Foster on trumpet or trombone, Vince Angell played acoustic bass, and Duane Thompson and Rod Pacini were the reed men. Our father sat in the back, surrounded by his drums, his cymbals, and all the other accoutrements needed to make his craft magnificent. All the musicians in town loved when our father played because he had a terrific sense of rhythm, and everyone knows that without a good drummer, you can never have a great band. We learned that from our mother.

Mom never sang at our jam sessions. Her musical dreams began as a young girl with classical piano and voice and moved to jazz as a performer. Her voice was divine, but it came with a stomach bundled in nerves. As a professional singer, she would get so nervous that she routinely threw up before each performance, but she continued with the hope that someday her comfort level behind the microphone would allow her to move past the threshold. In her wild days she performed in jazz bands as the lead singer; her demo records reminded us of what could have been. We have all imitated her recorded voice, even our brother Paul, who does an almost perfect impersonation of her. All the girls in our family raided our mother's trunks of costumes when we reached the age of reason; we each have pieces that have withstood the test of time and can be worn today as if they just came off the rack.

Although her professional singing career came to a screeching halt once she married, she continued to find ways to pursue her music. When our mother felt melancholic, she sat down at the piano and played the most beautiful "Moonlight Sonata." Never a night went by that the babies in our home missed hearing "Brahms Lullaby," "Blanket Bay," "Somewhere over the Rainbow," or a lullaby from our mother's repertoire. Her voice was pure and clear and magnificent; it was perfect. As the choir director at St. Mary's Catholic Church, she was able to keep her voice alive. At the same time, she was beginning to realize that her children had musical talent as well.

In the beginning, it was the four oldest girls—Debbie, Pam, Di, and Prissy—who performed, and within a couple of more years, Valli, at age four, completed our group. Our mother selected the songs we were to sing, taught us the lyrics and music, and made our costumes. We sang at church and community events; we sang at the county fairgrounds; we sang and danced whenever and wherever requested. We sang at St. Patrick's Day celebrations in our kelly-green felt skirts, white Peter Pan blouses, and matching green ties, and we sang in a local production of *The King and I* in our saris. But the most memorable engagements were singing for the patients at the Mendocino State Mental Hospital. Our entire family would visit the patients, who seemed fascinated by the little kids. They wanted to touch us and hold us, and as we sang, they would rock back and forth and try to sing along with the music. I'm fairly certain that my siblings were as traumatized as I was by these encounters. However, our mother thought it was important to reach out to these people who had very little family in their lives, and we knew the patients enjoyed it immensely.

Our days of entertaining continued for several years, with our mother at the helm. I'm not sure if she tired of working with us or if we grew weary of her, but as our voices matured, our church organist became our accompanist. We also began voice lessons with a singing coach and her daughter. They both were professionally trained, and considering their girth, their training was probably operatic. All of us were encouraged to play musical instruments, in addition to piano and, of course, singing. From oldest to almost youngest, we played drums, clarinet, flute, clarinet, drums, trombone, saxophone, and trumpet. Paul, the baby, played nothing, but he loved to dress up and do impersonations, so maybe that was his act. We entered competitions at the Mendocino County Fair, and one year we actually came in third place. It was a particularly exciting moment, due to the fact that one of the judges was Johnny Mathis, who grew up in the Ukiah area. Our mother told us that the whole thing was rigged—we were obviously the best—and the only reason that the other two participants placed ahead of us was because they were students of Johnny Mathis's singing teacher. Maybe she was right, maybe she was dreaming, but the whole experience was surreal.

As we approached our teenage years, our willingness to be "on stage" faded and was replaced with a greater desire to be the typical adoring fans of other stage personalities, such as the Beatles. The last thing in the world that we wanted was to be publicly associated with each other as a singing item, and letting our mother choose the music titles was becoming a huge embarrassment. Thus ended the "Wilson Sisters."

We did, however, continue in music, at least throughout high school, either in the band, the choir, or theater and dance. We had to. There was no other outlet for our time since we did not have a television. Television in the '50s was visionary, in the '60s it was more widespread, and by the '70s, it was commonplace. But television in our home was not to be. Television was a boob tube; it would "wreck young minds, turning them to Jell-O" (something else that we never saw at our house). If our father wanted to watch something on TV, he was relegated to the fire station down the street where he would always go to watch the University of Nebraska football team, wearing red to show his true colors.

There probably wasn't a single issue more debated in our household, but it never grew to more than a debate. It did, however, prompt us to develop social skills and work skills outside of our special commune. If it wasn't for our craving *Mannix* or *Gunsmoke* or *The Man from UNCLE*, we wouldn't have had to leave our four walls. I began babysitting, just so I could watch television. My sister Debbie may have never met our next-door neighbor, Loelia, and started her gift shop, if not for her desire to find a spot to watch the Beatles on *The Ed Sullivan Show.* As luck would have it, we were allowed to rent a television for a short period of time; sadly, it was to watch the devastating series of events during the death and funeral of President Kennedy. Although no one was aware of it at the time, this event was singularly the gravest sign to portend things to come. Our simple lives in the 1950s were changed dramatically by the social transformation of the 1960s and 1970s.

When we first moved into the home where we spent most of our formative years I was seven and our next-door neighbor, Mr. Bell, was probably seventy-seven. I don't remember what possessed me to go to his home to visit at my young age; I only remember that I loved it. He had a wonderful home; the wood-paneled walls were dark brown and lent a sense of closeness and security. He spent his days at the task he loved most—tending to his lovely garden. Everything in his house was perfect. It was also old. He had lots of books and beautifully carved mahogany tables, the marble tops carefully draped with crisp white doilies. The table next to his front door was like this, with a little ceramic dish in blue and white on top, meant to hold his keys and an extra pair of glasses. Mr. Bell's house was exciting because he had a television. I had never seen one before, and when I would visit, he would turn on Disney cartoons and treat me to sliced pimento cheese and Ritz crackers. I could fold the slice of cheese into fours and have a quarter slice of cheese per cracker. None of my siblings ever joined me, and I felt very special, being able to share our time together, just Mr. Bell and me.

It wasn't more than a few years before he died while working in his garden. Someone, probably the postman, found him slumped over in one of his many flowerbeds on a glorious summer day, doing what he enjoyed most in his old age. When a new family moved in, I made sure to stop by. Upon seeing the little table at the entrance with the wire-rim eyeglasses, I took them, knowing that Mr. Bell would want me to have them.

We climbed trees to keep watch over the neighborhood. We could climb the pomegranate trees and see Mr. Bell's garden next door. Probably one of the reasons that Mom allowed me to visit him was she shared his aesthetic for anything that blossomed. Our front yard was a constant source of magnificent blooms, from the flowering crabapple, to the camellias, to the pyracanthea bushes lining the street; we were surrounded by beautiful flowers nearly year-round. His garden was maintained in the manner that he would have expected after the new owners moved in. Not only did they maintain the garden, but they remodeled his whole house—and added a new wing.

There were three kids total. The son was my age, one sister was a year younger, and the third was a girl, four years her junior. The whole family was exciting. After a previous marriage produced the first son and daughter, their mother divorced, and remarried, and she and her new husband had their last child together. We were raised Catholic, so this relationship was likely the first divorce and remarriage to which we had ever been exposed. My mother raised an eyebrow, as she tended to be on the intolerant side in matters such as this. My father most likely advised her to mind her own business. Our mother, no doubt, knew that her own children were absolutely perfect in every way and seemed confused when the young man next door enjoyed the chance to get under her skin. Every evening, when Mom would call outside for us to come in for dinner, the new neighbor boy would echo her calls. Not only was he about fourteen years old, he was probably astute enough to know just how crazy this made her. She would seethe at his disrespectful behavior—positively seethe.

"Every time I go outside to call the kids, there he is, imitating me. Jesus, Mary, and Joseph, he is the most obnoxious ..." Mom said through clenched teeth. "If he was standing in front of me right now, I swear I would give him a piece of this knife!" This time, the knife got way too close to her fingertips as she continued to cut up the carrots. "And the next time I see him hanging around the alley behind our house, I'm going to either call his mother directly or the police. You know, you girls need to close those curtains in your room when you're changing at night. Anybody can see right into that room when it's dark outside and your bedroom lights are on."

All pleadings to the mother next door were to no avail. Whether or not she saw fit to reprimand her son, she probably felt if my mother were a little more diplomatic, perhaps her son would actually treat her more respectfully. As if all of this was not enough, the neighbors were Democrats, and our parents were Republicans, and although we seldom discussed politics, we knew beyond a doubt where our parents stood. Although it added more fuel to the fire, it didn't prevent us from socializing with the kids next door.

They were absolutely great. The son was a bit obnoxious yet intriguing, and the older daughter was popular, fun, interesting, and had a great wardrobe. We became good friends—my just-younger sister, Diana, our neighbor, and I. I spent a lot of time next door and enjoyed every minute. I never knew it was possible, but every Christmas their tree was a different color. One year it was pink with silver and blue ornaments. Another year it was completely white with only red ornaments. Our neighbor's mother also taught me how to make the most fabulously delicious lemon meringue pie, which goes unrivaled to this day.

The years they occupied the house next door began to fill with contention. At one point during their stay on Oak Park Avenue, the mother next door found a friend. He was a contractor, with nice biceps squeezing from under his rolled-up red-plaid flannel shirt. His truck generally showed up about the time the father next door drove off to work. And then, one day, life became difficult. The mother wanted her guest to leave, and he pulled a gun. He held her at gunpoint, calling the father to come home from work and pass judgment on the case unfolding in his home. It all turned out well— at least as well as those awkward situations can turn out.

The incident faded in the months that followed, but our girlfriend next door had some questions and uncertainties about the past events. Luckily, Mom was there for guidance. Our mother's life as a practicing Catholic forced her into a moment of truth. She was obligated to help our girlfriend understand that her mother would be going to hell. "Hell. Anyone who commits a mortal sin is destined for hell." Mom remembered the nuns explicitly describing the sinful nature of such immoral behavior. I cannot imagine telling a child this, but diplomacy never ranked very high on her parenting list.

As with all normal human beings, our mother was not infallible. She was, however, when she wanted to be, the best advocate for her children. She had a certain spot for me, I think, because she was not quite sure how my future would turn out. Although I was the second born, I lined up fourth in height among my siblings. My physical development was an issue for her, and she took care that certain exceptions were made on my behalf. Telling the story of my first few months, she said, "You always slept; it was the strangest thing. I wanted to let you sleep, but after ten or twelve hours, I began to worry that you weren't eating enough."

By the time I entered elementary school, she insisted that each day after lunch, "Pam should not return to the classroom with the other kids. She simply can't make it through a full day. She needs to take a nap in the nurse's office, if only for fifteen or twenty minutes."

Her insistence mandated that the principal would follow her directions to a T. My academic development seemed not to suffer, but as I fell farther behind physically, her concern grew exponentially. Adults were enamored with me; my size tricked them into thinking I was incredibly precocious, as they assumed I was younger than my years. But as I got older, I began to fall behind socially—and emotionally as well. By the time I finished eighth grade, I was four foot six and was light-years away from adolescence. My mother began taking me to San Francisco to see an endocrinologist, with the expectation that growth hormones could be administered if I was seriously in danger of being too short. After some months and several tests, it was determined that even though I was an eighth-grader who was the size of a third-grader, my parents shouldn't be alarmed. First of all, I hadn't approached puberty; another important consideration was that neither of my grandmothers ever reached five feet tall. Obviously, there was only one solution: I was not ready for high school, so I would be held back.

"Don't worry, honey," my mother said. "No one will tease you and say you flunked eighth grade. You'll be fine; you need this time to grow." She comforted me, "You know, the best things come in small packages. And besides, challenges like this build character."

So the next year, when I changed schools and was enrolled in the public junior high school to repeat eighth grade, instead of my old classmates tormenting me about my size, my old classmates' younger siblings did. "Why are you wearing a bra?" they asked. "You don't even need one." Such was the torment I endured.

As it turned out, my mother was right. I quickly made friends, moving on to high school where all the teenagers in town were enrolled and where my previous classmates attended. By the time I began as a freshman, I had reached the grand height of five feet, with my shoe size an overwhelming three. And I had character. Nothing anyone said to me bothered me one bit. I had learned to ignore the teasing, and I knew I was special. My mother had convinced me and for some unknown reason, I believed that everyone else knew it too. I also learned that the most important thing I could do was to treat everyone nicely—and it paid off. From then on, kids may have been mean to each other, but they were never mean to me.

Our mother struggled to ensure that her children were good Catholics and well educated—of course, in Catholic schools. I'm sure Mom dreamed that the money would just come rolling in, either from our dad's growing medical practice or from her father who, seemingly, had nothing else to do with his money. When the time came for us to start high school though, Catholic boarding school was out of the question, and so we ended up in the local public high school. I don't think any of us ever regarded this as a hindrance to a good education, but our mother struggled to come to terms with the fact that a Sacred Heart education was to be her own personal experience—not ours.

The one facet of our parents' marriage that was controversial was their religious differences. Our father lived the Ten Commandments every day, but it just wasn't quite enough to appease our mother, who worried that he would be lost in the afterlife. Although he professed Methodist as his religion, he never attended his church. He would, however, on special occasions, join us for Mass to attend sacramental events and always on Christmas and Easter. He never knelt on the kneeler, as if that was an admission that he was moving toward acceptance of our faith. That would have been just the slide down the slippery slope that would open the door for our mother's pleadings to convert. As a Catholic, our mother would never allow us to set foot inside a non-Catholic establishment. It would have been heresy; we were taught that such sacrilege was simply not acceptable.

As choir director at St. Mary's, Mom needed to be at the church a little bit early every Sunday. We were always rushed, scrambling to get ready on time. When the horn honking began, we would tear out to the car to see our mother fixing her lipstick while several children jumped from front to middle to rear seats, looking for the perfect spot. Upon entering St. Mary's, the older children grabbed the hand of a smaller child or two, but if they tried to wiggle away, it was their ear that led them to the front pew. Mom's whispers faded as we made our way down the aisle, "You girls remember: I want you to sit close so the little kids can see what the priest is doing on the altar. The usher knows to take you right to the front pew. Don't embarrass me; just go with him. I'll have my mirror next to me as I'm directing, so I'll be watching. Now go sit down. I'll see you after Mass."

When Mass was over, at least one or two of the little kids had tiny purple pinch marks on their inner arms where the big kids had to instill some discipline over the course of the hour. It was expected that our mother would have noticed a thing or two on her own from her eagle-eye perch a balcony away. During Lent, it was customary for us to attend Mass daily at the little chapel a block from our house. The problem was that Mass was at six thirty in the morning. Our mother would dutifully wake us all at six o'clock, and there was absolutely no excuse to miss it. We have built, each and every one of us, such a surplus of plenary indulgences that we will all be in heaven before our last breath cools.

Our mother used her silent Mass moments for prayer, and her devotion mimicked her father's; her faith was consummate. In prayer, our mother's choice was novenas. There were several options depending entirely on the request. If our mother found out that someone was in a car crash and in critical condition, the appropriate novena would be one as short as possible, so as to acquire that benefit immediately. If our mother was praying for one of her children to find the perfect mate or trying to move the Lord to get rid of the obnoxious boy next door, the novena could go on for several months. It took an incredible amount of discipline to find the time to say the novena, and then it took an incredible amount of discipline to remember to say it each night, or three times a day, or whatever the specific formula was. She learned this discipline from watching her father pray on his knees twice daily, and she learned from the nuns at the Sacred Heart boarding school and college she attended. Her devotion to both the Sacred Heart and the Blessed Mary gave her the strength she needed to manage her life. Religion was her rock; remaining constant, it was with her at all times. No matter what the incident, she always seemed able to draw from her soul the fortitude to pull through.

Our father was a product of the Great Depression and felt obligated to work constantly to provide for us. As was customary, he spent little time in the management of our lives, but we were guided by his example. It was rare to encounter people who, once they realized who we were, didn't speak accolades on his behalf. In hindsight, it might have been equally important for him to devote more of his time in helping to discipline us, but Mom carried on in his stead. After all, having a large family was a gift from God. Josephine considered it her duty and Lee seemed pleased, if not fascinated and sometimes overwhelmed by his children.

The miracle of birth was not lost on us, as we were always about to have a baby or just had a baby. Mom, in her matter-of-fact style, determined that her approach to teaching the subject of sex and reproduction with her children should be direct and transparent.

Our mother began our sex education at home by explaining conception through the example set by our pets. We always had several cats, and it was the cats that guided us through the process from conception to birth. We heard the mating screams in the middle of the night and watched as our mother cats expelled those writhing, peeping, wet creatures. Explaining procreation through the guise of our cats seemed like a natural way to lead into human reproduction. "Sex is wonderful," she told us in all seriousness. "But sex is determined by God to be between a husband and a wife. So once you're married ..."

Only a re-creation of past events could ever determine if this was the right approach to present to a house full of teenage girls, but it was the way our mother felt comfortable in allowing us to recognize the beauty of our changing bodies and enjoy, within boundaries, our sexuality. As the oldest and not knowing she could defy our parents, Debbie took all statements to heart, and since I was incredibly uncomfortable with my body, I was never going to even undress in front of a man. So the sexual revolution that exploded on the scene in the mid-1960s was left as the responsibility of the younger guard. I lived vicariously through the stories and the escapades and the conquests, and I was intrigued. Girls who were sexually active teenagers before 1965 seemed very brave, or else they allowed their boyfriends to dictate the degree of involvement. Those who were sexually active after 1965 were setting the pace for a new world order. And every baby boomer stepped up to do her American duty. With the development of the birth control pill and the onset of the sexual revolution, girls finally became masters of their own bodies, in control of their futures. I felt wedged in the middle.

At thirteen, I was caught, inadvertently, in a neighbor's yard with some neighborhood children. Their visiting grandfather, sitting outside to keep watch over his grandchildren, saw fit to call me to sit next to him, and instead of paying attention to them, he decided to fondle me as he sat with me trapped at his side. It happened only once, but once was all it took to keep me fully clothed and outside the sexual realm for some years after. Sexual mistreatment and abuse, regardless of the degree, has a way of lingering in memory's grip, and the blanket of fear permeated my behavior. My life continued without ever notifying my parents or siblings of what had happened, but my level of caution thereafter was heightened and dictated my personal space. I was okay with all of this too because it freed me to maintain my borders, and I never lost control.

It was also when I was thirteen that our growing family necessitated a larger home. It didn't take a feasibility study to determine that three boys in one bedroom and six girls in the other was a recipe for chaos. Our modest three-bedroom home had just undergone a facelift that added bedrooms, baths, a laundry room, and the space that we all loved—our new family room. Our dad had, with no coaching, brought home four train trestle beams for the ceiling and a fifth was to be mounted as the mantel for the fireplace. For weeks, our father worked on his contribution to the construction effort. The beams were charred to black with a blowtorch and then painstakingly sanded with a wire brush until the slate patina shone like pulled taffy.

Our new home was picture-perfect, except for the backyard. Ukiah's first swimming pool had been built in our yard in 1934, and for thirty years, it remained the same. Instead of renovating the pool and surrounding area, our parents chose to set aside that project for a later date. The result was a cement hole, complete with tires, algae, frogs, footballs, and whatever else may have been tossed over the fence into the abyss below. It was a great way to develop our large motor skills as well, suspending a foot-wide plank across the middle and walking, running, skipping, and bike riding to the other edge.

Josephine always spoke of wanting a family of twelve children and considered it her duty as a practicing Catholic to have as many children as the Lord gave her, although later in life, she would admit to being overwhelmed by the constant obligations in rearing so many children. Her desire that our father take a more active role was never realized; his first obligation was to his patients. "Doctors are like priests; they should never marry," our mother confided. "Their job will always come first."

Our dad, setting aside his less-than-hands-on approach to his children, had a way of making us feel that we were all important. No one had a bear hug like Dad. Expected each time he came home, he would just grab us up in his arms and squeeze us so tight. There were no heart-to-heart sessions, but I think we were okay with it. I probably would have liked it if he had discussed his views on the world or current affairs or hinted at his own life growing up from time to time, but his nature was quiet, save for a hysterically funny joke or witty aside.

As firstborn and well read, Debbie preferred her role as mentor and intellectual, imparting knowledge to any of us who would listen. She enjoyed the discussion, but shied away if it turned to an argument, unless the argument involved her position as head of our clan. Debbie, as protector, was my shield against the bullies on the playground. Nobody could wield verbal assault and stand ground against injustice like she could, the injustice being a few bigger classmates pushing me around. She was obliged to protect our family name with a few quick barbs like "How *dare* you!" and "You should be ashamed of yourself, picking on someone smaller than you. Try that again, and I won't be so nice the next time!"

Only once did she have to physically fight for my honor. It landed her in the principal's office, but I secretly think she was proud—and maybe a little surprised that she was willing to go, literally, to the mat for me.

Unlike me, she was not a fighter but instead preferred a quiet setting to dream. As roommates during our teen years, Debbie and I maintained a more symbiotic relationship, I was viewed as the younger sister, and she was always the teacher. In addition to the aesthetic aspects of life, she coached me about makeup and fashion, but most important, she taught me to dance. I mean, she really taught me to dance. To this day, I am regarded as likely the best dancer on the planet.

Diana was the third-born. Bright, fun, and compassionate, she opened her arms to everyone without question, conveying warmth, and closeness, and loyalty. During my childhood, I was more emotionally connected to Di. In elementary school, when my list of close friends was zero, Di included me without hesitation. I don't know if I was really that much fun or if she just felt sorry for me, but there was never any question that I would always be included. We ran away from home together once and took only a loaf of bread and a carton of orange juice, expecting this would suffice on our escape to San Francisco. We also took Prissy with us.

Priscilla was the fourth, and she was beautiful, with her huge blue eyes and blonde hair. We teased her that she was way too pretty and probably not our real sister. She was born on April Fool's Day, and had inherited Dad's droll sense of humor. She was quiet, but you could see in her eyes that she missed nothing.

Valerie was girl number five, another redhead. She smiled— always. The twinkle in her eyes could coax anyone into thinking that she was smiling constantly. She was adorable, with tons of energy, and she was small like me. Finally, I was bigger than one of my siblings.

David was a "God damned good-lookin' baby," as one of our neighbors pointed out at his premier. He was a brunette and being the first boy, we all fawned over him, but he never seemed spoiled or bratty. Divining so much attention from a bunch of girls was a mixed blessing. Instead of a focus on sports, he was encouraged to draw and play games; to use his brain instead of his brawn. It probably was not the best way to prepare him for his role as "boy." Unfortunately, we were part of the learning curve too.

Rebecca was number seven and had David's coloring but with a more serious and guarded demeanor. She was probably the most determined of all our siblings, graduating from high school in three years. "Why would anyone want to waste another minute in high school if they didn't have to?" She left Ukiah to work a summer job in Michigan before beginning her college career at Loyola University, but only lasted a year before the bitter cold in Chicago got the best of her. At the first sign of spring, she packed her belongings and dragged her bike to Carbondale, Illinois, where the Bicentennial Trail began. With only a brave notion that she could manage it alone, she hopped on her bicycle and rode all the way home to California.

Our parents named our eighth sibling Zachary, because he was intended to be the end of the line. He managed his youth with a charming smile and true grit, standing up to whatever got in his way and protecting all those he loved dearly. Probably the most emotional of all of us, he will cry because he can't help it. He should have been the last child because he would have loved all the extra attention, but as his luck would have it, he was to be just the second to last.

As the ninth and final child, Paul, possibly a surprise or an afterthought, was named Paul Shannon, or PS—for postscript. He turned out to be anything but an afterthought. He was sweet and adorable from the day he was born and nothing seemed to bother him. His platinum-colored hair looked like he had a halo resting atop his head—our own little angel. Appeasing us all by doing whatever we asked, he was so hysterically funny that no matter what he did, we laughed uncontrollably. His early days of being forced to perform became second nature, and he developed a love for stand-up comedy.

When Paul was ready for grammar school, Josephine needed an escape. Raising kids was fun, but this level of fun was becoming exhausting. The solution was that our mother would work days at our father's office and someone would fill her spot at home, cleaning while everyone was at school and then babysitting and cooking after. Our mother recognized the value of order in our surroundings but abhorred the routine of housekeeping. She also abhorred the idea that any of her children would be of such idle mind that they would want to be bothered cleaning.

When our grandmother once complimented me on how neat and tidy my room was, "Pam, what a nice job you did. Jo, Pam's quite the little housekeeper." My mother snapped, "*None* of my children are good housekeepers!" Since our mother took issue with housekeeping, finding someone to take her place in this role was the only way out.

There was one unsuspecting young woman who had graduated from high school and was looking for a job. Margie started running our household at eighteen and stayed on for about twenty years. For some strange reason, she never married, probably because she loved managing our crazy lives so much. Stepping into this job as surrogate mother to mostly adolescent and prepubescent kids presented a number of challenges, yet she fit into our family beautifully, instinctively knowing when to stay behind the scenes and when to take matters into her own hands. I think each of us loved her equally; she never took sides or treated one differently than another. She was the embodiment of her Pomo tribe, her gentle nature the antithesis of our rowdy Irish American upbringing. The slurred intonation and quiet inflection as she spoke could be easily drowned out by nine or so children running up and down the stairs, slamming doors, and out-talking each other at every turn. Once a week, Josephine mapped out the schedule for the five oldest girls, and the duties rotated between making dinner, cleaning up afterwards, washing the laundry, folding the laundry, dusting, and garbage. The scheduling was the easy part; it was up to Margie to see that we fulfilled our weekly obligations. When finally presented with the inequities of forcing the oldest five into doing most of the chores, and all girls at that, the schedule quietly slipped into oblivion.

High school was liberating for me. I enjoyed academics almost as much as my social life, and I began to develop friendships for the first time—friends who were completely unrelated to my family. A few remained close from my second trip through eighth grade, some were musicians and actors in the band and musicals, and those closest to me were the girls I spent hours with after school as cheerleader and song leader. My world grew exponentially, and I loved it. I spent all my extracurricular time during my junior and senior years on the songleading and cheerleading squads, and although now considered a rather dubious distinction, it was, without a doubt, the most memorable part of my teenage years. Hours outside of the classroom were dedicated to practice, pep rallies, games, radio spots announcing the upcoming sports events, and all things associated with promoting school spirit. The more activities I could cram into a day, the more I liked it. I attended anything and everything relating to high school, and my dates for dances were always friends.

It was also about this time that I decided to let down my guard and start dating. My sweet and gorgeous boyfriend at sixteen was the first relationship I had, and it was what every parent would want for their teenager—not too serious, but a good start. At times, my mother discouraged particular associations; some friends didn't display any intellectual curiosity, which was the kiss of death in our house. Our father's standard was more closely guided by who held down a job, so if they missed out on the IQ factor, some could still pass the litmus test. More important, as siblings we influenced each other, and our closest friends were traded among us.

Audrey didn't even enter at the closest-friend level. She simply went straight to sister status. From the time she was five and in kindergarten with Di, Audrey was "in" to the fullest extent allowed by law or by our parents. I loved going to her house; it was interesting, crammed with fabulously overstuffed chairs, and the creek running through the backyard was filled with pollywogs and lizards. For some reason, though, it wasn't as fun as being in our house. The level of commotion in our home that permeated every floorboard to every ceiling beam was immense. Loelia, an only child and Debbie's best friend, lived for eight a.m., when she could drop by on a school morning and experience the chaos firsthand. It was noisy and hectic, and somehow, we all managed to get to school on time, with the necessary books and homework and a bite or two of breakfast for sustenance.

Friends also accompanied us on our summer trips. It was customary to spend one week each summer on a vacation that included our father. He liked the Mendocino coast, partly because it was the most beautiful scenery in the world and partly because he had friends who volunteered to let our entire family spend the week in their cabin. Summer days on the northern California coast were overcast, allowing our fair complexions to bask somewhat worry-free from sunburns and blisters. Our cabin hung at the precipice of the most magnificent and dramatic rocky cliffs at the ocean's edge. Morning and evening, we explored the tide pools that brimmed with a collection of crustaceans, sea anemones, and urchins; the crabs homesteaded an assortment of vacated shells, sometimes oversized, sometimes so tight that the crabs looked like their claws might pop off at any moment. If we were lucky, we could find starfish and abalone shells and sand dollars, which we collected to take home, hoping they wouldn't be crushed in travel. Some of these vacations were more memorable than others; one stands out in particular because what was intended to be a prank was misinterpreted and remains the second most significant vacation of our youth.

We totaled thirteen on this particular vacation. The cabin slept all of us comfortably. The second day we were there, one group of teenagers from our crowd needed supplies, possibly snacks or cigarettes, and left on their mission. Those staying behind became restless and determined that a practical joke was in order; they would make it look like there had been a break-in while those unsuspecting were gone. And so the planning ensued. It may have been the influence of Alfred Hitchcock or simply our twisted teenage minds, but with the support of our mother, our plan was more realistic than anticipated. We knocked over furniture, spilled food, and tied up a couple of kids as well as our mother, and waited for the unsuspecting carload to return.

As they approached, we could hear them talking and laughing, but as they drew closer, we could hear their voices fade to gasps as they entered and saw the unthinkable. It took several minutes to calm them down and convince them that it was a joke, that we had done it all by ourselves to trick them and that everyone was safe and no one harmed. We instigators, never thinking that it could possibly have shocked them as it did, have endured stories relating the sadistic nature of our prank for years.

Our trips to Mendocino through the redwoods continued for many years, until our father decided to rent a houseboat for a two-week vacation on the Sacramento River Delta. The greatest challenge was that none of us knew the first thing about boats. Each night, when the sun went down, our inability to maintain the function of the generator meant that our day was done. It also should have been obvious that we were in the sun constantly for twelve hours, and bare heads and bare feet were game for the fair-complexioned. In addition to the blistering sunburns, we were grounded on sand bars no less than a half a dozen times during this excursion. Regardless of the setbacks, it was a great experience, remarkable for the blinding sunrises against the wakening sky and the brazen orange sunsets as the sun fought against falling into the earth for the night.

Our most memorable vacation was the brainstorm of our mother, who determined that her children needed to see the two most important things in the world: our extended family and the United States. As planned, a small U-Haul trailer was attached to the rear of our station wagon to accommodate all our belongings as we toured the United States for six weeks during the summer of 1967. For the first two weeks, our father accompanied us, which meant that our station wagon housed eleven people and our dog, Coco, the poodle, whose role was headrest for the driver. Our travels routed us across Interstate 80 through Denver, Omaha, Chicago, Detroit, the New York City area, down the Eastern Seaboard to Miami Beach, and then continuing back west along the south, around the Gulf of Mexico, through Texas, New Mexico, Arizona, to Los Angeles, and back up the coast of California. Our station wagon could be spotted at any time during this journey with legs and more legs hanging out of the windows.

We napped, read, played games, and had to agree on the radio station, and our mother liked none of the music we enjoyed. We stayed in motels, sleeping two to three to a bed, and every morning, after a quick breakfast from the assortment of cereals packed, we prepared sandwiches so that our midday stop was time-efficient. We visited aunts and uncles and cousins, some we had never met before, as we embarked on a whole new world. We toured major cities and saw the Great Salt Lake and the Rocky Mountains, the Great Lakes and Niagara Falls. We were awed by the skyscrapers and lulled to sleep by the Great Plains. In Chicago, we were introduced as an interesting storyline on the *Don McNeil Breakfast Club* at the Allerton Hotel's Tip Top Tap. New York's Ellis Island greeted us as we lazed on the ferry, and we listened to our mother's college classmates tell stories of life in Manhattan. Our trip included the nation's Capitol and the White House, and we couldn't make it through Washington, DC, without a visit to the Smithsonian and Arlington National Cemetery.

As we drove south through Savannah and Charleston, the trees changed, and the mysterious moss meant we were in a different place. We recognized the magnolias and the dogwood, but the Florida palm trees we knew only from pictures. The dead-calm water of the Atlantic improved a little when we reached the Gulf side of Florida, and the beauty of Biloxi, with its magnificent mansions, would stand only until the hurricane a few years later. We all considered our time in Texas as purgatory, with nothing to break the hours of monotony except the oil derricks against the cloudless sky. The Southwest faded into more travel days, until we miraculously came upon our very own California, with its mountains and valleys and rivers and oceans and agriculture as far as the eye could see. We unanimously chose our very own home state as the pinnacle of beauty. Although we had a vague sense of how remarkable our vacation had been, we returned home eager to see our friends.

Life began to speed up, with so many events happening to so many people in our household. Try as they might, our parents' firm control over our activities and acquaintances began to erode as we were learning to challenge the purpose of those authority figures around us. Debbie managed to graduate with great grades and without making too many waves before her next journey into the world of higher education.

As my consciousness opened to the realization that I would soon be moving on to college, my fear and anxiety of the unknown began to overwhelm me. San Francisco College for Women was close enough to visit my family on a whim, and since Debbie was already a student there, my decision was easy. The ten nervous pounds I had lost the week before I left on my journey was regained within the first quarter as I began to adjust to my new home.

My dorm mates became my surrogate family, and this quaint little institution situated on the top of a hill in the center of San Francisco was our playground. As I became less homesick, trips to Ukiah were reserved for holidays, and I was always accompanied by a few classmates who could not visit their own homes half a continent away. They would meet, for the first time, my dad at his drums, surrounded by the other musicians on their instruments, and my mother welcomed everyone with her big, beautiful smile. There was nothing I enjoyed more than bringing new and unsuspecting visitors to our house and watching their expressions as they crossed the threshold into my world.

THE 3RD VOICE ~ DIANA MARIE

Those who are the hardest to love are the ones who need love the most.
—Jo Wilson

EVERY FAMILY NEEDS ITS NEUROTIC CHILD. I GRACEFULLY, YET unwittingly, slipped into that role in 1952 in San Francisco's St. Mary's Hospital, where my dad was an intern. I was named Diana, like the powerful mythological goddess of the moon, the hunt, and, as luck would have it, fertility. My middle name, Marie, is in honor of the mother of Jesus. Now if that is not a heavy enough load for a child, I was born after Debbie, the overachiever, and Pam, the socialite and darling of the family.

When we moved to Eureka shortly after my birth, I took my heart with me but have always maintained a fondness for the city by the bay and was to return numerous times during my adolescence. From Eureka, I have a foggy notion of steps rising to a lawn held by a rock wall, a chocolate cake with candles, and two babies—one a blonde angel (Prissy); the other so tiny, with the brightest, sparkling eyes (Valli).

Life in general—and my fears, phobias, and obsessive habits in particular—become more vivid: in 1956 we settled once again into a new home, this time in Talmage, on the outskirts of Ukiah. It was a great spot for children. We were located right near the Russian River with a large alfalfa field behind the house where I had many happy times constructing forts and studying insects and reptiles. We acquired a few cats, leading to many more kittens, and I grew attached to them all. This proximity to nature provided me my earliest awareness of death. One cat left her litter behind to search for food in the field but was cut down by a tractor mowing the alfalfa. I can still picture her dragging herself across our yard a few days later on her bloody stumps, attempting to return to her kittens. My dad said she could not survive so he euthanized her.

I think another cat also met its demise by my father's hand. This one was a stray who came at night to steal our cats' food, to mate, and to fight. It seems so unlike my dad, but I watched him sitting in wait with a shotgun. I am not sure whether he finally succeeded in ridding us of this bothersome tom, but I know it seemed wrong to kill the cat for just doing what was in its nature to do.

The most traumatic cat death for me, though, was when my favorite was hit by a car. While my dad buried my pet, I listened for what seemed like hours, tears pouring down my face, as my phonograph played over and over, "Zip-a-dee-doo-dah, zip-a-dee-ay! My, oh my, what a wonderful day."

Dead cats were not the only creatures I wept over. I ached for the dead fish along the banks of the river, the withered snake and frog bodies that lay on the dry, cracked earth in the middle of summer, and even the tiny black ants swept off the window sill and down the kitchen drain. I stared silently, in morbid fascination and horror, as my mom sprayed a pesticide on a particularly valiant spider that had run to hide behind a door. Reminiscent of *The Incredible Shrinking Man*, that spider appeared to grow exponentially as he refused to die. He kept fighting and fighting for his life as Mom sprayed and sprayed until, finally, his legs buckled and he surrendered to the inevitable. His courage loomed large in my mind's eye, especially as I had been unable to find my voice in time to save him.

I'm not sure when my fear of water began—possibly when I was caught in the undertow of the Pacific Ocean at about three years old. More likely, the onset was in the winter of 1956 when heavy rainfall caused the Russian River waters to rise so dramatically that my family had to be transported by boat from the house. It was exciting but terrifying as well. From that day on, I had regular nightmares involving water and drowning. One was a reenactment of an event

I witnessed at Lake Mendocino, where the locks were opened and water went rushing into the reservoir. I accidentally dropped a tennis shoe and red sock into the churning water and was overwhelmed by the power of the water as it swallowed the shoe whole and only allowed me a brief glimpse or two of red before the sock as well disappeared forever. In my dreams of this event, it was most often I who followed the clothing into the water to be lost forever, but occasionally, one of my siblings took my place.

Another recurring dream involved the Russian River. I see my mother driving our Ford station wagon across the bridge over the river. Debbie is in her plaid school uniform, and I am in the backseat. As we reach the middle of the span, the bridge transforms into the Golden Gate Bridge, and we're crossing the San Francisco Bay. Suddenly it converts once again, this time into a drawbridge. My mother is unable to stop the car and over the edge we plummet into the shark-infested waters below.

After only a year, we pulled up stakes again and moved into Ukiah to a big house on a beautiful street. My awareness of our social status developed through both my father's elevated position as a small-town doctor and our involvement in St. Mary's school and church. Diligently cultivating her first-rate garden of children, Mom routinely reminded us of the need to behave in a manner appropriate to our position as children of the much-loved and admired saint, Dr. Wilson, as any misbehavior would reflect poorly on him. My self-consciousness blossomed as I began to notice the attention I received outside of home. Because of my red hair and freckles, I was easily identified and frequently had strangers inquire if I was one of the Wilson girls. I was particularly intimidated by adults and could barely put two words together when addressed directly. I proceeded to develop many nervous habits.

What am I, an idiot? – Don't answer that. As I entered elementary school at St. Mary's, my mother tried to address some of my more obvious issues, like thumb-sucking, hair-pulling, and nail-biting. She tried Tabasco sauce on my thumb and when that was ineffective, she sent me to the dentist to get a retainer with teeth to prevent me from putting my thumb in my mouth. I adjusted to the "rake" by hanging my mouth open so my thumb would still fit inside. I hooked my index finger over my nose and continued to use thumb-sucking for comfort and stress release.

Mom had more luck with my hair-pulling. Since I had large bald spots on my head, she managed a Ted Koppel-style pullover with adjacent hairs and held them in place with bobby pins. The utter humiliation of having to attend school looking so pathetic seems to have broken me of that habit. Or perhaps it was transferred to my poor fingernails. I bit them—nails, cuticles, surrounding tissue— until they bled and throbbed. It was not a pretty picture, but one, like thumb-sucking, to which I clung like a security blanket.

Luckily, I was able to avoid thumb-sucking at school, and for the most part, I loved attending. I often slept in my uniform so I could leave for school early on my bike. I liked the routine, the pens, the pencils, and clean sheets of paper. One of my favorite scents was that of a new book, especially a textbook—even an old textbook. It seems I always knew how to read and write. I must have learned at home from my mother and maybe my older sisters, because I was already able when I began St. Mary's. Academics came easily to me, and I received the Academic Excellence award when I graduated eight years later.

Ask a stupid question, and you'll get a stupid answer. Unfortunately, I still lacked self-confidence. My success always felt like a fluke—that I was going to be found out as a fraud, that I wasn't really smart enough, that I was undeserving. My fears led me to dread being singled out for attention. If a teacher addressed a question to the entire class, even when I knew the answer, I would not volunteer it. If I was singled out to answer, my heart rate would accelerate, the question would ricochet about in my head, and the only response available to me was a barely audible, "I don't know."

On paper, it was a different story. Mom liked to say, "You can always do better," and I took it to heart. I practiced printing and cursive writing. I was such a perfectionist that if I needed to erase something I had written, even nearing the end of the page, I would throw out the entire sheet of paper and begin again with a clean, unsullied piece. I even tortured myself for hours because my handwriting wasn't right: the stem of the "g" the exact length, the "t" crossed in the proper place or the dot of the "i" not its precise distance from the stem.

Writing became exhausting, but I did find something that was clear-cut and controllable. Early in my academic career, I began my lifelong infatuation with numbers. I began to count everything I came across—tiles in the floor, leaves on a plant, steps I took to cross a room. I favored odd numbers especially and tried to do everything in threes.

My love of numbers was a source of joy for me. I could always be assured an easy A in math classes, and I especially relished solving equations. During my high school years, when I was into drug enhancements, I would swallow some speed, grab my textbook, and complete page after page of problems. One year I received my math book in September and read it cover-to-cover—including completing every exercise and test—before November. My head was full of numbers. I thought about them as I fell asleep at night and worked math problems in my dreams. I even had a favorite formula—the quadratic formula, $x = \frac{-b \pm \sqrt{b^2 - 4ac}}{2a}$, (hmm, how odd that it is so even).

My dad liked math also. Mom told me that he took calculus just for fun. She said I was like my dad in many ways. She even called me a saint when I was still young, which made me extremely uncomfortable, because I knew better. She also thought I should be a doctor like my dad, and so did I. But in fifth grade, when we had to present an oral report on our career choices, I floundered. A chubby classmate told the class that she wanted to be a stewardess when she grew up, and all the boys burst out laughing and made rude comments about her weight. I took that as a warning and when my turn came, rather than face their mockery, I reported that my intention was to become a nurse.

With all my anxieties and insecurities, I found friends who loved me anyway. I met Audrey in first grade at St. Mary's School. Perhaps we met earlier at the Talmage house—I was the one wearing the worn overalls and the striped beanie with the propeller on top who peeked out from behind my mother. Either way, not only did we become fast friends in school, but she became part of my family. Always clever and loyal, Audrey's verbal acuity complemented my taciturn nature. Though both of us would get nervous in social situations, I could always count on Audrey to inadvertently cover for my shyness. As I became more and more tongue-tied, she reacted to the contrary, relating increasingly elaborate anecdotes to our attentive audience, while I oohed, aahed, and laughed at the appropriate times and threw in the occasional one-liner. We had numerous adventures over the years, and she was one of my greatest assets, enabling me to substitute her verbal curtain for my mother's skirts.

Julie was another "friends4ever." She was bright and pretty and loved to laugh. Though other friends came and went, Audrey, Julie, and I remained a solid threesome throughout our school years. The fact that we were all musicians kept us connected to each other as well as set apart from others.

You girls have a god-given talent, and it is a sin not to use it. I suppose my musical life began in the womb, since my mom and dad were both musicians. I cannot think of a moment when music was not being played on the radio, the record player, or a musical instrument, or when someone was not singing, humming, or whistling—even at the dinner table if willing to get bonked on the head with a butter knife handle. Mom said at five or six months old, I sat and rocked in time with the musical beat. I loved when Daddy came home at night after making his hospital rounds, put on a recording, and then sat down at his drums and played until the wee hours, while I, upstairs in bed, fell asleep to his jazz lullabies. And I was awestruck when Mom sat at the piano, her fingers flying over the keys, as I soaked up the sounds of one of her amazing classical pieces. I always dreamed of playing piano that fluently.

I began my keyboard studies at seven years old. I loved the

piano—it was such a passionate instrument—but in my third year of lessons, I had to study with a German teacher who had a strong accent and a style of teaching that was unfamiliar to me. He was oblivious to my sensitive nature and would knock my hands off the keys when I did not lift them high enough. I also had to confront another of my phobias as I rode my bike to his house for my weekly lesson past the home of a dog with a zeal for chasing bicycles. I rode as swiftly as possible, sweat pouring and heart racing, with the dog barking, growling, and nipping at my feet. By the time I reached my teacher's house, I was in the midst of a full-fledged panic, not at all conducive to a productive lesson. My dreams during this time were traumatic: The Nazis came to our home in the middle of a stormy night. They came inside, corralled us all, and led us to their waiting garbage truck, where we were to be compacted. I was the last in line and trying desperately to escape, but I was wearing roller skates that were stuck in a mud puddle in front of our walkway. The wheels spun round and round in place while I watched my family annihilated one by one as they were tossed into the back of the truck. I awoke with a pounding heart, only to relive the experience the next night and the next and the next. I reluctantly told my mom I no longer wanted to play piano but omitted the part about the dog and the Nazis.

In addition to playing piano, Mom was a professional singer. When I was about eight, she put together a vocal quintet consisting of Debbie, Pam, Prissy, Valli, and me. Mom directed us as we sang Christmas carols, popular tunes, and classical pieces. We performed for school functions, social functions, and at rest homes. One Christmas we were invited to sing on a radio program, and another time we performed for the Mendocino County Fair talent show (we lost to Holly Near flying across the stage as Peter Pan). When I was in high school we took private voice lessons from Esther Munroe whose adult daughter was an opera singer. Mrs. Munroe and her daughter were large women whose huge operatic voices contrasted drastically with the scene upon entering their home—their miniscule Chihuahuas yipping and snapping at our heels. I think Mom wanted us to be the next Lennon Sisters, but we were on another planet altogether—I would have preferred John Lennon. After a few years, and with Debbie off to college, we stopped performing together.

For many years, Mom was the choir director at St. Mary's church. Singing in the choir was a blast, especially during Mass, when we sat in the balcony and, between hymns, dropped spit wads down onto parishioners below. Then we got the giggles, and as we tried so hard to laugh silently, one of us – usually Audrey – would inadvertently snort, setting us off on a new bout of laughter. The glaring eyes of the adults burning into us made it next to impossible to stop.

Audrey and I began studying flute when we were nine. Luckily, St. Mary's had a band with about twenty members, including Debbie on drums; Pam, Prissy, and Julie on clarinet; and Audrey and me on flute. I had fun playing in that band, as well as later in the high school band. I sat first chair through most of high school, which was much-needed validation for my innate insecurity. Unfortunately, during my teen years I was too busy rebelling to practice regularly, leading to the reasonable fear that I would make horrendous mistakes in front of the entire band or audience when I had a solo, which detracted from its enjoyment. I can still hear that painfully dissonant high B-flat screeching throughout the auditorium during my final concert with the Ukiah High School band.

Audrey and I frequently played duets and sometimes performed at rest homes, hospitals, and the like. We usually were so nervous that on more than one occasion, we completely abandoned our professionalism and got the giggles in the middle of a performance, once to the extent that we had to leave the stage and could not complete our piece. We loved playing together, though, and like singing with my sisters, Audrey and I were so in tune with each other that we played as one with minimal effort, raising our expectations to outrageous levels for working with other musicians.

Dance was another musical endeavor in which I participated with my sisters. We studied ballet and tap and also danced around at home for fun. I loved dancing the twist, and I was great at it. I could twist to a squat on two feet or just one. But then my mom unintentionally spoiled it. My dad drummed with a jazz band for years. Often, they would play at our house just to jam or for parties. Hearing them perform was one of the best memories from my childhood. We children would just listen or play around or sometimes dance a bit when we thought no one would notice. I was always self-conscious about dancing in front of others, even in a group. One evening when I was maybe ten or eleven, my mother decided I should show the adults how well I could dance the twist. I declined the invitation, but she insisted. I wanted so badly to be brave and perform, to have them all applaud me, and to make my mother proud, yet still I resisted. I was embarrassed at being singled out, but she wouldn't give up. So I ended up in a no-win situation, where I either had to perform under duress or live with the humiliation of cowardice. I chose humiliation for myself and embarrassment and frustration for my mother—a hint of what was to come.

You just have to have faith. Religion was a huge part of our family dynamic. I thought about marrying Jesus off and on throughout my early years, admired most of the nuns I knew, and seriously considered joining a convent a few times. I thought it was pretty cool that on the first Friday of every month, all the students went to Mass in the morning. Then we walked back to the school, chatting with our friends, and upon our arrival were treated to hot chocolate and doughnuts. I always got a stomachache afterwards, but it was worth it. The combination, though, of Catholic catechism and a mother who was a religious zealot can cause a highly sensitive, neurotic child to come awfully close to falling over the precipice. By seven or eight years old, I was suffering from insomnia. I tossed and turned in bed at night, while my mind wrestled with theological and philosophical dilemmas, such as *always* was and *always* will be—how could God have no beginning and no end? Why were wars acceptable if God said not to kill? Why did animals have to go to a different heaven? If God was perfect, how could he be so unfair as to ban the little pagan babies from heaven? Were these the same little pagan babies for whom we saved our pennies? Night after night, I cried tears of panic and frustration until, exhausted, I finally fell asleep.

I watched a movie about the life of Jesus, *The Greatest Story Ever Told*, with Max von Sydow playing the lead. I tried to be absolutely perfect for a few months afterward. I definitely did not want to be responsible for the death of Jesus because of my sins. But no matter how hard I tried, I could not attain perfection. And to ensure that imperfect state, when I attended confession, I made up sins so as not to share my real self with this stranger, the priest. Then, of course, I had to live with the guilt of my dishonesty.

My fears were multiplying rapidly. I was frightened of bees and horses, which caused me problems when I played in the tree house at Audrey's. Her playhouse was built among the branches of a large tree in the middle of the pasture where her horses lived. Not only was there a beehive preventing me from relaxing and enjoying myself, but she also had a horse who liked to chase us as we ran to and from the tree. I was once "treed" by that evil beast for an entire afternoon until Audrey finally escaped and found her sister, my savior.

Of course, I was also afraid of the cosmos and the ocean. They were so massive and overwhelming. When my friends or siblings and I lay outside and looked up into the heavens or sat on the cliffs overlooking the sea, I became dizzy and nauseated and felt lost as I contemplated their vastness. When our house was being remodeled and we lived down the street, night after night I dreamed I was in the other house, the one under construction. There, as I descended the stairs to the basement, a monster began chasing me. I turned and climbed back up, only to find there was no end in sight. I climbed and climbed, faster and faster, as the endless stairway stretched into the firmament, with the unrelenting monster close behind. I awoke terrified and exhausted.

My mother realized I was rapidly becoming a nervous wreck and gave me tools to help me deal with my anxieties. She taught me to meditate by reciting rosaries or Hail Marys. She also taught me to breathe slowly and deeply to calm myself. "Hail Mary" became my mantra and when combined with the breathing exercises, I reached the point where I could remove myself mentally from stressful situations. I became so adept at it that I could be in the middle of a severe panic, and no one around me would have the faintest idea. It came in handy at dentist appointments—and also when Audrey and I ran into the sheriff, a family friend, as we exited the local five-and-dime, our pockets stuffed with contraband. ("Hey, Tomato! Doing your Christmas shoplifting?")

You can catch more flies with honey than with vinegar. Despite my early-onset angst, I think I had a relatively happy childhood. I thought we were special because my parents were highly respected, there were so many of us, we were smart, and several of us had red hair. We also laughed a lot, loved each other immensely, and enjoyed each other's company. My family played more than just music regularly; we also played games. After large holiday or birthday dinners, we played Murder or Dictionary. When just a few of us were available, we played Scrabble or cards. Mom began teaching me card games when I was about four or five. I was mad about cards. One of the first games I learned was Russian Bank. It was a rather complex game, and I felt so proud of myself when I first beat Mom. Bank was a two-player game, so I got Mom to myself, which was a bonus. She also taught me a gazillion solitaire games, to which I became totally addicted, playing for hours at night after lights-out. I frequently played card games with my mom, my sisters, and Audrey over the years, and my favorites were the late-night games. Sometimes the fun expanded to include my brothers and/or an additional friend or two, but usually it was the girls laughing, chain-smoking, and drinking endless cups of coffee (I was never a coffee drinker so had to stay awake of my own volition), as we played Hearts deep into the night. Usually about the time that Mom asked "What was led?" when only one card lay on the table, Daddy would enter the room and look at Mom as though she were crazy for letting us stay up so late—even on school nights, sometimes—but then would just leave the room, shaking his head in resignation.

We had exciting Christmas celebrations, and gifts were in abundance. Over the years we acquired a trampoline, a unicycle, a bicycle with a very large front wheel and a small back one, a surrey with a fringe on top that seated two, a tandem bicycle, stilts, and copious books, puzzles, and games. After staying up late for midnight Mass, where we sang and sang all those great Latin hymns and carols, we had eggnog with friends before falling into bed and trying to sleep, while listening to Dad/Santa putting together bikes, wagons, and other large toys. We never had a television in our house, but none of us would have had the time to watch anyway, with all the other amusements available to us.

We received loads of books for Christmas. Our parents put a premium on reading, and I was one of the lucky ones who enjoyed it and read profusely. Many nights after lights-out, in the middle of a good book, I turned the light back on, or used a flashlight to read through to the final page before going to sleep, sometimes as the dawn was leaking through the curtains. My love of reading came in handy when I was sent for a timeout on the chair just inside the living room door. There, next to the red-cushioned seat, was a bookcase filled with a wonderful assortment of books. It hardly felt like punishment as I sat there and pored over material like *The Iliad and the Odyssey for Children,* Alcott's *Little Women,* London's *Call of the Wild,* and a fascinating book, the title of which escapes me, that was filled with earliest history—Stone Age and Ice Age, Neanderthals and prehistoric animals; I was awed by the pictures of the woolly mammoths and saber-toothed tigers. It was also while sitting in that chair that I devoured *The Lives of the Saints, Saints for Girls,* and *Saints for Boys.* Over one summer, possibly more than one summer, I tried to read a book a day. I don't think I reached my goal, but I came close.

Summer as a child was great fun. We had scores of sleepovers. We and our friends set our sleeping bags up on the lawn and waited until the neighborhood was quiet. Then we snuck out of the yard to play games like hide-and-seek in the dark and then danced and sang under the streetlights in our nightgowns. We stayed up talking and laughing until the wee hours and woke at dawn, with dew on our faces and the sun in our eyes.

For the most part, I got along well with my sisters and brothers. My mother relied quite heavily on Debbie, the eldest, to help maintain and control our unruly horde. She was placed in the unfortunate position of authority over the rest of us, making her appear bossy, critical, and distant. When Debbie, Pam, and I shared a room, Debbie did not often want to join us in our fun and games, and when I had friends over, she just seemed annoyed with us—the bratty little sister and her friends. I have to admit, we could be bothersome. Once, shortly after Debbie got her driver's license, a friend and I were in the backseat as my cool big sister cruised around town. I realized a policeman was driving directly behind us, so it seemed the opportune time to begin jumping around, yelling, dancing, singing, and basically acting goofy. Debbie asked me to stop but instead, my friend joined in. When her request to cease and desist went unheeded, Debbie pulled the car over to the side of the road, parked it, and walked home, putting a big damper on our little fun-fest.

I admired and looked up to Debbie, though I am not sure she knew it. She was very serious but so confident and articulate. She quarreled frequently with Pam and my mother and usually won. The three of them liked sitting around the table after dinner, arguing religion and politics. I always wanted to join them, but if I stated my opinion, they would turn to me as one, to inform me that I did not know what I was talking about, successfully shutting me up.

I was especially impressed by Debbie's artistic talents. She and her friend, Loelia, who lived across the street from us, opened a boutique in Loelia's basement. They sold homemade gifts and crafts, like painted jars and pet rocks. I thought they were awesome. I took all of my friends over to show off Debbie's talents. Debbie spoke with a convincing British accent too, and I just knew the Beatles would think she was groovy.

Pam and I were almost always congenial. We were good friends as well as sisters. Mom worried about Pam's diminutive stature early on, but by high school, she had everything my mother thought best: petite figure; cute looks; long, thick red hair; feisty personality; and taste in fashion similar to Mom's. I loved Pam and thought she was wonderful, but I was rather envious of her relationship with Mom.

Pam and I did have one fight. As a teenager, I walked into the bathroom where Debbie and Pam were doing their usual arguing. The peacemaker in me felt the need to butt in, so I said something sappy like, "Now, let's not fight, girls," whereupon Pam spun around and punched me in the face. I was absolutely shocked! I don't think I had ever been hit before. Not only did it hurt, but I was dumbfounded, and it occurred to me that Pam was completely out of control. I was afraid of what she might do next, so I socked her back, thinking I would knock her out so she could not do any more damage, and I could go get help. Of course, my plan failed. In fact, I think she burst out laughing. I felt so ashamed that I had resorted to violence that the following day, I put makeup on before school to camouflage my black eye, but, as Mom proudly told the story, Pam wore hers like a badge of honor.

When Debbie, Pam, and I shared a bedroom, Mom considered us the "big" kids and the others the "little kids." After our house was remodeled, Prissy and I became roommates, and she joined the ranks of the "big" kids. We had similar interests and tastes, especially in music, books, candy, and games. We sat on our big brass beds for hours, listening to music and reading or playing solitaire, our mouths stuffed with M & M's. Though I shared a room with Prissy for years, not a single fight or argument comes to mind. I certainly had an easy time getting along with her, and if she had any complaints about me, she never let on.

Valli was never allowed to become a "big" kid. I think we older kids would have been fine with it, but Mom was not agreeable. Mom was often mean to Valli, and I could never understand why. Val and Becky shared a room and quite frequently fought and argued, and Mom always took Becky's side, regardless of where the blame belonged. It really offended my sense of justice. As far as I know, Mom never hit the older kids. Maybe she became overwhelmed by the numbers, since I know she did hit at least Valli and Zack. Once, when I expressed my disquiet at her behavior, she said that she spanked Zack nightly because he liked to cry himself to sleep. I don't know if she spanked David or Paul. I think she might have had Dad take care of that. I was never spanked, though. Mom said I punished myself enough.

Mom must have felt David was special, since he was the first boy born after five girls. She was very protective of him because he was an artist rather than an athlete, in an era when boys were more valued for their physical abilities. He hated to do any work, so instead he spent hours rigging up fancy contraptions that were meant to do the work for him. He was very clever, and his procrastination would have been fine with me, except that on Saturday mornings, the entire house had to be clean before anyone could go anywhere. I could not bear to wait all afternoon for David to clean his room, so I invariably went in and cleaned it for him. At least that way I could get out of the house to meet my friends. I once had a dream that David played with a hot electrical wire that was hanging from a telephone pole and he was killed. When I awoke, I immediately ran to his room to make sure he was safe, but he was not in his bed. He just happened to rise early that morning, but I was devastated and worried about him thereafter.

Mom may have routinely taken Becky's side against Valli, but I do not think Mom and Becky were very close. It seems Becky was always lumped in with the boys. She may not have been very happy about that, but she certainly learned to be tough and stand her ground. Becky had a stubborn streak, and Zack liked to punch his siblings as he passed us. Becky and Zack presented tough façades that protected their sensitive inner lives. Zack also had a philosophical bent, and I enjoyed discussions with him in my search for truth.

The youngest is often the clown, and our family was no exception. Paul found humor in everything and enjoyed entertaining us all with his observations and tomfoolery. When he was young, he had a friendly bee to pal around with. He carried on in-depth conversations with his insect companion for months—or maybe years. Another time, he stood, pencil and notepad at the ready, to take dinner orders from our myriad feline pets who sat at attention at his feet. Paul mimicked every movie he saw and every comedy skit he heard. Mom always crowed with delight at his theatrics, but Dad seemed more often annoyed.

One side or a leg off. Growing up enmeshed in this big, rambunctious, loving family led me to test boundaries. Probably being lost in the crowd and suffocated by religious dogmatism necessitated my frenetic search for identity and self-expression. My rebellion began subtly, with no one big event as catalyst, but rather growing gradually over the years as I became aware of injustice, first in my own narrow universe and then in the world at large. Early on, maybe around age nine, Audrey and I decided it was not fair that boys were not required to wear shirts but girls were. So we spent a summer removing ours whenever we thought it was safe to do so—jumping on our trampoline, hanging out with her family, and running around my house and yard until my mother saw us and immediately put a stop to it. I was disappointed in my mother for that. After all, she was a feminist, emphasizing that she was one of the first women to work at *Life* magazine and for American Airlines and railing against the double standard that allowed men to get away with things for which women were pilloried. But she remained adamant in her belief that we must wear tops. Before long, our burgeoning pubescence changed our outlook, and we quite willingly acquiesced.

In 1963 the Beatles entered my life. My friends and I owned all the Beatles albums, and I spent hours consuming them and memorizing all the lyrics. I bought teen magazines and clipped newspaper articles to learn everything there was to know about the Fab Four. I cut pictures out of magazines and wallpapered my entire bedroom with them. I felt an affinity for their message of love, pacifism, and revolution. My favorite was John. I liked his looks, of course, but more than that, I was drawn to his intelligence and wit. He wasn't afraid to speak his mind, and for the first time I was conscious of the way the media twisted words or took them out of context in order to exaggerate or warp them. Mom did not like the Beatles' music, but at first, she was willing to accept it as a passing fancy. She even allowed me to attend the final Beatles concert at Candlestick Park in San Francisco when I was just thirteen. I was ecstatic, screamed at all the appropriate moments, and was certain John looked right at me through the window of their armored car when they were transported off the field at the end of the show. I continued to admire the Beatles as they matured and began their religious/consciousness search in the East, and delved into drug experimentation. My world began to expand as well.

During my last couple of years in St. Mary's, my attitude toward religion started to evolve. I still believed in Jesus' teachings—turn the other cheek, love your enemies, do unto others—but not so much in those propagated by the church. When the bishop came for our confirmation, we each had to kiss his ring, an expectation that seemed much more king-like than Christ-like. And the fact that women were not allowed to become priests was utterly unacceptable to me. I showed my disdain by running and laughing in the sanctuary (which was off-limits to women) and by lifting my skirt to moon the statues and the chalice. I enjoyed the excitement, the adrenaline rush, and the admiration I perceived coming from my peers in the face of my daring. I was not really all that brave, though, for I only behaved in that manner in front of my friends or classmates. If an adult were anywhere in the vicinity—particularly, god forbid, a priest—I wore an ever-so-pious countenance and bowed my head.

It's as easy to fall in love with a rich boy as a poor boy. High school began innocuously enough, though the pressure to excel was beginning to overwhelm me. For the most part, I worked diligently throughout my freshman year. I enjoyed my classes, loved playing in the band, and got along well with my friends. I also disappointed my mother terribly by receiving my first C. History had never been a favorite class, so I found it easy to put my time and attention on a boy rather than my studies. I had enjoyed quite a fondness for boys throughout my youth. In fact, my first "marriage" took place in the rock garden of our Oak Park home. Debbie officiated and choreographed the ceremony. I didn't know Peter very well—he was a distant neighbor, and his mother was acquainted with mine. I was five and he, my lucky groom, was six. Our marriage lasted all of about ten minutes, and we parted amicably. Another of my early beaux, and my favorite, was Bruce. He and I were a "couple" off and on throughout elementary school. Bruce was sweet and gallant, always happy to tote my books, and no doubt would have plucked my fallen handkerchief from the ground had I but carried one. More important, he was hilarious and acted as though making me laugh was his highest calling. Even when I was grounded—for some simple infraction, I am sure—Bruce and his good friend, Leonard, would arrive outside my house to serenade and entertain me as I gazed down admiringly from my second-story window until my mother heard my laughter and chased them away. But nothing and no one prepared me for Robbie, not my father or brothers, not my friends' fathers or brothers, not even Daphne du Maurier, the Brontë sisters, Mary Stewart, or Frank Yerby and their romance novels, which I devoured on a daily basis. My mother tried, but her approach was to send me to Catholic school and then prevent me from attending my eighth-grade graduation party at Audrey's house because it was coed.

The lessons learned from *The Lives of the Saints* meant nothing in the face of this Adonis look-alike. Robbie had dark curly hair, a beautiful smile with impeccable white teeth, and light brown— almost amber—eyes that sparkled with humor and wit. A good kid from a nice family, he was athletic and intelligent, and we flirted blatantly throughout the year. At fourteen we were still too young to date and even too shy to openly admit our attraction to one another, but we definitely became friends, at least on the school grounds.

We were separated by summer break, and my family took an extended vacation around the country. It was quite an education but probably not the one my mother had in mind. The year was 1967. We saw many "important" sites, but none of them impressed me much. I was more interested in people, like the cute boys in the garage band next door to my aunt's house in the Chicago suburb of Evanston, who took my sister and me for a ride about town. Unfortunately, we forgot to ask permission prior to leaving, so we were met with sour faces upon our return, but it was worth it.

In Jackson, Michigan, we visited Uncle Ted and Aunt Bev's. I sat in their basement with my cousin Chris and listened to the newly released Beatles tune, "All You Need Is Love." It fit right into my philosophy. In Detroit, I became aware of the civil unrest facing our country at the time. I learned of the race riots and noticed my mother locking our car doors as we drove through certain areas. In New York City, we stayed in a hotel in Greenwich Village. Debbie had been smoking cigarettes for a while, and I had claimed I would never do the same, but now I wanted to be cool too. I sat on the hotel windowsill and choked my way through a cigarette or two until I felt nauseated. Debbie taught me to tap my cigarette over the carpet and rub the ashes in with my shoe, because she alleged the ashes were good for the carpet.

In New York I saw beatniks and hippies up close and personal for the first time. They presented quite a contrast to the Rockettes or to Florence Henderson in *South Pacific* at Rockefeller Center. I wanted to know what they were about, so I bravely left our hotel room by myself and went to the park to talk to one. There, I met Jacoba. He was a guitar-playing black hippie. We sat and conversed about life and society for an hour or more before my mother showed up, quite agitated, and hauled me back to the hotel. She kept a much better eye on me throughout the rest of the trip.

Another awakening I experienced was the severe disparity between where we spent an afternoon swimming and visiting friends of my mother at the luxurious home in Connecticut and the dilapidated shacks housing families along the Mississippi Gulf. I had been utterly ignorant of the gross inequality in this "great" country of mine. I could not quite mesh the Christian country of my classroom textbooks with this obviously un-Christian reality.

Nothing else really stands out for me from that trip besides the huge, gross bugs in Georgia and Texas, hanging my leg out the car window as we drove and getting second-degree burns from the sun so that I was unable to put any weight on it, and having the dubious honor of unpacking and repacking the U-Haul on a daily basis. At the end of the six weeks, I was eager to return to my friends.

Near my fifteenth birthday and within a month of our family trip, my friend Julie and I decided to run away from home. That's not quite accurate. We were not running away from anything as much as running *to* something. That something was San Francisco's "Summer of Love." It was a spontaneous moment when Julie was spending the night at my house. There was no discussion of should we or shouldn't we. One of us just said, "Let's go," and the other said, "Okay," and we were off. It was past bedtime, so we snuck out of the house, walked to Highway 101, and headed south. Immediately a semi stopped, and the driver offered us a ride, which we accepted. He lectured us about the dangers of hitchhiking, drove us to Santa Rosa, and put us on a Greyhound for San Francisco. We arrived at dawn and asked for directions to Haight-Ashbury. En route by foot, we ran into a young man willing to escort us. High as a kite, he sang the entire distance until we reached Golden Gate Park, where he wished us well and went his own way. An awesome scene awaited us. Live music played nonstop in the park. Every person we passed smiled and wished us peace; hugs flowed freely. Marijuana and psychedelics were in widespread use, but no one cared that we did not participate. So as to save my mother from worry, I telephoned her to let her know we were safe but that no, we were not ready to return home. We wandered all day, soaking up the music, warmth, and freedom. A big woman wearing a long flowery dress and beads in her Afro took us in for dinner and to spend the night. The next morning, her elderly neighbor paid us to sweep his driveway so we could buy food. While we were hard at work earning our keep, I heard my name. Looking up, I saw my mom's friend Martha, leaning out of her car window. The funny thing is, when I was five and angry at my mother about something, I actually did run away from home, and I ran to Martha's house, which was about a mile down the road from mine. So it was kind of ironic that Martha, who now lived in San Francisco, had found me on the street. She talked us into getting in the car with her and returning to her house. We waited there until my parents arrived from Ukiah. I ran away a few other times in the ensuing years—once to Eureka for a week and a couple more times to San Francisco. I probably got grounded for those little escapades; after all, I was grounded throughout most of my high school years.

The Summer of Love ended, and I returned to school where

I began to have difficulty focusing on my work. Math, music, and English were still fun, but my mind was elsewhere. Our family's age limit for dating was sixteen, but when an older guy named Cree asked me out, I convinced my parents that at fifteen, I was old enough. He was pretty cute, and since Robbie still had not asked me out, I thought I might as well go with Cree. We went to a movie or a party or something else not very impressive. A few days later, we went to his house on our lunch break where I enjoyed my first massive make-out session. When we returned to school, my legs were so wobbly that I could hardly walk, though no one seemed to notice. Shortly after, Cree and I went on our final date. This time, he tried desperately to convince me that kissing and groping were good fun, but it was time to go "all the way." I can still picture him, stripped down to his underpants, alternately begging me to give in or singing "Hot-diggity, dog-diggity, boom, what you do to me ..." I, on the other hand, was staring at his crotch, where his boxers were unable to camouflage the first, live, man-sized erection I had ever seen. I thought, *Are you kidding me? I'm not getting anywhere near that thing!*

It was early in my sophomore year. Debbie was off to college, and Pam was busy with cheerleading and her social life. I was, as usual, searching for my niche when I began experimenting with drugs. The first one I tried was speed. It was great. I could practice my flute for hours, read book after book in no time at all, and whiz through my math work. In fact, I did math assignments I had not yet been assigned. Then one Sunday morning I feigned illness to avoid attending Mass. After Mom and the others had left to do their holy duty, Julie came over with a big fat joint—our first. We had seen people stoned on marijuana before, and they seemed cool and mellow, so we knew we could handle it. We went out in our yard and began smoking. We finished the entire joint and then decided to take a walk around the block. We were so high that we laughed until our stomachs ached. And then we laughed even more. We tried to sit on a fire hydrant at the end of the street but could not keep our balance and fell onto the sidewalk. We laughed some more. We tried to converse but could barely put our words together, which again sent us into paroxysms of laughter. Everything looked, smelled, sounded, and felt funny. We laughed until we could no longer inhale and thought we would die. Circling the block only once, we managed to use up the entire time until my family returned home. We had come down from our high some by then, and they treated us as usual. Maybe the neighbors were all at church also, because to my knowledge, not one of them ever said a word to our parents or to us about our strange behavior. I felt my world had changed dramatically and no one else had noticed a thing.

This was an emotionally tumultuous time for me. I did not want to disappoint my parents, but I felt completely overwhelmed by their expectations and feared I could never live up to them—not just the academic ones but the moral standards as well. I particularly doubted my ability to die for my virginity like St. Theresa did. I no longer had much control of my impulses, and perfection was definitely out of the picture. I was uncomfortable expressing my feelings to anyone, especially my mother. Her standard responses were "Offer it up for the souls in purgatory" and "If you can't say something nice, don't say anything at all." She repeatedly told me I was too sensitive—counterproductive, I know, but I guess that escaped her. I never doubted her love for me, but she was so busy that it seemed she just wanted me to toe the line so I could have the life she planned for me, go to heaven when I died, and not embarrass her while she lived.

Mom began working at my dad's office when I was a sophomore in high school, affording me a freedom of which I was eager to take advantage. Mom hired a housekeeper/general helper at this time. At first Margie came to our house once a week to clean. She shortly became like one of the family, and I loved her and held her in high esteem, even though, because she was a figure of authority, I did not always treat her very respectfully. After a while, Mom became more and more dependent on Margie, and she began babysitting, and then it seems she was always there. One day, Mom informed me that while Margie was cleaning my room, she found two home-rolled cigarettes. Suspecting they were not tobacco, Mom took them to the police station where the police confirmed her suspicion that they were marijuana. I was then grounded but did not hold it against Margie and did not take my punishment seriously. Mom was at work, and I had better things to do. I was expected to go home right after school, but as long as I had dinner prepared on time, I felt my afternoons were mine to do with as I wished. So I did what any curious, rebellious, extremist teenager would do in the '60s—I filled my afternoons with sex, drugs, and rock and roll.

Hey, handsome, you spoke for? I started dating Robbie when we were fifteen. Unable to wait any longer for him to gain the courage to ask me for a date, I asked him out first. We got along famously and talked about our hopes and dreams, our fears and feelings. Not only did he listen, but he accepted me as I was and loved me no matter what I thought or felt. When I was around Robbie, I saw myself through his eyes: I was smart and talented, sexy and beautiful, clever and funny. My brothers and sisters thought he was great. When he spent time at my house, he played with them and enjoyed showing off his athletic prowess, like walking on his hands across our long front porch and riding a unicycle, sometimes with Paul or Zack on his shoulders. After several months, I was rather overwhelmed by the intensity of our relationship and so broke it off.

Music was still a big part of my life. My friends and I listened to all the latest pop tunes on KFRC and spent hours searching through record albums at Hayes Music, where I spent most of my allowance. Besides the Beatles, I bought Cream, Janis Joplin (who performed at our little high school with Big Brother and the Holding Company), Dylan, Chicago, Otis Redding, the Rascals, the Doors, Marvin Gaye, and Elvin Bishop, to name but a fraction. We attended numerous concerts in San Francisco, most of them without my parents' permission. I snuck out of the house and joined my friends in the back of Julie's pickup truck or her huge Chrysler sedan. Other times, we rode in Audrey's car or with our friend Fred in his Volkswagen convertible. We passed around joints or acid, and I shared pills of various sorts that I had pocketed from the storeroom while cleaning my dad's office the previous weekend. It is amazing that we survived those crazy days, because by the time we arrived in San Francisco, we were loaded to the gills. Sometimes we ended up ingesting too many downers and sleeping through a concert, but usually, we had a great, fun time, and the music was fantastic. We saw Mike Bloomfield; Donovan; Crosby, Stills, and Nash; and Charlie Musselwhite, among others. Once we even saw Santana as an opening act so remarkable they put the headliner to shame. After our two-hour return trip at the end of the evening, I faced the challenge of climbing onto the swimming pool fence and then shimmying up the balcony post and over the railing before sneaking through a bedroom window and back into the house, often without my parents ever discovering my absence.

Many of my friends were musicians. I belonged to the high school band and spent much of my free time with my bandmates. We took part in music competitions and went on band trips out of town to march in parades and reviews. We put our music director, Mr. Nielson, through quite a bit of torture, like the time we were to put on the half-time show at the annual East-West game in San Francisco. Julie and I became bored watching the first half of the football game, so we wandered away, smoked a joint, and did a little sightseeing. Upon our return, we realized that the half-time show had begun, and our band was already in formation on the field. The television cameras caught us as we grabbed our instruments and dashed out to our positions in a most unprofessional manner.

Rocky was one of my close friends. He was a great saxophonist—smart, hilarious, always late, and Julie's boyfriend. He was also our sophomore class president. Maybe because of the emphasis on peace, love, and tolerance that the late '60s represented or perhaps because of the camaraderie enhanced by marijuana, it seems our class was not made up of many small cliques as is usual in high school but rather was connected in a larger way. For the most part, we all got along really well, though we did not accomplish a lot as a class. In fact, at the end of that year, the student-body president presented Rocky with a special award for our class—a large, yellow lemon.

We held many parties throughout those years, parties consisting of a diverse group of jocks, musicians, artists, intellectuals, cheerleaders, and a plethora of oddballs. Sometimes the parties were held inside, but more often, we spent our time in the amazing outdoors around town, like in the lush redwood forest at Montgomery Woods, in the rolling hills of MacNab Ranch, at Mud Lake, Lake Mendocino, the dams, or our favorite skinny-dipping spot, Cold Creek. (Well, maybe only some of us went skinny-dipping—mainly the boys—but I, always one to take things to extremes, had to join in. I liked that they thought I was daring.)

Through Rocky, I became friends with his mates: the twins Stan and Steve, and Robben, and Mike. They were all quite talented musicians who played in the school band and also formed a rock group. I once rode with them to San Francisco, where Mike filed for conscientious objector status to avoid the draft. I was so proud to go along on such a significant mission. In the city, we stopped by Debbie's apartment, where she was living in sin with her boyfriend. When Mom learned I had taken my friends to that den of iniquity, she was aghast. Not only did my friends now know of our family's unspeakable failing, but she was horrified that word would spread throughout the Ukiah Valley. The generation gap was so wide that she did not realize that my friends did not care enough to notice, much less mention it to others.

Stan and I dated for a few months, and Audrey conveniently dated Steve. I loved to hang out with the band when they rehearsed and would have enjoyed singing with them but never had the guts to ask. Stan was an exceptionally nice guy and very funny. He and I lost our virginity together. We were at my house at the time, upstairs in my bedroom. My parents were not home, but many of my brothers and sisters were downstairs. It was the middle of the afternoon. We were taking part in our favorite form of entertainment, necking and groping, when suddenly I felt not just the desire but the need to go all the way. I was tired of constantly aborting the passion, delaying the inevitable, and being unable to satisfy my curiosity. When I suggested to Stan that we go through with it, he hesitated—there was no lock on the door and many people nearby who might enter the room at any moment—but not for long. I suppose he was a well-endowed young man because physically, the initial penetration was a rather painful experience. I did not know I would bleed like crazy, and that kind of freaked me out. I even went to Julie's doctor to make sure I was all right. Emotionally, though, I was quite excited that I had finally taken the ultimate step.

A couple of days later, I broke up with Stan, not because of our experience, but because I was still in love with Robbie. I was eager to have the relationship with him that we had been heading toward earlier. It was especially handy that both of our mothers were working daily—I had a lot of freedom, and his house was available to us every afternoon. We made love every chance we got and every place imaginable. Often, Robbie borrowed one of his parents' cars, and we discovered all the secluded places in our little valley and some not so isolated, like downstream from our friends on the sandy beach at Potter Valley's Cold Creek or the closet of Audrey's family's vacation home in Tahoe, with our friends just beyond the closed door playing games and chatting and our chaperones, her parents, downstairs. Once, when we were parked just outside of Ukiah near the old state hospital grounds, in the middle of our enjoyment, we heard a knock on the window of our car. Unable to see through the steamed-up glass, Robbie rolled it down. There stood a middle-aged gentleman who, seemingly unruffled by catching us *in flagrante*, inquired, "Do you have the time?" We burst out laughing and abandoned our activity for the afternoon.

Another time, Robbie's parents were away from home for the evening so of course, that is where we headed as soon as we knew they had left. We were enjoying our evening in his sisters' bedroom when we heard his parents enter the house. I jumped out of bed and into the closet, where I waited, stark naked and heart pounding, until we heard them retire to their room about two hours later—an eternity.

I was shy around Robbie's mom, but I was fond of her. She was kind and smart. She once gave me Kahlil Gibran's *The Prophet* inscribed with the words "To Di, with wishes for your heart to say in silence, 'God rests in reason' and your heart to say in awe 'God moves in passion.'" My mom, on the other hand, seemed to like Robbie well enough at first, but after we had been seeing each other for some time, she began to discourage our relationship. She maintained that we were far too young to be dating each other exclusively; that we were not really in love but just thought we were and that when I was older I would recognize my feelings as merely puppy love; that teenage relationships never lasted yet marriage was forever and thus mistakes were inadmissible; and—probably the most ominous— Robbie not only was not Catholic, but he did not even believe in God!

Obviously, I was not behaving according to plan at all. In addition to dating the wrong boy, I cut classes on a regular basis, and my school work suffered—my grades generally alternated between As and Fs. One of my English teachers had the students stand and cheer when I returned after cutting his class daily for three weeks. I either slept through math class or skipped it and only showed up for the tests, even though Marvin T. Elder, my math teacher throughout high school, was my favorite teacher. It is unlikely that he knew it, though, as I was quite rude to him. Once, after hitting another car while exiting the school parking lot in my dad's green Ford Galaxy, I sped down the street and away, disregarding his request that I stop. Another time, friends and I piled into Audrey's car to leave campus during school hours when Mr. Elder appeared at the car window. "Go! Go! Go!" we yelled to Audrey and then laughed and hooted as she complied. I felt ashamed as I saw the look of frustration and disappointment on his face. He knew my parents, since I had been friends with his daughter in grammar school, but I do not think he ever told them of my indiscretions.

I also refused to take classes that required an oral presentation and so quit attending them. For a week, I tried dropping acid in the morning before school with the hope that it would enhance my interest and curiosity but to no avail. In other classes, I either did not bother taking tests, or I turned them in with drawings or poetry instead of appropriate answers. Worse yet, when my mother went to school to discuss my difficulties, my French teacher had the gall to call me a flower child! I thought my mom was going to have apoplexy.

It just ain't fittin'. Mom hated the way I dressed, and she confiscated some of my favorite clothes, like the pink leather sandals with thongs that wrapped around my legs and tied at the knees, my knee-high moccasins, and my long dark-green scarf with the black tassels that I wore wrapped in a band around my head, tassels hanging down one side to my elbow. I also liked to draw black Twiggy lashes under my eyes, but Mom made me wipe them off before leaving for school. (I learned to dress in a way she found acceptable when I left the house but carried a different outfit and makeup to put on around the corner.) She threw my Beatles albums into the garbage, because she decided that my hero, John Lennon, was the devil. Once, Mom tried to call me at Audrey's house, where she thought I was spending the night, to tell me that our dog, Coco, had died. When she realized that I was actually with Robbie, he too joined the ranks of Satan.

What followed was the first of only two meetings I was to have exclusively with both my mother and father. My dad looked like he'd been dragged in, and it was the last place on earth he wanted to be. I do not think he said a word the entire time. My mom asked if I was sleeping with Robbie, and I confirmed it. She told me that making love was wonderful and fun but was intended solely for within marriage. She then moved on to religion and fornication, and that is when I lost interest and tuned her out. Apparently she and Dad subsequently had a meeting with Robbie's parents, who suggested my folks send me to Europe, which irritated Mom to no end.

Robbie and I liked things the way they were, so we decided to ignore our parents' concerns. When I was grounded, I simply snuck out of the house. At seventeen, I took up drinking, which loosened me up quite a bit. I really enjoyed it. Instead of the quiet, introverted pot/acid head, I became much more outgoing when I drank. Robbie and I kept up our socializing, with each other and with friends. Audrey and I frequented Johnny's Market, where our parents had charge accounts. We took advantage of their tabs and, without their consent, bought picnic supplies for ourselves and our friends, including good-quality steaks and cigarettes by the carton. We took many trips to the coast. Along the way, we stopped at the market in Boonville, where I grabbed a jug of Ripple or some other cheap wine and stuffed it under my jacket. As a distraction, the others paid for snacks. I spent hours at the beach, high on acid, watching Robbie and his friends throw knives at targets.

Basically, life after the "conference" went on as usual—with one exception. Dad started paying attention to me. He took me to the coast, where we spent the day wandering the beach and watching the fishing boats. We also attended a Miles Davis concert in San Francisco, where we sat together on the floor of the pot-filled concert hall and let the music pour over us. It was awesome, but I guess his interest came too late, because I could not really talk to him.

Since grounding clearly did not have the desired effect on me, before long I was required to visit a psychiatrist. Not many people went to shrinks in those days—certainly none of my friends did. I had no idea what to say to him. I reverted to my old technique of deep breathing and removing myself from the situation, like an out-of-body experience. I attended four one-hour sessions without uttering a single word. I guess my parents finally came to the conclusion that this was perhaps not the wisest way to spend their money.

As the end of high school approached, the proximity of adulthood began to close in on me. I desperately completed enough school work to enable me to graduate with my class. I took the SATs and actually sent out applications to colleges—only Catholic ones, of course, since they were the only ones Mom would allow me to attend. I was still in rebel mode, though. I attended antiwar rallies and heard of sit-ins on campuses around the country. At a party shortly before graduation, I suggested that we all boycott the graduation ceremony (as a symbolic gesture of our antiwar sentiment, maybe, but more likely of basic rebelliousness). Many of my friends agreed, and I informed my parents. As graduation day drew near, though, my friends changed their minds. Ultimately, I was the only one who refused to walk with my class. I sat in the stands with my parents while all my friends and classmates received their diplomas. As much as my behavior hurt and frustrated my parents, I was too stubborn to capitulate.

Mom and Dad were relieved that I had actually graduated, and I am sure they eagerly anticipated my departure to college in the fall, but I was not finished torturing them. Our graduation party took place at our friend Fred's house and lasted all night long. There, high on acid, pot, and alcohol, both of us only seventeen years old, Robbie and I conceived our child. We had discussed having children someday, but this was a bit earlier than intended. We were both quite excited, though, and Robbie proudly boasted to his friends of his upcoming parenthood. We spent the summer making plans for our future together and chose names for our baby. Robbie wanted to get married, but I was hesitant. For one thing, marriage was so establishment. I was also completely drug-free and mostly alcohol-free due to my pregnancy, and without the substances to prop me up, I was back to my doubting, insecure self, deathly afraid of making mistakes. I thought living together for a while before committing to marriage seemed a good option, or even living with my parents a while longer and continuing to see Robbie until we could afford to live on our own. That way, I could postpone a ceremony where I would have to speak in front of others, especially of something so profound and intimate.

I felt sure Mom would not concur, and so I could not muster the courage to broach the subject with her and my dad. I knew my parents loved me, but all those years of having my feelings dismissed taught me to hide them and even be embarrassed by them. I was definitely not going to cry or speak of how scared I was. Instead, they learned of my predicament through the grapevine.

The three of us held our second summit in the kitchen. My mom proposed marriage or adoption; I rejected both. Dad attempted to suggest abortion, but before the words were out of his mouth, Mom rebuffed the idea. Instead, she vehemently believed I should go away to consider giving my baby up for adoption. Since this way I could defer making the ultimate decision, I reluctantly agreed and let Mom take control. When I told Robbie I was leaving, he was devastated and broke down and cried. I was horrified by my actions, and my heart shattered with his pain and mine. I was filled with such shame at my cowardice but felt paralyzed with fear. I shed not a single tear.

Within a couple of weeks, I found myself on a flight headed for Chicago. There, I lived with my Aunt Jane, my senile grandfather, and my cousin Peter in my mother's family home in Evanston. I studied flute for a bit at Northwestern University, played pool and board games with Peter, and isolated myself in my bedroom with books. Robbie wanted to fly out for Christmas, but my aunt—or more likely, my mother—quashed that idea, though Audrey was allowed to visit me. I was required to attend therapy sessions to discuss giving my baby up for adoption. My obstetrician also encouraged me to give my baby away, even going so far as to line up an adoptive couple, friends of his. But that just did not seem the right thing for my baby or for me. Instead, I began to read parenting and child-development books.

On March 2, 1971, I headed to the hospital, escorted by my aunt's son-in-law, with whom I was barely acquainted. Aunt Jane had left town two weeks earlier to visit her daughter and maybe to avoid having to accompany me to the hospital. Giving birth in a teaching hospital felt like being in a circus. What I really wanted was for them all to leave me alone, but instead, a large group of strangers surrounded me and watched and chattered as my son entered the world. They all disappeared from my consciousness, though, when I held my perfect baby, Joshua Eli. I stared at this miracle in my arms with awe and an upwelling of love. All my doubts vanished, and I knew he was the best thing that had ever happened to me in my eighteen years. He gave my life purpose and meaning and beauty, and I intended to give that back to him one hundredfold. My mother flew out to be with me, and five days later, the three of us headed back to Ukiah. I was ready to provide Josh the ideal childhood. I would be the perfect mother.

Carrie Ann Wilson at 56 years old.

Livingston James Cullen

*Leland Blaine Wilson
Medical Boards Photo – 1952*

*Josephine Ruth Cullen Circa 1937
Manhattanville College Graduation*

Mom and Uncle Buddy 1919

Mom poses on Thunder on her
family farm in Dublin, Georgia

Mom in her Prom Dress.

Family Portrait- Grandma Carrie with Dad and Uncle Lyle in 1914

Brothers – Uncle Lyle, Uncle Ted, and Dad

Dad jams on the drums   *Dad's hands and cymbals double exposure*

On their Wedding Day

Uncle John with Debbie and Pam

Typical Daddy

Di steers, Pam pedals

Diana, Pam and Debbie

Debbie holds Prissy for the first time   *Debbie and Prissy dress up*

Our family portrait 1955
Pam, Debbie, Di (standing),
Mom holds Valli and Dad holds Prissy

Cherished moments with Grandma Carrie

Mom takes Prissy and Valli to the beach

Daddy holds David and Diana watches

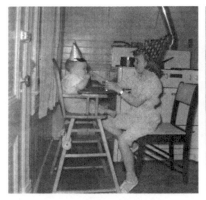

*Debbie feeds David in
their party hats*

Valli, David and Prissy posing

*Valli and Prissy down in front
Di, Debbie and Pam seated on couch*

Daddy holds Becky

Prissy and Valli share
a seat at the table

"How big are you, Prissy?"
"Soooooo Big"

Valli leans on her own

St. Patrick's Day Recital -
Valli, Pam, Debbie, Diana and Prissy

Di and Valli are feeling groovy

Gathered together – Becky, Valli, David in front;
Pam, Di and Prissy in the middle,
and Debbie is alone on top

Pam, Prissy, Di, and Debbie are ready for baseball

The Greeters

David at 2. Guess I hadn't
better fall on my chin again

Becky ready to party

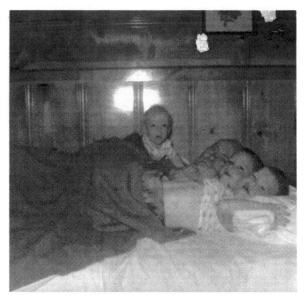

Lazy morning boys

Debbie and Pam entertain Zack

Pam gives Paul a piggy-back ride

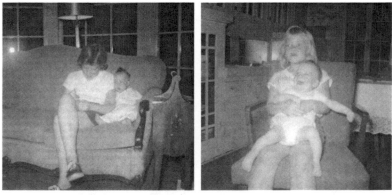

Paul watches Debbie solve the puzzle   *Prissy holds Paul tightly*

Valli cradles Paul and Zack
is comforted by his thumb

Becky is almost big
enough to hold Paul

Di, Pam, Debbie and Prissy are ready for Mass

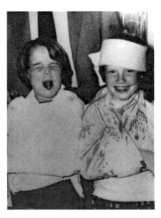

Audrey and Di clowning around

Zack and David on church steps

Pam and Di modeling

The musical end of our living room

Singing with Mom – Prissy, Di, Debbie, Pam, and Valli

Deborah

Pamela

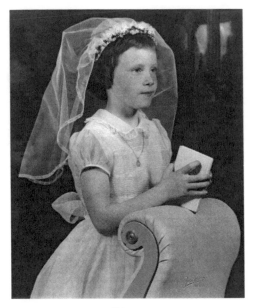

Diana

Priscilla

Valerie

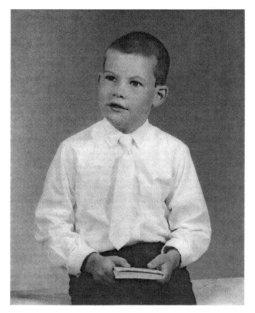

David

Rebecca

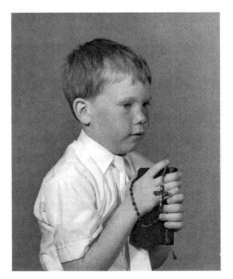

Zachary

Paul's first communion photo is missing.
Mrs. Gulyas probably has it.

THE 4TH VOICE ～ PRISCILLA LOUISE

o

WHEN I WAS 0, WE LIVED IN EUREKA, A TOWN OF NOW ABOUT 26,000 on the northern California coast, which still looks and feels like a very old salty dog kind of place. It has a naval yard and is in the middle of the redwood logging industry. The highway still runs right through it along the coast, making for a sluggish drive at any time of day. It's full of gigantic Victorian buildings that are protected as landmarks and delicious seafood restaurants, but other than that, it seems far from the rest of civilization and reminds me of a place a person would go to get away from it all forever.

My dad got a job there, so he and my mom moved from San Francisco with my three red-headed sisters. I was born at the old St. Joseph's Hospital and my next sister, only thirteen months younger, was born at the new St. Joseph's Hospital. Though now aware of the improbability of a hospital actually being built or even just rebuilt in only a year, that's the story I remember my mom telling me, at an age too young to even guess at.

1–3

Most kids start walking at around one year of age. I imagine that's when my younger sister started walking also, which would have made me barely over two. Mom told us that when Valli started walking, I went over and pushed her down. I don't remember that, of course, and I don't recall ever feeling unkindly toward her or my other little siblings. The pecking order—nature's way of playing our cards for us, like parents do, until we understand the game. I don't think I ever lifted a finger to anyone at any other time in my life, except, I admit, as a young mother, but it was discomfiting and short-lived.

When the family moved to Mendocino County, we first lived in Talmage in a farmhouse that I have exactly three memories of. One is of a flood and a man, a friend of my parents, carrying me to apparently higher ground; another is of being on the back enclosed porch with two siblings younger than I and dropping a huge water jug on somebody's foot followed by loud crying; and the last is that my older sisters got to ride the bus to school. I couldn't wait until I was old enough for school so I could ride the bus, but it was never to be. We would move into town soon and I would walk, ride, or bicycle to school for the next twelve years.

4

"They say it all started when Gerald was two. That's the time kids start talking, least, most of them do."

Gerald McBoing -Boing is one of the books I really liked as a kid. We had tons of books in our house, always. The original *Mary Poppins* was so much better than the movie. *The Peterkin Papers*, A.A. Milne, poetry books with and without pictures, Nancy Drew and the Hardy Boys, Trixie Belden, and the Bobbsey Twins all kept me occupied when I was young. Every Christmas, we were delighted with piles of new books for all ages—one of the perks of a big family. Our built-in bookshelves were crammed with classics, controversies, nonfiction, sets of award-winning novelists, and so many others. Mom enjoyed religious books, mostly on the history of the Catholic Church and the popes. (When we were teenagers, she bought a book called Deliverance, which she put on the shelf with the others and strongly suggested we read. Assuming it was another of her boring religious tomes, we passed, until sometime later, when the movie came out.)

There were huge coffee-table books with pictures and photographs from museums and great places around the world, famous artwork that we might or might not get to see in our lifetimes, and close-ups of the finest pieces of jewelry and clothing and other designs since the beginning of time. A set of books on the five great religions— Catholicism (funny I put that one first), Judaism, Islam, Hinduism, and Buddhism—I took with me when I grew up and left home.

> *I'm so sorry for old Adam*
> *Just as sorry as can be*
> *For he never had a mammy*
> *For to hold him on her knee.*
> *And he never had a childhood*
> *Playin' 'round the cabin door*
> *And he never had a pappy*
> *For to tell him all he know.*
> *And I've always had the feelin'*
> *He'd o' let that apple be*
> *If he'd only had a mammy*
> *For to hold him on her knee.*

Mom read us stories to go to sleep, almost as much as she sang to us. She had made some recordings as a young woman and we now have copies on CD, thanks to Pam. Mom was the classical to my dad's jazz. They were nicely complementary in that regard. He admired her musical abilities and she was more than happy to open the house with host bar to his swinging friends when the opportunity arose.

She also played piano quite well. She had studied piano her entire young life; she practiced something like four hours a day during the week and eight hours on the weekends for many years, and it paid off, not financially but in our enjoyment of it. She was fortunate enough to inherit the family piano, a Steinway, which was a staple in our house and now sits in Di's house in Santa Cruz. That piano really has an excellent sound, so excellent that it makes playing a lesser piano very difficult. The favorites were Mendelssohn's "Fox

Hunt," a number called "Enchanted Cascade", which I think was a practice piece, and a French song ("Bien Ami"), a happy lilting number in 6/8 time.

Along with Dad's collection of jazz and swing 78s, our record supply rivaled our book supply. We listened to beautiful classical pieces, the great Broadway musical soundtracks until we knew every word, comedy albums—Bill Cosby's *To Russell My Brother Whom I Slept With* was one of my favorites—and so many others, including some obscure but marvelous albums. None could compare to Copp & Brown, two English fellows who produced hilarious stories starring mostly animals, like the kitten who gets separated from its parents at a music recital and wanders the aisles until the helpful MC asks its name ("The kitten's name is Meow"); the unforgettable Ric and Gic, who picnic on the highway, not understanding the speed limit sign and pulling the wig off a woman whose cries for help lead them to Quicksand Bog; the clever pot whose owner teaches it to run home from a gambling den once it's filled with money ("I skip I skip"); and the slow-witted Mr. Hippity, who is tricked into believing his toy duck will die without junket, until they are both taken in by a kindly rich old man. An entire album was dedicated to the journey of the Glups (including their cow, who sat in the front passenger seat) from Kennebunkport, Maine to San Francisco to collect an inheritance from an estranged relative. All the voices and sound effects were made by Jim and Ed. We quoted those stories in their silly voices constantly through the years and anyone who enjoyed them as much as we did was a true family friend indeed.

5

I went to kindergarten at Yokayo, the largest elementary school in town, because St. Mary's didn't have a kindergarten then. It was within walking distance of home—about six blocks, a wonderful learning experience in itself for a five-year-old. Imagine all the details of life a child can pick up from just walking along the street. So I walked back in 1959, with so many other kids, to kindergarten and home again. One day I showed up at home crying because a boy had followed me and kept pulling my pigtails. My grandfather Papapa was at the house when I got home that day and I think he and Mom chuckled about it. I can't remember ever not liking school, even that first year when I would have been alone without my sisters to guide me, as they already were at the Catholic school. Mom says I got an A in scissors and her sister who was visiting laughed about that. Her sister didn't have any kids and apparently didn't realize the importance of getting an A in something, in anything.

Our house had a big fat pink cement porch across the front with cracks in it that turned it into a giant skewed hopscotch board, or better yet, a blueprint for a two-dimensional playhouse of our own, each outlined area a different room. Someone would be the mother, someone would be the father, and the others would be newly invented children or friends. I always chose to be the dog, crawling palms flat to the ground if a male and on fingertips if a female. A crabapple tree grew right next to the porch facing the street, overflowing with buds in the spring and then with crabapples a month later that fell to cover half the porch and the ground surrounding it. The yard was enclosed with a fence in the back and a hedge in the front. We had a Gravenstein apple tree toward the back of the house on one side and had homemade applesauce every summer. A plum tree grew near the front gate and we made jam from it, though most of it, to my recollection, ended up sauce. In the summer, we often slept outside in the yard in sleeping bags to stay cool. One evening a stranger wandered down the street and Pam climbed up into the crabapple tree to have a look and a holler. To our amazement, he responded by opening the gate and coming into the yard. We ran into the house and he left, and nobody ever hollered from the crabapple tree again, though we continued to spend our summer nights outside.

6

We all went to St. Mary's, the Roman Catholic elementary school, still standing at the same place, though a new church was built closer to it from the old one in the middle of town. The old church was beautiful and warm. It's still standing also but is no longer used as a church. The Catholic community in Ukiah was our second family. We never missed a Midnight Mass and rarely a Sunday one. Mom directed the choir for a number of years and was a member of the Silver Ball committee, an annual benefit for the school, which eventually became Mardi Gras and is, to this day, their largest fundraiser. Mom went to Mass every day during Lent and tried to drag us along, sometimes successfully and sometimes not. There was an orphanage run by the nuns a couple of blocks from our house and we would walk there at 6 a.m. for those forty days, chilly that early, for Lenten Mass. The nuns would sing a cappella and the priests took turns giving the service. I'm sorry I never took my kids to Lenten Mass for forty days straight; it's an accomplishment, and how much spirituality do we get in our lives without a little effort?

The first day of school brought brand new white oxfords, bright white socks, and uniform jumpers, or skirts for the seventh and eighth grade girls, sometimes new and sometimes hand-me-down. I would see my sisters and brothers around the playground and had lots of friends in my class, especially Kathy and Diane, and Janet, whose mom played organ and smelled like sweet flowers. St. Mary's was so much fun, most of the time. A couple of harsh memories won't escape me. I saw my brother Zack get his head opened during a baseball game on the field and to this day I feel a gut wrench when I watch the game, as friendly as it is; and I saw my brother David get beat up in front of school. The assailant eventually became an upstanding member of the community but not to me. I had to continue to blame him for that misery; I hadn't done anything about it except watch.

My dad had a reputation in the community for being a great guy. I don't remember talking to him, but I remember the sound of his voice from hearing him talk on the phone to people. Rarely he would end up on the phone during dinner, which meant somebody else had not answered it, and he was caught by a patient, or maybe hospital personnel trying to get him to cover when he wasn't on call. We were supposed to answer the phone "Dr. Wilson's residence" – or my mom would. She knew how to put off patients. One of Dad's patients, a very nice woman who taught at St. Mary's, told him she was tired of her family and friends telling her to quit smoking. He told her to break the filters off her cigarettes and stick them in her ears.

Dad had one habit that was awful, one of those things you grew up with, and so didn't know it was weird until you'd been in the world a while. He never used napkins when he ate. He would wipe his hands in the armpits of his shirt, his hand between body and arm, then pull it out. He also didn't use deodorant because apparently he was allergic to it. I don't remember him smelling bad ever, except for his feet, and our darling little poodle Coco would lie on his socks to sleep.

7

Mom took us clothes-shopping in San Francisco twice every year because Ukiah didn't have any good stores except for the Palace Dress Shop for women and MacNab's for men (still there), but those were for grownups. We came home with the most stylish clothes, and the shoes! In high school, we traded outfits (except for Pam; she was too small) and I got shoes then that I wore for a good twenty years, real quality stuff. I still love the city, any city, not just the stores but the hustle and bustle, even the smell of the traffic. After shopping, if there weren't too many of us, we'd sit near a window at a downtown café, play card or dice games, and observe the people walking by as we discussed events of the world. Greatness, we came to learn, comes not from achieving excellence but from caring for it.

I can only give you love that lasts forever
And the promise to be near each time you call
Say it's me that you'll adore for now and evermore
That's all, that's all.
I can only give you country walks in springtime
And a hand to hold when leaves begin to fall
And a love whose burning light will warm the winter night
That's all, that's all.

We five oldest sisters sang and danced together. We also played in musicals when there were parts for children. Mom made our wonderful costumes and we entered recitals and talent competitions with other local kids, and sometimes entertained at convalescent homes and the like. Rick and Dave Kleman had a little rock band, Ginger Sarber (Jesse McCartney's mom) sang, and Holly Near swung across the stage as Peter Pan. We tap-danced in sandwich-board clocks with gold mesh alarm heads or head-to-toe black ballet leotards sewn all over with bright-colored satin streamers, among our various costumes.

Our house was on a one-block street, Oak Park Avenue, lovely with trees down both sides. At the north end lived a highway patrolman and his three kids. I don't remember a wife. His mother, Mrs. Sousa, ran Westside Grocery, the neighborhood market, which was close enough that we could walk there and back after dark as long as we didn't dawdle. It was directly across the alley from the back of their house. His two little boys, Teddy and Marty Hair, were my first playmates besides my siblings. Teddy was blond and Marty was dark and always had a runny nose. I have often wondered what happened to them. Toward the south end of the block lived a mother with her daughter and son, Kit and Norman. Kit was a fat girl who probably was tormented for it throughout her youth, by us as well as others, but I remember her as one of our best friends.

At the very south end of the street was a small church with a driveway all the way around it, which was one of our cycling spots away from the house when we were little, any day except Sunday, when they congregated. When older, we would continue a block farther to McPeak Street and circle back down, and older still, continue on to the Mendocino Avenue area where could be found many of our friends' homes as well as a back way to Dad's office, or we'd head down Clay Street to heavier traffic. At the church, Oak Park meets Jones Street. Mom sometimes rode a bicycle to Dad's office and back, panting by the time she reached home from the ride up "Jones Street hill", a grade unnoticeable to anyone under age forty and nonexistent when compared to the real hills that rose only a mile or so to the west. The stretch between McPeak and the foothills was empty land. We watched it fill in row by row as the years went by. A friend of my brothers taught me to burn rubber on Eastlick Drive, one of the first of the short dead-end blocks to fill up with young families.

8

When Becky was a baby, she was sitting in the highchair at dinnertime one day and the tray fell off, and her along with it. She cut her tongue right down the middle. Dad asked if the chair was okay and mom said, what about the baby? He said, I can fix the baby, but I have to pay to get the chair fixed.

Her tongue did begin to heal, but it did not heal together, instead becoming forked. Dad had to scale it down and sew it back together. When Zack was a toddler, he cut his nose and it had to be stitched. I went with them to the office, where Dad put a four-hole button on the little nostril and sewed through it just like you would on a shirt. Once the cut healed, the button was snipped off. Dad would take us on house calls with him now and then. He carried a doctor bag and we played with the otoscope more often than the stethoscope, maybe because the rubber ends came in so many different sizes (and it was way more fun to look at giant-size nose hair than listen to heart beats). Our living room shelves contained a large number of medical encyclopedias. That was how we learned about anatomy. Body parts were simply what make up a human physique. What more needed to be said?

I went to summer school at Yokayo Elementary one year and took a class taught by a teacher who called me Razzy the entire six weeks. My friends giggled about it, but I was too shy to say anything. At the very end of the program, he asked me where I got the nickname Razzy. I told him that actually it was Prissy and he said I've only known one other girl named Priscilla and they called her Razzy too.

9

Nine years old is a great place to be. You can spend time with friends away from the family and still have so much innocence that it is just pure enjoyment. Coming home on your own when the church bell rings is almost like being a grownup. Skipping in public; finding miniature frogs in puddles by the park; falling asleep in the sun with your shirt rolled up and waking with a nasty sunburn, then learning that the large Noxzema jar has all the letters of the alphabet on it. (In high school, one of my friends could hold a jar of Noxzema under her breast in the what-can-you-hold-under-your-boobs bathroom competition. We considered her the loser because her breasts were so big.) At age nine, I got glasses. I hated wearing glasses so much that I didn't for the first few years except when absolutely necessary.

In the fourth grade, I liked a boy in the second grade until I saw him throw up on the merry-go-round. That was the end of that. I moved on to another second-grader who came from a family of all boys, nine of them. Mom would ask us in church why couldn't we be more like the Hendersons, always so well behaved. He gave me my first kiss outside church – right in front on the steps!

Pam would feed the little frogs to our pet turtles. She also pulled the wings off flies and locked us in the basement when she baby-sat, a much scarier place than it already was when told the lights would be turned off and we'd be alone down there. We weren't completely wary of the basement, however. We were sent down when necessary to restock. It was a small basement reached via a trapdoor in the family-room floor and used to store bulk products like toilet paper and paper towel as well as mustard, mayonnaise, and ketchup. It also housed boxes of our parents' past and other things normally found in the storage rooms of a home. Whenever one of our many cats was due to have kittens, she would disappear and we knew she and her litter would surface in the basement crawl space. Then within a few weeks, they would show themselves safe and healthy through the coverless vents that entered into the yard.

In 1963, President Kennedy was assassinated. We had never had a television in our house, but mom wanted to watch the news about that so got hold of one somewhere. We were living in a house down the street at the time while our house was being remodeled, finally adding on a couple of bedrooms and a family room. Until then, we had slept the three oldest girls in one room and the other six of us in another room with two sets of bunk beds and a single bed, which I slept on. Zack and Paul shared a bed sleeping a head at each end, sometimes tied in with a harness so they wouldn't be able to get up after they were put to bed. The harnesses were actually made to fit around the mattress and secure a child. You'd be hard pressed to find one of those in a store now. Truman Hayes did the remodeling and Al and Leno Valentini were the painters. They were great guys, the nice way they treated us kids running around when we just couldn't contain our curiosity any longer and wandered in to watch the work. They gave us nicknames. Mine was Sunshine and I bet my siblings could remember theirs, too.

So we tread quietly through those somber days after Kennedy's death, the first Catholic president. Is that why he had been shot? Maybe it was just that this was the biggest, most outrageous event the public had ever been able to experience en masse that so galvanized us, but the TV was gone again before the shock had passed.

10

When Christ our Lord was born in Bethlehem afar
Although 'twas night there shone as bright as noon a star
Never so brightly never so whitely
shone the stars as on that night
The brightest star went
away to call the wise men from the Orient.

We had the most wonderful Christmases growing up, exactly what you imagine with the big family in the big house and all the presents. The main door into the living room was a thick heavy wood sliding door that was always open (unless someone in the rest of the house wanted to drown the noise from the piano, drums, or stereo), but on Christmas morning, it would be closed. However old we had become, we had to line up by age, oldest to youngest, in the hallway facing that closed door. I can remember how dark it was in that hall on such a rare occasion. Then we all went in at the same time. We received an Irish mail, which is a vehicle that you steer with your feet and pump to accelerate with your hands, a surrey with a fringe on top, a tandem bicycle, and every other kind of bicycle including a unicycle, which nobody but David ever learned to ride.

David was an unhappy boy. He always seemed to be moping or angry and took a lot of grief from the tough kids at school. Ultimately he would take it out on the littler boys at home, particularly Paul, since Zack was pretty feisty and would give back as well as he got. Paul sat, stood, and lay through a lot of experiments of various kinds, especially if they were risky. Once he was shot at with a bow and arrow, which went into his shirt collar, and he was tied up a few times too. As a teenager, he became quite the clown, amusing and sweet natured, while David spent a good part of his high school days in the garage playing hooky and dreaming of bigger and better things.

My dad would sometimes barter with patients who didn't have money to pay for his services. Fresh produce was certainly welcome and he was always happy to get new music. He had a reel-to-reel tape player and once in a while got a tape we all enjoyed, like Trini Lopez ("Lemon Tree") or Dean Martin or Perry Como. We weren't to touch his drums or hi-fi—his one true passion, which he collected in pieces over the years, literally wearing cardboard in his shoes at times rather than spend a penny that he could use on his stereo equipment—but he was at work until dinnertime and little by little, we all learned how to feed the tape reels and adjust the amp controls to our preferences, then put them back again before he got home. Debbie, Valli, and Zack all learned to play the drums and, since Dad was playing them late at night while we slept on oblivious, they must have picked that up during the afternoons while he was at work.

When we moved back into our house, we had four bedrooms upstairs. Deb and Pam shared a room, Di and I shared a room, Valli and Becky shared a room, and the boys had a suite of their own with a walk-in closet and a small bathroom that had a square bathtub with a lowered showerhead because they were still so little. The big bathroom had two toilet stalls, two sinks, a tub-sink combo, and a separate shower, exactly what was needed for six girls. We did call the bathrooms the girls' bath and the boys' bath, and the bedrooms were called by color, since each had been given a different color carpet drawn to a neutral in the hallway. The windows of the two backyard-facing bedrooms (the red room and the blue room) accessed a narrow balcony that could be climbed down in case of emergency. Of course everyone used it to climb down as well as up for other than emergencies – what else would be the fun of it? I only climbed down once. Sliding down one of the posts scratched up my stomach and I decided if there ever really was an emergency, I'd just climb out my own bedroom window onto the roof, then jump onto the front lawn, even though there was a tree right outside the room with branches that stretched onto the edge of the roof and would have been the obvious choice for climbing down if ever need be. We climbed out that window onto the roof many times, to lie in the sun, to sneak drinks with friends, to spy on people down below, or just because it was there. From the first level, you had to hoist a foot onto the drain gutter to get onto the top roof, which with time left the gutter bent and useless. If that roof could talk, it would have some unique stories to tell.

Di and I had an understanding that whichever of us was second into bed would have to turn off the light, so she made a point of jumping into bed at the very last second when she saw me heading to get into mine. Always the trooper, I turned out the light.

11

I got pretty good grades in school. I was a very good speller and in junior high, I made it into the finals of the town spelling bee. I lost. The caller had a cold that day and gave me 'hemoglobin' as one of the challenge words. I said h-e-b-o-g-l-o-b-i-d.

Grandma Carrie, Dad's mother, moved into a little house in the alley behind us when she became old enough to need someone nearby to care for her. She had a piano and went to the Methodist church regularly with the wife of one of Dad's Jazzberry Jam band mates. She planted plastic flowers in her front yard. I thought they were pretty. Of all of us, Di spent the most time with Grandma. Eventually Di and her little family would live in that same house after Grandma died, until they became too many and had to move on.

Helen and Kathy Thies lived in a second little house right next to Grandma's. Helen was a sad old mother who just stayed home most of the time and her chubby daughter Kathy was her connection to the outside world. Kathy was Zack's age and always came out to say hi and chat when we were within hearing distance. She had a crippled arm and walked with a limp for reasons unknown to me and seemed a little behind other kids her age in development. Helen treated Kathy like an invalid, apparently to keep her from leaving her mother alone, but Kathy still managed to make herself a happy life. Someone got her a tricycle when she was a teenager and she loved riding that thing to the corner store, (George's, we called it, even years after George had gone), though it was cumbersome for her. One day she tried to turn the corner on it and fell over, and after that she just went back to walking. Despite her mother's dependence, Kathy grew up, slimmed down, and went on to marry and raise three stepchildren, moving out of that little house on Barnes Street never to return.

12

When Paul started first grade, mom went back to work. She became the office manager at dad's office. At that point, we were ages 18, 16, 15, 13, 12, 11, 10, 8, and 6. Mom had hired a housekeeper, Margie, who was only nineteen when she started and stayed with us until we were grown. She became a friend and confidant when we were older. When my parents went out of town for a medical convention, Margie would baby-sit. I know at least once she reported to them upon their return that that was the last time she would stay with us, apparently having gone insane during that seventy-two-hour period.

Debbie, as the oldest, was the obvious surrogate mother when necessary. She certainly did her share of babysitting. One evening when my parents were out, she got into a battle with Pam and Di and locked the house so they couldn't get in. I happened to be outside also and they told me to ring the bell so she'd open the door. When she did, however, she tossed out a cup of hot water, angry enough not to care who received it and forcing my hand to join the ranks of the outside camp. We decided to run away. Where would we go? San Francisco, KFRC radio, the ranking hot station of the day. It was only one hundred and twenty miles away and we would say we were friends of the Beatles and talk with British accents. They would be so excited to meet us. Plan set, we coaxed the little kids up in the second-story bedroom into throwing us down clothes and food, which they did, and we headed south, following the freeway but staying low and out of sight off the shoulder. A long time later, maybe two miles out of town, we started getting tired and feeling that maybe we had been hasty in our getaway. We sat and ate, giving ourselves a chance to confirm our change of plans, then grudgingly headed back toward home. I remember my best friend Kathy's older sister driving up to us and asking what the heck we were doing, saying that people were out looking for us including the police. Wow! We'd caused a stir! That attitude would've fit in great with our trip to KFRC, but reality set in when we got back home and saw all those glaring grownup faces staring down at us, not caring to discuss our futures in rock-n-roll, just our presence in our bedrooms right now.

13

Our family vacations were few and far between. We occasionally went to the coast for two or three days during the summer and slept on the beach, which was allowed at that time. Mom and dad would sleep in the car. We went to Konocti Resort in Clearlake where we swam and played. These days it has grown to quite a popular resort and concert venue. We drove up to Brooktrails in Willits and rode horses for an afternoon. Di got bored with the canter and held her horse back until she had enough space between herself and the rest of us to gallop a ways.

In the summer of 1967, we had a real vacation. Mom took all of us kids and the dog Coco on a six-week trip across the states. Debbie was getting ready to leave for college and had not seen much of the country nor many of our relatives, whom mom wanted us to meet. Mom had always cut our hair herself and before this trip she cut our hair really short, except for Pam's, the girl scout in mom planning ahead for time efficiency, no doubt. Dad went for the first stretch of the journey but left to go back to work after a couple of weeks. (Nobody ever complains on their deathbeds that they spent too little time at the office...) We had a fabulous time. We went to Nebraska to see our paternal uncles, aunts, and cousins, stopped in Texas a time or two and saw the biggest bugs we'd ever seen, and passed through Mississippi right after Biloxi had been hit by a hurricane. We went to the house where mom grew up in Evanston, outside Chicago—1017 Lee Street, then she married a man named Lee who died on October 17—and saw Papapa and Aunt Jane and cousin Peter (who looked like David and Becky). The best part of the trip, however, was New York City. We saw so many different colors and styles and worlds of humanity. It was a people-watcher's paradise. We stayed at the St. Albert Hotel and really took the whirlwind tourist route. Then we went upstate to visit mom's college friend Mimi, who lived next to the Skakels of Kennedy in-law fame where we were invited to go swimming. We visited Mt. Vernon and saw a show at Radio City Music Hall, and I got yelled at by someone on the street to "curb your dog". He didn't slow down to tell me what that was supposed to mean, but it didn't take long to figure out. Somewhere during the trip, we tried out a stockade. Paul was so skinny; his whole body could've fit through one of the holes. We traveled in a station wagon pulling a U-Haul trailer with all of our luggage. We slept in motels where they would let us all stay in one room and have a dog, though sometimes mom would use her instincts about whether to ask if the dog was allowed and just carry her quietly in. She was such a good smart poodle, never caused any problem.

14

I saw a newscast recently about elderly people having trouble getting their medications and one old woman was screaming at the reporter about how angry and upset they all were with the plight they were facing. Shockingly, she reminded me of my mother. The tone of voice was so familiar, I realized I had heard it many times as a youngster. I wasn't the least bit fearful of mom, but I can see that she was very critical. She told us that her family didn't always get along and it was very important to her that we all love each other and be agreeable. We weren't allowed to argue and certainly weren't supposed to fight. Once, Debbie, Pam, and Di got in a fight. Apparently Debbie and Pam were going at it and Di, the peacemaker, tried to stop it. They ended up with black eyes, which they wore to school the next day. Val says we are too non-confrontational and boy, is she right. We rarely discuss personal or other matters close to our hearts, especially about each other, but the family grapevine always proves itself healthy with the discussions we have forwarded to other members. Round and round the story goes until the only one who needed to hear it in the first place finally does.

Mom was so funny. She had a subtle sense of humor that came out in little spurts throughout the day though generally avoided dinnertime. Her family had owned a farm near Macon, Georgia and every now and then that southernness would show. When we were in the car and she saw a cute man, she'd say "Hey, honey, you spoke for?" with the windows closed, of course, and "One side or a leg off" to anyone who might put her in the position of having to slow down when she had the right of way. "Offer it up for the souls in Purgatory" was her way of tranquilizing an unnecessary whiner. How many times we heard that in our young lives, I couldn't count. When she had something to discuss that she considered distressful or uncomfortable, she would start the conversation with "Now, how can I put this nicely?"—so-called diplomacy making a beeline for the jugular. Her schooling had included elocution class, and she still remembered one of her favorites, which she taught us, all Ts aspirated: *"Betty Bota bought some butter, but, said she, this butter's bitter.*

If I put it in my batter, it will make my batter bitter, but if I buy some better butter, it will make my batter better. So Betty bought some better butter and it made her batter better." She was a stickler for proper English ("Enunciate!") and would correct anyone anywhere, feeling it just part of the job of making this world a better place. Dad had a patient, a woman whose name was spelled E-u-l-i-n-i-d but called herself Ilunid. Mom would tell her directly when she announced herself for an office visit, "It's U-lin-id."

Across Clay Street, at the end of our block, lived the nicest man and his six kids, five boys and one girl. They lived right by the Albertinum, the orphanage run by the nuns, which included the school, chapel, and children's and nuns' dormitories. The Nicholsons would occasionally take in one of the kids from the school as a foster child. One year they took in a boisterous boy named Johnny Gaines, who outside the school was able to be just one of the neighborhood kids. He kissed me as I sat on the back of our car one sunny afternoon, the first and only kiss I ever got from a black boy. I think he probably kissed a number of girls those days, including at least one of my sisters.

15

I remember fifteen as being one of the best years of my life. I had the kind of contentment amid the terror of teenage-hood that from never having been not cared for, the contentment that, twenty or thirty years later, protects you from demons in the real world invading your personal space because you never knew they were capable of getting in. I had steered away from most of my grade-school friends and was hanging out a lot with my seventeen-year-old sister and her friends, smoking pot, taking speed, driving without a license, that sort of thing.

If you're going to San Francisco
Be sure to wear some flowers in your hair
If you go to San Francisco
You're going to meet some gentle people there...

A lot of us from town would spend summer days at Cold Creek near Potter Valley. It's a narrow stretch of river that was perfect for keeping cool and occasionally inner-tubing for miles to the other end of town. The local kids still go there. There's one spot where the water can pull you under a large rock, and I believe a boy drowned out there not long ago, but it is otherwise quite idyllic. One summer we piled into my dad's old car and as soon as we got there the car collapsed, just like in a cartoon, unable to make it through one more 100-degree trek over the river and through the woods to Cold Creek to get stoned we go.

The best place to swim was the Mill Creek dam. You turn right at the end of Talmage Road then left onto Mill Creek Road. You go about five miles and come upon three dams. The last one has a picnic table and a couple of parking areas. It's long and narrow and every couple of years the Army Corps of Engineers trims back all the greenery and cleans it up. There's not really any beach to speak of. Kids just lie out right on the dam and sometimes they fish, sometimes they swim, sometimes they swing out on a rope swing that hangs from a tree on the woods side of the dam, not the street side. A few people died from jumping off that rope swing too close to the edge and every time, the ACOE goes out and puts up a Danger sign. The next day some kid pulls the sign out and everyone starts swinging on the rope swing again. You can swim the length of the dam to the shallow end. A lot of people think it is too far, but you just have to relax and enjoy the journey. I did it a number of times and back. I'd have to say it is my absolute favorite swimming hole of all time.

I started smoking cigarettes when I was fifteen. We all smoked. Mom and dad smoked Camel nonfilter, though mom didn't start until she was in her forties. She told us it wouldn't necessarily cause cancer, that some people were predisposed to developing cancer and it had nothing to do with any bad habits. Dad tried to tell us not to smoke, but what could he say, really, smoking at least a pack a day himself at a time when you could even smoke in a hospital or a medical office and the first thing we put out getting ready for a party were ashtrays. When we went shopping at department stores, the dressing rooms always had ashtrays in them. Mom and us kids and our friends would smoke and drink coffee and play cards for hours at the breakfast room table. The table was a rectangle that fit in the breakfast room just right technically, but the room was at the angle of an L formed by the kitchen and the dining room, so one corner of the table prevented smooth access through the area. Mom had a carpenter chop the corner off and leave it a three-legged table. It worked fine. We ate most our family dinners there, with whoever got there last sitting at the kitchen counter, unless someone had already chosen to eat at the counter for that particular meal to avoid the dynamic at the table.

16–17

My brothers built a fort in the backyard. It was there for years. They took shingles off the garage of the house next door to use on the fort to protect it from the rain. It worked. The little lady that lived next door was very sweet about it—she told my parents, but the shingles stayed. A cherry tree grew right on the property line and when the cherries were ripe, we would pick them and bake pies or whatever else we thought of. The cherries stay on the tree when they're ripe. You have to get up a ladder and pick them off before the birds get them. One day you'll notice the tree is full of cherries and the next day the crows and jays will have eaten almost every cherry off the tree. We would share the pies with Mrs. Cox since we considered her half owner of the tree. She was so old and frail, we would take her one slice of pie and she said it was too much, she'd never eat it all.

My first mate, Alan, was cute and charming, a high school football player who dated the popular girls and looked great in whatever style the kids happened to be wearing. He lived with his sister and father on the Mendocino Avenue curve beyond our house and walked home with me sometimes, hanging out at the house for a few hours before heading home. Many years later he told me our house was like a second home to him, which I had not considered as a teenager. I taught him to play Puccini on the piano and let him drive mom's car when she left it home in one of the older kid's care. We played games and listened to music, and started making out on a regular basis, but the first time we slept together was at his house, not mine. His father was a mailman, divorced, and would leave the flag up on the mailbox as a code for his kids when he had a woman over. So one day we proceeded to venture into the unknown world of sex, the first time for both of us and, looking back, a perfect first time—not intimidated or scared or out of control, just inexperienced. We heard his father enter the house and both jumped up at the same time. He grabbed my belongings and tossed them after me into the closet, where I dressed, wide-eyed and trying to comprehend the day, then left as fast as I could when the coast was clear. I walked all the way home and discovered when I got there that my clothes were on inside out.

I played clarinet in the high school band and loved it. My closest friends during high school, Elaine and Nina, came from band class. We marched in parades, not just locally but also out of town for competitions. We played half-time shows during high school football season and in the next couple of years even showed up in uniform a time or two drunk and fell in the bleachers, but we always made it through the shows just fine, music and steps memorized. Four of us friends played in a clarinet quartet. We were really very good. We took private lessons and had the privilege of being recorded on an album from a concert the band put on. Di won a couple of marching trophies during high school. I won a couple of honor band awards, the first entries into my Special Things wooden box that sits in my office.

Band, in fact, carried me through the emptiness I experienced when my sister became pregnant and went to Chicago to live with an aunt during the pregnancy. She had just finished high school. I have never missed anyone so much in my life. I did have a breakup with a boyfriend once that left me lonely and hungry for a while, but that was more a matter of having to break a bad habit than the simple loss of a loved one that gripped me when my childhood better half was suddenly gone.

All my bags are packed, I'm ready to go
I'm standing here outside your door
I hate to wake you up to say goodbye
The dawn is breaking, it's early morn
The taxi's waiting, he's blowin' his horn
Already I'm so lonesome I could cry...

I was the one who told my mother that Di was pregnant. I don't think she asked me directly to tell mom, but she didn't tell me not to, and I knew it was serious enough to have to speak up about right away. I went into her bedroom and sat on the bed, then I don't know if I told her straight out or if I said "I have to tell you something" and she said "Di's pregnant", but the truth came out. Then she must have talked to dad and her family in Chicago. I don't recall hearing any discussion about it, but Di packed up and was gone by the time I started junior year in the fall. At Christmas that year, we all got something made by her personally out of suede in different colors and designs. They were very nice. I got a blue suede dress that I wore many times, I think until it fell apart.

After the baby was born, the two of them would return home, and a new, more grownup time would begin for us both.

The 5th Voice ～ Valerie Jean

—The middle child

I WAS THE QUINTESSENTIAL MIDDLE CHILD—INDECISIVE, INSECURE, low self-esteem, "too little" for the big kids and "too big" for the little kids. I remember sometimes feeling as if I really wasn't a part of the whole thing, growing up as if I was an outsider. Even now, as an adult, when my family gets together, I still have a feeling of being somewhat distanced from all the goings-on. Actually, I think I lay that little trip on myself after we've all parted, perhaps because I never feel as though I've made the most of the gathering.

I was born in Eureka, California, where my older sister, Priscilla, was also born. My father was county physician there in Humboldt County, and, because there were already four other children, Mom was a busy housewife and mother. I don't remember much about my first few years, but I understand I was a smiley little girl. I know there was a lot of love around, because in all those old photographs of us five oldest kids, we were usually smiling.

I adored my father and his mother, Gramma Gigi, but my mother and I seemed to butt heads from the beginning. She once told me that her pregnancy with me was probably the most difficult and stressful time of her marriage, and her life. I got the impression that she was unhappy, and with four little kids already, I'm sure she was stressed to the limit. Because my father worked late every day, she was really raising a family by herself. She believed that the stress, frustration, and anger she felt was transferred to her unborn child— me. Considering our volatile relationship through the years, I'm sure that had something to do with it.

When my mother was ready to deliver me, she had to go to the bathroom, but the nurses wouldn't let her because she was dilated so much. She told me that when I finally came out, so did all that poop, and we gave each other crap from then on! I'm sure I must have loved my mother, as most children do, but we just never seemed to agree on anything. Even as a little girl, I felt angry a lot of the time.

I loved it when Gramma Gigi came to stay with us. She was a whirlwind bundle of energy packaged in a tiny frame, and she had a substantial bosom that any little child would love to fall into—warm, soft, and comforting. She would do some silly little jig now and then, and she used to leave little notes around the house, especially one in our bedrooms that read, "Cleanliness is next to Godliness." She was truly what one would call a God-fearing woman; my impression of her was that she never would have done anything to tick off God! It seemed my mother didn't appreciate her the way the rest of us did. Whether that was because my gramma came from a dirt-poor family or Mom just didn't like her very much, I don't know. I do know, because my mother told me, that I thought Gramma could do no wrong. When she was around I wouldn't let anyone else help me dress or do just about anything for me, only Gramma Gigi. Perhaps that upset my mother. Now a mother myself, I guess that would irritate me if my boys treated me like they didn't need me.

When I was three, my family moved to Ukiah from Eureka. By then I had a little brother, David. My father was a physician out at the Mendocino State Hospital and so we lived on the grounds in a little house. Evidently, there was quite a storm the winter that I was about four. I don't remember the storm and flooding, but my family, like so many other families, had to be taken out by boat to drier ground. We ended up living in a large house near the hospital, not far from the Russian River. I remember hearing the crowing of a rooster many times early in the morning, out there in the country, and also seeing tall fields of corn out in front of the house. At some point, we moved into town and ended up on possibly one of the most beautiful streets in all of Ukiah. Back in the '60s and '70s, Ukiah was a sleepy little town where everyone knew each other quite well. There were no stoplights and certainly no big-box stores or "low income" housing. Of course, as I got older I couldn't wait to get away. Now I long for those wonderful days when Ukiah was small, surrounded by pear trees that blossomed beautifully in spring; the hot, dry summer days and nights; the crisp, cold mornings in the dead of winter; the windy, balmy autumn season, when you could actually smell the pears that still hung on the trees before picking. We'd hang out at the river near Potter Valley, where the freezing cold water numbed our toes.

We were free to roam the streets without fear, to ride our bikes anywhere we wished, and during the school year we walked to the elementary school where we were enrolled, St. Mary of the Angels. I wasn't a very studious child. I remember going to kindergarten at Yokayo School, and when I was left there on my first day I was scared to death. At St. Mary's I had many fun experiences, but I also had some traumatic ones. In the first grade, I scribbled in my *Think-and-Do Book* and got an F. The school actually called my mother and my teacher was very upset. I think my mom thought it was a bit ridiculous that she had to come to the school for that. I was afraid I was in big trouble, but not so. It was in the third grade that I really started struggling as a student. We had a teacher, Miss Kraukmann, who was a real terror. Looking back, I think it may have been difficult to understand her because she had a very strong Dutch accent. I had a terrible time with math as well as some other courses. That was the start of my big block against math, which has stayed with me to this day.

As it turns out, I'm quite quick at figuring things out in my head, mathematically, but over the years I had convinced myself I was rather stupid. It was also in the third grade that possibly the most traumatic thing happened to us students. Something upset Miss Kraukmann and she ended up beating up a student in front of the entire class. I can still picture the occurrence and it just seems incredible. It took my mother and some other parents over ten years to get rid of that teacher. I think Mom and Miss Kraukmann had a few different run-ins, and one of them left a lasting impression on my mom. She had to give Miss Kraukmann a ride home one day because the teacher didn't drive. Mom took her home and after she dropped her off, she backed up—right into Miss Kraukmann. The teacher sustained a serious injury to her leg, I believe, and she was in the hospital for a while, needing surgery and skin grafting. My mother felt obligated to help her rehabilitate after she got out of the hospital. I think Miss Kraukmann thought my mother hit her on purpose, and Mom dreaded going over to her house. I guess at some point she must have felt that she had paid her dues and stopped going.

The whole Catholic school experience was a real mix of fun and dread as well. The classes were small, and in my graduating class there were about nineteen kids. The girls far outnumbered the boys, and for a somewhat introverted, flat-chested, bespectacled girl, life was not always a bowl of cherries! Once, in seventh grade, a boy upset me quite a bit when he said to me, "What pirate sunk your chest?" Talk about humiliating! I left the room in tears. Funny how a person hangs on to that sort of bad experience.

When I was in about the fifth grade, I wrote to a nunnery. I was sure I was going to be a nun. Nuns with the Dominican order wore a habit, or uniform of sorts, and they were quite completely covered. I just always assumed that they were flat-chested. Since some of the other girls were starting to develop and I wasn't, I figured I must be destined to become a nun. The only problem was that I wanted to get married and have a huge family; I thought it would be great to have ten kids. Obviously I figured the whole thing out eventually.

The first real memory I have was from when I was about four. My parents went out of town to a medical convention and some of us kids had to be sent to stay with family friends. I ended up going to the home of a close friend of my father. They had a daughter about a year younger than I, but I had to sleep in a crib of some sort, and in the evening after we were put to bed, the lights were turned out so it was totally dark. That completely freaked me out. At least one other time, my mom wanted me to stay there again, but when she came to get me and take me to their house, I was nowhere to be found. It turned out I was hiding behind a toilet in her bathroom and absolutely refused to go. Years later, my mother asked me what the problem had been but, honestly, I couldn't remember why I didn't want to go. Now I just assume it was because I was freaked out by the dark.

I had nightmares for years, actually up until about the time I went away to college. I was afraid I would have them while I was away from home, but I didn't. My mother said that she would be downstairs at night, after we'd been put to bed, and she would hear whimpering. It started out sort of soft and quiet, but if she didn't get upstairs before the dream was fully developed, I would be in a complete state of panic. The dreams were weird, sometimes abstract things, as I recall. One of them, though, was a product of the old drill "duck and cover." We used to have to do that in elementary school and some of my dreams were triggered by that whole scenario. In the dream, I was standing upstairs in one of the bedrooms and huge planes were flying overhead. They were close enough for me to see the pilot and there were huge bombs being dropped over Ukiah. What a thing to teach your children—we have enemies in the world and they just might come bomb the living daylights out of us, so this is what we have to do to protect ourselves.

One claim to fame in my childhood would have to be that I was the first in my house to be strapped into a harness in my bed at night. Evidently, I absolutely would not stay in bed when my mom put us to bed. I guess it was easier to strap me in than go crazy spending the evening running me down to put me back in bed. I could move around in a circle and turn over, but I was not able to actually get out. Good thing there was never a house fire!

My sister Becky and I shared a room for many years. We shared a room and a double bed. That was quite an ordeal. We used to fight like cats and dogs. She was the slob and I was the neatnick. And I may have had the more volatile temper. Our favorite memory is of the night she and I had been fighting and when we finally went to bed, she told me to watch out, do not go to sleep. Well, at some point I woke up with her actually choking me! In bed, in the night! At some point, she decided to stop. Perhaps she realized if she did me in, there would be no one for her to torture. We are great friends now, of course, and have lots of laughs about the good old days.

If we wouldn't go to sleep when we were supposed to, my mom would make us wait up for our father so that he could "punish" us. I think he was annoyed at the idea that he had to be the disciplinarian sometimes. More than once Becky and I had to go outside late at night and play Chinese jump rope until Daddy came home to relieve us of our punishment. I think we may have even been locked out. Of course, that didn't happen in the cold winter months, but it was tough, nonetheless, having to stay up late when we really wanted to go to bed.

As I said, I had quite a temper as a young girl. Who knows where that comes from.... perhaps because there were so many kids and we all didn't get the attention we wanted. Then there was always the crazy relationship between my mother and me. For some reason I took the brunt of her angry outbursts. We would get into some sort of confrontation and it often led to her "spanking" me. The problem was that she just couldn't seem to control herself once she started hitting me. I remember many times just being huddled up against the wall while she wailed on me with her fists until she was worn out. I know she felt awful about it, but somehow it happened over and over again.

At some point she quit. I don't even know how old I was, but it ended. I do remember her slapping one of my sisters across the face once, but there was not much physical confrontation other than that.

I used my mother as a model of sorts for when I became a mother myself. I wouldn't do this and I wouldn't do that. One thing I didn't do is spank my children much. The first time I spanked my older son, Kenny, he was probably about three or four. I smacked him hard across the bottom and he looked at me with such a look of astonishment and hurt that it made me cry as well as him. It cut me to the quick and I never spanked him like that again. My second child, Zack, was a different story. He was already in little-boy undies and I was upset with him for some reason. I gave him a spank across that thinly veiled little behind. He just looked up at me, pulled down his pants, and said, "Is there a mark there?" So that was it with him. Also, I just knew as a stressed, working mom that if I spanked my children, I might not have been able to stop either. I loved my children with all my heart and more, but there were times that I felt such rage, I must have really scared them with my outbursts. I said some things now and then when I was upset, when they were young, that made me want to just cut my tongue off, but I usually apologized and tried to make them realize it was my fault, not theirs, and I hoped hugging and kissing them would make them feel loved.

The house in which my family grew up over the years, 416 Oak Park Avenue in Ukiah, was on the loveliest street on the west side of town. It was known to possibly be the most beautiful street in town then, and could be one of the best even now. The houses were all fairly old with large yards and lots of trees surrounding them. There were pomegranate trees in the yard next door to our house and we often would grab a few pieces of fruit when they were available, hanging out over the fence, waiting to be plucked and eaten. Back then I thought that was such fun, eating those messy poms, staining red everything I touched in the process. I wouldn't even think of buying the fruit for my kids when they were little, knowing what a mess they could cause.

Our house had a beautiful crabapple tree right in the front yard. It was absolutely lovely when it was in bloom. And when the crabapples were hanging, we used to pick them and eat them now and then. That is a bitter fruit, but somehow I ate them again each year. If we weren't eating them, we were trying to blast each other with them. For some unfathomable reason, the people who bought the house from my mother cut that tree down. That was one of the saddest things about losing that home.

There was also a daphne bush in the front yard and, I must say, the scent from a daphne is unbeatable in its pure, sweet aroma. (I purchased one myself recently and am hoping for blossoms soon, so the memory of my home on Oak Park is available at a sniff.) The blossoms are quite delicate and beautiful also.

In the backyard of our home—a huge two story with a balcony on the west side and huge windows on the east—there stood a Gravenstein apple tree. We climbed that thing and picked and ate the apples she produced. We carved our initials in the trunk, hung upside down from the limbs, and sometimes just perched on a branch, looking out over our little kingdom. My mother had an old-fashioned applesauce maker with the crank handle. It had to be clamped down on the edge of a table or counter and then, once the apples were boiled and softened, we got to help crank the machine, watching as the sauce poured out of the holes into a bowl. Mom added cinnamon and some sugar and *voila*—there sat the warmest, most inviting, tasty pile of applesauce one could ever want to eat.

On the west side of our house was an in-ground pool. It was put in in 1934 and I believe it was the first pool in a private residence in Ukiah. It was actually a lap pool for the previous owner who needed to do physical therapy. Since the pool and pump were old, my parents didn't want to have to pay to have them updated. So instead of a pool, we just had a big cement hole in the ground bordered by a wire fence. The fence was handy because if you wanted to get out of the house but couldn't get permission from Mom or Dad, all you had to do was go to one of the upstairs bedrooms, climb out the window, slide down the balcony, and jump down onto the fence, then the ground, and you were free to go. Getting back into the house was easy also, as long as you could shimmy back up the balcony post and no one had locked the window on you while you were gone.

The boys enjoyed the pool more than the rest of us. When it rained they could jump bikes off the edge into the water. As dirty and disgusting as that water was, they didn't seem to care; they just wanted to be wild. There were rock-throwing contests, and in winter, that deep water was the perfect place to hide and destroy things that someone else really wanted. My mother planted tulips along the fence inside the pool area, so even though there was a lot of dirt and cement, it still looked colorful during springtime.

There was an alley along our house, behind the pool and garage area. At the end of the street was a little market, Westside Grocery. For sugar fanatics such as ourselves, it was the perfect place to spend our allowance, or the money we sometimes stole from my mother's dime piggy bank. That store had every kind of penny candy one could want. We bought and shared gum, candy, soda, and lots of other junk food. My siblings and I actually had something we called ABC gum. Once you chewed your gum for a while, you would pass it on to someone else and that person could chew it for a while and so on. Of course, the poor sucker who got it last didn't really want it because all the flavor had been chewed out of it!

I used to run errands to the store, but I never took a list with me for some reason. I would ask what was needed and then say ok, and go down to the store. I think that every time I came back from the store, I had forgotten some items. Now and then, I would have to call to see what the heck I was supposed to get. That became a big joke: what is Valli going to forget this time? We had a charge account at Westside and we were only supposed to charge necessary items to my parents' account. We got away with charging goodies now and then, but George and Pearl Knight, the owners, were pretty smart. They knew exactly what was okay and what wasn't. It was tough to get away with anything when they were around.

There were a few other mom-and-pop stores around when we were growing up. One was on Dora Street, and we passed it on the way to school each day. One day when I was in third or fourth grade, I was walking home from school. I went into the store and was looking around. I decided to steal a gumball; it was grape flavored. I got caught stealing that gumball and it was a most humiliating experience. I had to take some money back to the store the next day to pay for it, and that one little experience cured me from stealing for many years. Once when I was in high school, I was on the coast with a few girlfriends and we went into a store to get some food. One of my friends and her sister stole some bread and lunch meat and maybe even a bottle of booze. I was so freaked out by the whole third-grade gumball experience that I immediately left the store. I just could not steal anything. Fortunately, they did let me eat some of that stolen food! These were the same girlfriends I would get drunk with and drive through the vineyards in their dad's Bronco. We had an absolute blast, especially when we were running from the cops. Back then, the police took away your beer and sent you home. Life was simpler then.

Our home had some unique and wonderful features. It was a two-story with a basement. The living room was huge with high ceilings and lots of windows on the front. There were French doors at one end that opened up onto a large front porch, and about four sets of French doors that faced south. There was a large fireplace, which rarely held a fire but held eleven Christmas stockings every year. On the wall above the fireplace was a framed picture. A picture that wasn't a picture, but actually a jigsaw puzzle that had been put together by my mother and her siblings the year she graduated from high school, which would have been about 1935. The puzzle had been framed and hung in my mother's family house, until she inherited it. I am lucky enough to have it hanging on my own wall now. At the far end of our living room was a beautiful Steinway grand piano and a set of drums. Our parents were both musicians, which is how they met. The story is that my father was playing drums at the Airplane Club in Denver, and my mother was the singer...the rest, as they say, is history.

I would have to say that my fondest memory growing up is of going to bed at night listening to my mother play the piano. She had such talent and was quite good at playing classical music. My favorite song was called "Enchanted Cascade", a rolling, flowing, melodic number that might remind one of being on a rollercoaster, without the nausea. Mom could sit down and play and a person listening would feel completely drawn in.

Playing piano at night and soothing children to sleep is one thing; coming home late and putting on headphones to have drum accompaniment is another altogether. My father would do exactly that, though he played old-school style—smooth and quiet, if needed. I think that was his true calling—music—but he must have known that playing music wouldn't feed a family of eleven. He came home late, dealt with us kids if we needed it, and then sat down to play drums, to relax, and to reconnect with himself. My brother, Zack, was the lucky bugger who inherited the drum set. But he was the right person to get the drums. He is a skilled drummer himself, with a love of jazz, like my father.

My father was a wonderful, compassionate, good-hearted man. I don't remember his ever saying anything bad about anyone. He believed in truth, honesty, and hard work. He was a veteran of World War II who put himself through medical school. He grew up dirt-poor in Nebraska, one of three sons of an unmarried woman, Carrie Wilson. She raised three wonderful men on her own. I'm not even sure if they knew who their fathers were, but she managed to instill in them a sense of right and wrong, Christian morals, and kindness.

Daddy was a hard-working physician who would help people regardless of whether they had money to pay him. A local Ukiah woman once told me a story about my father. Her own daughter was quite sick when she was a child, and she and her husband had to take her to San Francisco for care. While they were in San Francisco, they came to know a young Hispanic boy about the same age as their daughter. Because he had no family in the United States, they decided to bring the boy back to Ukiah when they returned with their daughter. At some point, the boy had to see a doctor, but their family doctor was out of town. So they got the name of my father and he agreed to take care of the boy. He treated him at no charge, and wouldn't even consider taking any type of compensation for his time. It was not uncommon for him to do that. People remembered him and his great talent for medicine, his compassion, and his acceptance of people in general, no matter what their status in life. I worked at the local hospital when I was in high school. At that time, Ukiah General Hospital was small and, of course, we employees all knew each other. The housekeepers used to tell me how wonderful my dad was and how he was the only doctor who would have no qualms about sitting down to eat lunch at their table.

Unfortunately, being a popular physician in a small town also meant having to deal with needy people out in public. There were many times when the family would be out for an event or to have dinner at Fjord's Smorgasbord and a patient would approach us to get medical advice or complain about some ailment. Of course, Daddy would take the time to talk to that person and give advice or a pat on the back, but I know it drove my mother crazy. My dad died in

1977, but for years I have had people approach me to talk about what a wonderful person and doctor he was. Unfortunately, as time goes by, and as the town has gotten bigger, the number of people who knew him has gotten smaller. I dream about my father now and then. I believe that is how we stay in touch with those we have lost. Those dreams are little reminders of our past.

I often dream about our old house also. Of course, the house is never exactly the same in my dreams, but I can still picture it in my head. Besides the large living room, there was a large dining room with windows everywhere and more French doors to the outside. The breakfast nook was not large, but we always had an odd-shaped table in that room where we ate most of our meals. It was wide at one end and had a straight side and an angled side that ended in a small end. My father almost always made it home for dinner around seven p.m., and he sat at the head of the table, the wide end. He would have the plates stacked up in front of him and he served each person a helping and then passed the plate down to the far end. People think that is a very odd routine, but I guess when there are nine kids, one can't expect them to serve themselves and still have enough food to go around.

Dinner was a time to eat, not mess around, and if you burped out loud or screwed around or made rude noises, you could expect to get bopped on the head with the handle of a dinner knife—and believe me, that will make you see stars! I don't recall my dad spanking us, but there was that bop on the head at the dinner table. Every now and then, we kids got out of control and at any given moment there could be peas flying or mashed potatoes flung. I believe there were even peanut butter stains left on the ceiling of the kitchen by the time we sold the house.

We had a wonderful and dedicated housekeeper/babysitter while we were growing up. Her name was Marjorie Maize and I believe she started helping my mother out when she was only in her early twenties. She cleaned our house and spent many days watching over us when my parents went out of town. I'm quite sure we stressed her to her limits many times, but she continued to come back. Once, when I was about ten, perhaps, my parents were gone and Margie was watching us. For some reason, I was being chased by one of my siblings and I was carrying a perfume bottle in my hand. I ran up the steps of the front porch and when I hit the top step, I tripped. Unfortunately, when I landed, the bottle broke and I ended up slicing my hand open. The deep laceration bled like crazy and I had to be taken to the doctor's office to have my hand sewn up. Poor Margie felt awful, but of course it wasn't her fault. She had told me to stop running, but what are you going to do when someone is chasing you? She certainly had to put up with a lot of shenanigans when she took care of us.

It seemed like each time my parents went out of town, someone either got hurt, or a car got wrecked, or some other traumatic event took place. My dad loved fast cars, but so did my brothers. More than once they managed to find the keys when my parents were out of town. Lo and behold, there went another car, into some ditch somewhere or wrapped around a fire hydrant or some other object. Put a Wilson into a car and you could almost always expect something big to happen. That seems to apply to most of us. Thanks to my dad and mom, I still go for speed and sound when I buy a car.

I don't remember very many vacations while I was growing up. There were lots of weekend trips to the coast, though. My father had a patient who owned property south of Fort Bragg, a strip now inhabited by a place called the Pine Beach Inn. We used to go over to a cabin on the property and spend our days there, exploring and chasing each other around in the wilderness. Funny, the things we remember. There was an abandoned go-kart that we were sure we would be able to tow home and get running again. Just what my brothers needed—a little vehicle that they could race around the neighborhood and use to terrorize people! Another time we came upon a carcass of an animal, a goat, I believe. The thing was rotting and filled with maggots and bugs. It was very creepy, but we were drawn to it nonetheless.

Speaking of creepy, there was the time when a couple of us kids tied up one or two family members and trashed the cabin to make it look like someone had broken in. I don't recall the whole episode, but when the rest of the family got back from town, they came in the cabin and were completely stunned and horrified to find the poor "victims" bound and gagged. What a bent sense of humor we Wilsons have always had! Of course, it was funny at the time.

Because my father worked so much, we didn't get to take regular family vacations, but in July of 1967, my family went on our most memorable vacation, a trip across the United States. There were nine kids, my parents, and the family pet, a little brown poodle named Coco. We started in Ukiah and made it to Omaha, Nebraska, for a family reunion before my dad had to go back to California to get back to work. From there, my mother drove her brood all the way to New York City and back to California in a six-week time span. I particularly remember going to Williamsburg and Jamestown, and I recall that New York was an awe-inspiring and amazing place. We also went to Washington, DC and saw the Smithsonian Museum, then to Baltimore, Maryland, and Macon, Georgia, which is near where my mother's family owned a ranch when she was growing up. They spent many summer months there and my mother had many stories about "the farm", including tales of adventure and a little bit of romance thrown in here and there. I remember going to Connecticut, which was absolutely beautiful, and I was quite taken by the gorgeous neighborhood we visited near where Ethel Skakel Kennedy's relatives resided. My mother had a dear friend living in that neighborhood; I remember feeling that we were in a privileged part of the world.

Another place that stood out in my memory was Biloxi, Mississippi. I loved the smell, the Southern-style homes, and the abundance of large trees -- I believe they were willows -- which drooped and swayed like lovers in a trance on the dance floor. Florida was warm, too warm, I thought. The water didn't feel cool and refreshing, and I remember coming out of the ocean and thinking how humid the air seemed. As we traveled west, we all became excited about heading back to California. Along the way we encountered huge beetles covering the sidewalks in a small town in Texas. The vast expanse of Arizona and her Grand Canyon – another awe-inspiring sight - came next, and then...California. How we whooped and hollered at re-entering our home state. After a six-week trip, I think we were all ready to be home again. Surely a trip of such magnitude would be hard to match. As a matter of fact, we never did another trip like that again.

We grew up in a home with parents who smoked. Both my mother and my father smoked Camel non-filtered cigarettes. They both chain-smoked, but I don't remember smelling like cigarettes, or walking into our house and thinking how awful it smelled. I guess when you are used to that, it just doesn't seem to be a bother. I remember being sixteen or seventeen years old and smoking a cigarette in an upstairs bedroom one evening. My father came upstairs and, without knocking, came into the room. I was scared that I would get into trouble, but he just told me to put it out and not take up such a habit. Unfortunately, that very habit would eventually kill him.

Just outside that very same bedroom was a window that opened onto the roof of the house. There were many occasions I would sneak out of that window and go around the roof line to sit and smoke a cigarette. That rooftop spot was good for getting away, for sneaking cigarettes, for watching fireworks on the Fourth of July, and even for hiding out, away from everybody and everything.

During high school I went through all the usual stuff. There was school, which I still didn't particularly enjoy. I liked the social aspect of it, but overall I guess I just didn't care about learning anything. I was not a very motivated student at that time, either. I enjoyed the sporting events, the dances, hanging out with friends, and the weekend parties. I got into a little trouble now and then, but I wasn't a difficult teenager. I drank too many beers in a dry creek bed here and there around town. I drank too much Spañada one weekend night when I was a sophomore, which turned me off to red wine for about fifteen years. I experimented with pot, which was big in the '60s and '70s around here, as it was everywhere. I had a lot of laughs with my family and friends and experienced some heartache as well. The week before my senior year, a young man, who I liked, was killed in a boating accident at Lake Mendocino. I felt despondent over that for quite some time. I became good friends with his best friend, Bart. We hung out a lot together the last year of high school. When it came time for prom in May, we decided to go to the dance together. We were just friends, so we thought that would be fun. A week before the dance, Bart called and told me that he was going to take the girl he actually did like. I was very hurt and felt alone, but I realized why he wanted to back out.

That was the only dance I was invited to in my four years of high school. I even felt like an outsider then, during high school. I realized years later that I was like the ugly duckling, because eventually I turned into an attractive, fun, confident, and smart person. A few years after high school, I had two different guys tell me that they liked me in school. Knowing that during those difficult and awkward years might have made a difference in my self-esteem, but that is one of the ironies of life, isn't it.

There were some fun times during those frustrating high school years. Because my parents were both musicians, they had many friends who shared the same interest. My father had a group of friends who would come over now and then on a weekend, and they would have a jam session. Duane Thompson played the clarinet, Vince Angel played the bass, Barbara Curtis played the piano, and Ben Foster, a dear family friend, played the trumpet. Occasionally, there would be a "guest" musician, but generally the same group of friends got together to play and enjoy each other's talents. We kids got to invite a few friends to each jam session and boy, did those friends appreciate being a part of it. The atmosphere was full of energy, with people mingling and chatting, the sounds of music floating through the house, and food in abundance—and the alcohol flowed as well. The youngsters watched as the "old folks" drank and became more relaxed and danced the night away. Of course some of us teenagers managed to get our hands on the alcohol now and then, not really to get drunk, but I think we wanted to fit in, to feel like we were part of the adult group as well—and what a group that was. There were doctors, lawyers, neighbors who worked in city government, friends from all walks of life who loved to be a part of the Oak Park Avenue jam sessions. We became engaged in conversations with adults, listening to talk about work, politics, and even a little gossip now and then.

Many of the friends who were there at those music sessions talk about that when we see each other, even now. And my sisters and brothers and I still like to reminisce and imitate our mother, who would wander around the house at those parties, cigarette in one hand, screwdriver in the other, smiling and making a "tsk" sound to the rhythm of the music. She would smoothly dance around, by herself, weaving in and out of the people standing around enjoying themselves. What a wonderful experience that was for us.

My dad would also join some of his musician friends on weekends down at El 'n Lou's Restaurant, where people would hang out at the bar after they had eaten and take in the music. I think my mother got tired of going and having to hang out there by herself while Daddy played all evening. I remember seeing him once, at our house, playing with his friends, his eyes closed and his head tilted, a slight smile on his face, lost in the music. That summed it all up, how it made him feel.

I had many opportunities to learn to play an instrument, but unfortunately I just didn't want to practice, to stick with it, and I'm sure my mother got tired of pushing one child who didn't seem interested when she had so many others who kept at it. I tried the piano, the guitar, the trumpet, and the drums. How I wish I could play just one of those! Sometimes it is so obvious to me that if only I had stuck with, say, the piano, I could sit down right now and produce something beautiful. We are a musical family; how I wasted a God-given talent. But that is the story of my life, as I see it...if only.

My four older sisters and I did have singing lessons while we were growing up, and I did enjoy those days. We had a singing teacher, Mrs. Munroe, a sweet and wonderful lady who knew how to keep me motivated at every lesson. We five sisters sang at different events in town. I loved to sing, but going out on stage didn't seem to get any easier each time we had to perform. On the contrary, I felt more and more nervous about it as I got older and felt nauseated before each performance. Even now, at fifty-two, I still have a difficult time standing up in front of groups of people, even those I work with. I just don't like to be the center of attention.

I didn't like a lot of things when I was growing up. I had a lot of anger issues. I would get upset, not easily, but once I did snap, look out! I remember chasing my brother, David, around the house with a broken table leg. I planned on hitting him on the head with it. I used to lie in wait for my other "sister", Audrey. She was Diana's best friend and so she spent a lot of time with my family. I used to stand on the balcony outside the bedroom window and wait for Audrey to come over. Then I would try to drop a brick on her when she passed by underneath. I have no recollection of why I did that. She was like part of the family. Perhaps that's it; I treated her like I treated almost everyone else. It seems that I was always angry with someone or something. I don't think I was like that until I was at least ten, but once I started acting out, I went crazy. I even chased my little brother, Zack, around with some kitchen knives for some reason. I broke my mother's Mixmaster, broke at least one dining room chair, lit a fire in the wastebasket in the upstairs bathroom.... I'm sure there were many more incidents, but I just can't remember them all.

The upstairs bathroom was certainly unique. All of us six girls had to share one bathroom and the three boys shared the other. The girls' bathroom had a swinging door going into it. On the right were two toilet stalls with bar-style swinging doors. Then came a countertop with two sinks and lots of cupboard space down below, and two full mirrors on the wall. There was also a shower stall and in another small room, a tub. The whole bathroom was covered in wallpaper or tiny little one-inch tiles. All of our friends thought that was the coolest room in the house. It had to be big and cool; it accommodated a lot of girls. Unfortunately, we had to clean that big old room, too, and that was quite a chore.

We all had chores to do regularly. Of course the girls had to do the household work and the boys got to do the outdoor work. I always thought that was so unfair. How hard can it be to mow a lawn or pick up trash from the yard? We girls took turns ironing once a week and doing the dishes at night. That was a real challenge for me. After dinner, on the night when it was my turn to do dishes, I would immediately go to the bathroom for at least an hour and hang out. I still can hear my mother outside that powder room door: "For God's sake, Valerie, get out here and get those dishes done!" Although half the time she wanted to call one of us, she would go through the whole list of names. "Deb, Di, Pris, Pam, Becky Jo—oh, for goodness sake, you know who I mean!"

The bathroom was also a good place to escape to in order to get rid of unwanted vegetables. Brussels sprouts, in particular, were cleverly placed into a napkin at the dinner table. And then when one was excused to go to the bathroom—you had to ask to be excused—down the toilet went the veggies. How handy that was. But that is what happens when you expect your child to eat frozen instead of fresh vegetables. I swear I didn't know how delicious Brussels sprouts were until I tried them fresh. Now I love them, but back in those days, when my mom was trying to feed an army of eleven, bulk frozen foods seemed like the easiest way to go. And they were probably the cheapest. So was minute rice, boxed mashed potatoes, frozen peas and succotash, and fish sticks. I still eat Tater Tots, and my family loves them too.

My mother wasn't big on baking, if I recall correctly, but she did have some wonderful favorites. During special occasions or the holidays, Mom would make a fabulous cake called Icebox Cake. It took time, but was worth it. I think my sisters make that dish now and then, but of course, I never paid any attention to what my mother was making or baking, so I didn't learn much in the kitchen. She would also make a dish with whipped cream and chocolate wafers that we called Lincoln Log. That was another holiday specialty. If it was your birthday, you got to pick out exactly what you wanted for dinner. My brother David and I almost always picked ham, rice, and kidney beans. Zack like lamb shanks—I don't know why I would remember that—and Mom always completed the birthday dinners with devil's food cake, topped with homemade chocolate butter-cream frosting. It was absolutely divine and I think most of my siblings still use that as the standard.

We were all raised on sugary foods. In order for my mother to get us to eat some foods, she would top them with horrendous amounts of sugar—oatmeal in the morning with tons of sugar; cereal topped with mounds of sugar; white bread with butter—and lots of sugar! Many of us have dealt with sugar addiction over the years. It seems there were always packages of mint cookies in the freezer, as well as lots of ice cream. We would often sit around the kitchen, each with our own spoon, eating ice cream right out of the container. Sometimes we would have tomato soup and grilled cheese sandwiches for lunch or dinner, probably on Friday during Lent. In order for us to want the tomato soup, Mom would put a huge dollop of whipping cream, from the can of course, on the soup. Campbell's tomato soup slathered in Redi-Whip...try it, you'll like it!

As I raised my own children, I tried to keep their sugar intake at a minimum. Imagine my horror when I found out that when they stayed at their paternal grandparents, they got to eat oatmeal doused in chocolate syrup for breakfast!

Holidays were a real joy around a house filled with children. Easter egg hunts on Oak Park were such fun, and Christmas was my favorite time of year. There was always a huge tree in the living room, glittering and glowing with lights and decorations and presents piled high all around. We went to Midnight Mass every year, tired or not, and when we got home, we would have eggnog or hot chocolate if we could stay awake. In the morning we would line up in the hallway outside of the living room, which was always closed off in the morning. The order was always the same, youngest to oldest. We would stand and wait for everyone to get there, filled with anticipation and excitement, fidgeting and pushing, wondering what was waiting around the corner. There were always lots of presents, and every year there was also one big Santa present, something for all of us kids to share. One year we got a surrey with a fringe on top, one year it was a bongo board, and it was a wonder no one broke anything playing with that. There was a huge swing set with a double-seated swing on one end, and one year, a tandem bicycle.

We had such fun during the holidays, and I don't remember a lot of fighting over things. I think we were all so excited about the whole day. There was always holiday music playing, and each year we got an orange, candy, and some other little goodies in our stockings. Of course, Santa Claus always left a touch of milk and a crumb or two of cookies on the plate at the fireplace. Sometimes I long for that feeling I had back then because I think it felt like such a true family time. How can you hate each other when there is so much excitement and joy all around?

Thinking about times like the holidays fills me with such melancholy. The memories are so fresh it is almost painful. I have so many bad and ugly memories of growing up, but there are loads of good ones as well. And as we have grown up, my family has gotten closer. We get over the old wounds and feelings of resentment. Perhaps so many of us grow up in dysfunctional homes, some families with members who don't speak to each other for years, but I can't imagine that happening to us. We have survived through thick and thin—nine siblings with reasons not to get along, but I love and admire my brothers and sisters. Debbie has so many amazing accomplishments and such good advice and wisdom to share. I've always looked up to Pam because she always seemed so positive and upbeat and fun, the cheerleader in high school, Miss Popular. How I envied her seemingly easy way of getting along with everyone. I love Diana for her big heart. She has always accepted people, opening up her heart and her home to anyone in need. Perhaps that has had its downside, but she has a wonderful extended family and great friends because of it. Priscilla is independent with a great subtle sense of humor. She has struggled through some parts of life, but always seems to hold her head up high and keeps pushing on with a positive attitude.

I love myself! After all these years, I really do. I love David, the incredible artist and philosopher. He has an amazing mind, although sometimes I just can't keep up with his thought process. I love Becky, my roommate, my enemy, my pal. I always envied her because I thought she was so much smarter than I – and she even tried to tell me that when we were growing up! Besides, Mom always liked her best. There is Zachary, with all his boisterousness and bravado, the rowdy one, who people in our town always assumed would never get anywhere. People still ask about Zack and say jokingly, "Is he in jail somewhere?" I respond proudly and with much respect, "Of course not. He grew up and is a wonderful person, a father with a wonderful family and a successful career." And I love Paul, the baby of the family, with his charming and very funny personality. Those three boys kept us laughing over the years. We've been a very lucky family: lucky to be healthy, to remain friends, and to love each other tremendously.

When my father died, when I was twenty-two years old, I was quite devastated. I was stunned and saddened by our loss, literally sick the day of the services and wake. He was my hero. But when my mother died, despite the tremendous feeling of loss, I was able to unload all those built-up resentments. It is a unique experience, the loss of one's mother, that connection we have to the world as we know it. But to be able to let go, feel free, and feel good about it... what a joy.

The 6ᵗʰ Voice ~ David Blaine

IT WAS WONDERFUL BEING AN INFANT. ONCE THE WHACK ON MY butt brought forth the first burst of voice, it had all begun. Wrapped in swaddling clothes, bathed gently in warm water, being passed from loving sister to loving sister to loving sister to loving sister to loving sister and back. A warm, steady beat pulsing through the air. Fed mother's milk when I was hungry, stroked and nurtured when I called out, shown off like a circus freak when friends or relatives arrived. No doubt I was loved and doted upon during those early months of life. The soothing, sweet voice of my mother as she sang lullabies and rocked me gently to sleep was especially satisfying. I was given everything I needed and then some.

Life came into focus as I slowly began getting my bearings. I began to understand what my hands could do. They could grab at those objects hanging into my crib. With my hands I could grab at my feet, pulling on them, pulling on my toes. I could roll over and try doing push-ups. I could tug on my blankets or my dinky or whatever else was within reach. I grabbed at my mother or father when I was held, latching onto their fingers or exploring their faces. All of my family members received the same treatment as I explored my surroundings. Father was a medical doctor and my health care was as thorough and gentle as his bedside manner. Life was warm and tender, and Deborah, Pamela, Diana, Priscilla and Valerie made it even more so.

There was a point at which I was let loose on the floor and I took full advantage of the opportunity. As I lay there I felt the vibrations, then I crawled. Oh, I'm sure it was touch and go for a while, but like all young creatures following the natural order of things, I soon began getting a handle on my arms and legs. Under the keen eye of guardians, I viewed the world at floor level. Those days of lying on my stomach with a smile on my face and my arms and legs flailing wildly were over. I was mobile. Now my hands did more than just grab at everything within reach. Now my hands were moving me wildly from place to place. From cupboard to cupboard, room to room, light socket to light socket. If I saw something across the floor, I could move to it posthaste. If I was lucky, I could get it into my mouth before I was stopped.

In no time, I was being held upright. I wasn't always interested in who was holding me or why, but as I began to get my balance, life took on a whole new perspective. And I thought I was mobile before? Shoot! As I shook off the shakiness my wobbly knees began to stabilize, my nerves steadied, and I began to take aim at those same cupboards and doorways, finding new ways to move in, through, and around them. I felt reborn. I was unstoppable. Other than the occasional reminder of "who's the boss," I was free to roam, and roam I did—upstairs, downstairs, all around the house.

Soon I was introduced to the great outdoors. Ah, dirt. Not that dry, indoor dusty stuff but real, moist, tasty dirt, with things in it. Rich green grass to run through and all manner of bugs and birds everywhere. The rich aroma of country air was heavy from the nearby river, and its freshness could be tasted in every breath. It was this small house on the edge of town in which I spent the earliest years of my life.

Then another house became our new home and remained the family home throughout our childhood and beyond. It sheltered us and was a blessing to our family. We moved lock, stock, and barrel to this fine, big two-story in town.

A large yard with plenty of trees and bushes to play in and around made it seem like a world of its own. An old detached garage sat in one corner of the backyard, beyond which a paved alley separated our yard from more houses. There was a rough, gray, empty concrete pool in the backyard, up against the back fence. It looked like a huge hole just waiting to be explored. The surrounding chain-link fence with a gate at each end only added to the invitation. Along the whole front of the house was a concrete porch, three steps high, just wide enough to turn a bicycle around, with a ranch-style railing the length of it.

Inside the house was a huge living room with a very high ceiling, a fireplace, wooden floors, and a beautiful bay window. This large, cold room was beyond my reach. A heavy wooden door slid across one path, though I could look in through the French doors from the dining room, until Mother reminded me that that room was off limits as well. The kitchen was warm, like a kitchen should be, and the trick was to stay out of the path of the many chefs. It should be said that there was really but one chef and many helpers. The parents' bedroom was on the first floor and was always open to us, as long as the door was unlocked. Just inside their door was a closet under the stairs that housed all the board games one could imagine. The large enclosed back porch was for storage and laundry and could be fun, though work might break out at any given moment. The two bedrooms upstairs were assigned separately to the girls and boys (yes, there were more to come).

The summer days could be quite hot in the Ukiah valley and our air conditioning consisted of opening all the windows during the cool nights. In the mornings, Mother would call up the stairs to shut them again. There were large shades outside the front bay windows, and they would be pulled down as the morning sun began warming the day. This is the way the house stayed cool as those hot months were upon us.

As the next few years passed, another sister, Rebecca, and two brothers, Zachary and Paul Shannon, arrived. It seems I was always no more than a step ahead of my younger siblings as we all learned the ropes of childhood together. I can't say that I was a leader, but I would notice that I was being followed an awful lot. Before long, we were all running around and exploring the house, the yard, the neighborhood, and our limits. There were other children in the neighborhood but I'm unsure of when I met them or under what circumstances. Before any of us knew it, there were plenty of friends in our lives. Of course, there were already many girlfriends visiting my older sisters.

There was music, conversation, and laughter at our house. When you walked into our home it was understood that music was a part of the family. Mother was given a Steinway grand piano when she was a girl and it was at one end of our living room. That rich black thing was so stately and stable. It never moved from its station or lacked purpose. To the right of the piano was the Slingerland drum kit Dad played professionally as a younger man. All shiny metals and soft round shapes, its crashes and booms were exciting and contrasted so from the melodic sounds of the Steinway. When the pair of instruments were played together it all made sense. Dad would sit at his drum set and practice his chops. He would sometimes lift me up to his lap to join him as he played. Sometimes friends of his would show up for jam sessions. These fellows on the piano, clarinet, sax, horns and double bass really knew their stuff. Occasionally a guitarist would sit in. They played pre-war jazz and the music would fill that big room. We could be in the room if we behaved ourselves and dancing was always allowed. This scenario formed the basis of the parties our parents often threw and formed the earliest social experiences of my life. Initially these parties were given only for grown-ups, but as the years passed, our friends and the kids of our parents' friends were also welcomed.

Mother played classically and I was in awe whenever she was at her instrument. It wasn't often, but it was always memorable. I never took piano lessons though most of my sisters did. Some of my sisters sang as a group and Mother led them through their practice sessions, and they would occasionally perform around town. I wonder if by the time I came of age Mother no longer had the energy to press a youngster down that road.

I'm sure six girls and three boys could, at times, be somewhat busy. Yet there was an underlying structure that was laid down by the lawmakers. The parents. Mother was mostly the enforcer. The role seemed to suit her feisty disposition while father was more of the laid-back and reflective sort.

Father was reared in a Protestant community around rural Bloomfield, Nebraska, in the early years of the twentieth century, while Mother was baptized Catholic, in the shadow of Chicago, Illinois, one year before the official end of the First World War. From the stories she told I gauged her upbringing as quite strict. This is the manner in which she strived to raise our family, and church-going every Sunday was as important as anything. Father joined us only for Christmas services, but for the rest of the year, (and year after year), we would all pile into the Country Squire wagon without him. Dressed in our finest clothes, we would drive to church and find a pew we could call our own (all said and done, that would be over eight hundred walks down the aisle).

Outside the home life, it was church that most immediately interested me. The great room dwarfed our living room yet it was just as cold. The light was filtered through large stained-glass windows depicting scenes from some long ago time, akin to the pictures in the big book at our house. Several vaguely familiar statues graced the front area beyond a short wooden fence. Everyone was equally somber and dressed in what I would later learn was known as their Sunday best.

A man would enter while we, the crowd, were at our most solemn. He was dressed in a most peculiar fashion and spoke in a completely foreign yet quite beautiful tongue. A couple of boys followed this priest from the side door and waited on him throughout the service, wearing equally strange clothes and speaking in the same strange language. I understood him only midway through the service as he stood behind a tall narrow desk and glared at us, speaking of our lives and what we might do with them. Though it was in English, it made little sense to me. The boys served him drink and biscuits and he offered a small piece up to the huge crucifix hanging on the front wall of the church.

Beyond the big linen-covered table and decked-out gold box was the anguished visage of Jesus Christ hanging cold and alone. Every thorn and spike was larger than life. As my mind wandered, I could see the sweat bead up and the blood flow from His wounds.

The acrid aroma of incense only added to the enchantment of the experience. Everyone stood and sat and knelt as one. We shared from the little books placed in the holders in front of us. In unison, prayers were spoken or sung and an organ filled the room with magical sounds. The whole experience was so fantastic that it was many years before the ritual became tiresome to me.

Mother was completely involved, mesmerized really, and she made it her personal objective to convince me as to the value of it all. The success of this objective was greatly influenced by an experience I had one Sunday morning when I had become big enough to strike out on my own.

Services were concluded and I managed to break away from Mother's care for just a moment. It was long enough for me to go through the gate at the front of the room, beyond the limits of the commons of the church. Beyond even the sacred territory of the priest. As I grew older, the physical realities of the church building had begun to sink in. I realized that beyond the altar was a space, an area just out of my line of sight, an area into which I had seen others enter and then return.

Perhaps God himself could be reached through that portal. Hell, why not? Every other thing in this magical world was beyond me. Like Lot, I dared not look back as I made my way toward what would surely be a door to another dimension. My heart raced as I passed the altar. Imagine my surprise as I rounded the corner in great anticipation, only to find several large, empty ceremonial vases and a few two-by-fours lying about. A door did open that day, I will admit that.

Around this time in my life, I was taken by the hand and led several blocks to the school I had passed so many times before. Oftentimes I would see children of all ages playing in the big yard beyond the fence. All were strangers to me, but I was to be left in their care as Mother turned her back to me. Of course she explained how she would return for me later that day. It seemed strange to be in the middle of all this chaos.

Children running around like mad people with no reason or purpose. The boys would throw balls at one another, and the girls would smile or laugh, or snicker or scream. This was the first time or place any stranger would say something mean or raise a hand as if to hit me, and I found it very disconcerting. Inside there was a teacher at the head of the class, but I was put among the other youngsters. It was my peers that would share this experience, as the teacher busily explained all the rules.

We would start the day by reciting a prayer to a cloth flag hanging in the corner. We did some fun and interesting things. There were plenty of books to look through or color in, and posters and wall maps and a globe just like the one at home. You could find our small little town on the world globe because of the observatory substation located here. I've always found that fascinating. We finger-painted and did other crafts. We could be much messier than at home, but still I couldn't wait to return there.

We had a naptime, which I enjoyed. I've always enjoyed sleeping. Getting to sleep was sometimes frightening as closing my eyes would often conjure up all sorts of weird visions. Bugs and bees and other little monsters might show up and harass my pleasant state. Some nights at home I might close my eyes and drift through an abyss so deep and endless that I would feel lost and overwhelmed. When I could no longer take the greatness of it all, I would simply open my eyes and that would clear my head. Then I would close my eyes and try again. The fun never lasted long as I finally drifted off into slumber and dreamt the night away. Maybe that's why a lot of us young'-uns would rather stay up late playing than shut our eyes— even at the risk of facing Mom or Dad. Some nights that portal could be quite eerie and unfriendly.

After that first year at the factory—I mean school—it was off to more of the same in the form of eight years of parochial school at St. Mary of the Angels Elementary. It was only a mile or so from home, and in nice weather we would walk or ride our bicycles. Uniforms were mandatory and boys wore salt-and-pepper "tweed-a-roys", white button-down shirts, nice shoes, and a sweater when the weather demanded. The principal and most of the teachers were nuns and wore their own version of a uniform.

The first two years were much like kindergarten except that here nuns led the classes. A few laypeople were either teachers or staffed the office, and Mr. Mondine did the dirty work. This short, old, mustachioed Italian American would smoke his cigars wherever he chose and didn't hesitate to give a child a piece of his mind if need be. "Hey, don't a-you run in the hall" or "Take off-a-you muddy boots." There would be a whole lot of rules and new people to learn about in this new place, and I guess plenty of time too (although, as it turns out, eight years proved to be just not quite enough time). I would occasionally see my siblings in the hallways or playground during recess and would smile to myself.

It was about this time all of us kids were given jobs hauling everything we could carry to a house down the street. We were moving into the Turney house. They were horse owners, and Mother, who grew up around horses, told me they were moving to the country where they could be with their animals. Mr. Turney was a very big man but friendly. I heard that he had been in a car accident and had broken his neck. As he was alone he had to walk miles to the hospital holding up his head with his hands all the way.

So the Turneys moved out and we moved in. This was the only time our parents allowed a TV in the house until the youngest was a teenager. Tragedy had struck, and we were allowed to watch the black and white images of that most famous Washington family as they honored and buried their loved one while thousands of strangers, including us, looked on.

Down the street our old house was a beehive of activity. Trucks were there all the time now, and my curiosity got a real workout as the men on the job noisily and tirelessly changed the old house into a brand new place. I was allowed there with a parent or when I could manage to sneak there by myself, and I never tired of watching the construction.

The whole back porch was soon gone. In its place were several rooms on both floors. Downstairs a family room, a laundry room, and a small bathroom Mother called the "powder room" came to life. The living room looked pretty much the same, just shinier and more off limits than ever. The kitchen was all redone, modern and sparkly, with a huge matching set of fridge and freezer and a merry-go-round in the corner just under the freezer. I could just fit in there before it was loaded with goods and whatnot.

The laundry room shared a hallway all lined with closets good for many more hiding places. The family room was wide open with a great fireplace at one end—all brick with a long hearth and a wooden mantel. Next to it was a padded bench that could be opened for firewood storage. We boys would become familiar with that box as it was up to us to keep it full.

One wall was all glass and light and a view of the mountains to the west. It looked out at the swimming pool just a few yards away. Unfinished and unusable, the pool remained a wonderful and never-ending source of interest and fun for us kids. In the milder winters frogs would take up residence there and their chirping drew us into the deep end to search for them.

Up the still-creaky narrow staircase were two new bedrooms and a huge bathroom for the girls. It had two sinks, a bathtub, and a shower, and two toilet stalls with these cool swinging doors. Now the girls would be two to a bedroom while we three boys would continue to share our own bathroom and bedroom directly over the parents' room. We could hardly get away with any late-night shenanigans as our heating vent was just up from the folks' master-bath vent. As we became carried away with our nighttime rowdiness, we would hear Mother's hairbrush scraping the vent cover and a weird version of her meanest voice echoing up a warning. If our play escalated we might hear those slippers slap the stairs and then we knew the fun would soon end.

We occasionally made excursions into "the city" a hundred miles or so to the south of our little town. The Redwood Highway still winds its way through Mendocino, Sonoma, and Marin Counties on its way south. Along the Russian River the scenery is spectacular. My favorite sight, however, is leaving the southbound tunnel and viewing the arches of the Golden Gate Bridge with San Francisco in the distance.

The excitement of what was about to come could be almost unbearable. We would try to hold our breaths crossing the bridge, and the way Mother drove we could almost do it. The Christmastime trips were especially exciting and colorful with the city all dressed up for the holidays, and we would usually catch a showing of *The Nutcracker Suite* at the opera house.

We always stayed in a nice hotel and ate at nice restaurants, and we shopped at fancy stores for nice clothes. I didn't pay much attention to how I was being dressed, but the girls seemed to enjoy voicing their thoughts on the matter. The trips were mostly about getting the girls clothes anyway. I enjoyed all the traffic and all the people, and the escalators and the elevators, and the TVs in the beautiful rooms so high above the city streets. Friends of our parents sometimes joined us for dinner out and we would try to behave.

Back in Ukiah the new house was like a new start. The new start included a new regimen of chores. They included filling the firewood box in the family room. Chores like that were for boys. That's the way the work was designated. Inside work was for the girls. Outside work was for the boys. Lining the garbage cans with old newspapers, and cleaning the garage, the empty pool and the yard.

Before you shed a tear on our behalf, I should introduce you to Otto Ermer, our gardener. He only came once a week, but in this big old yard that left plenty of work for us boys. We didn't own a lawn mower, but we had plenty of rakes and brooms. In the front yard was a huge blossoming crabapple tree, and it left a mess on the porch and front yard during the summer and fall months. The clean-up was our duty. Why we didn't just do the chores right away is still a mystery to me. I don't know where I learned to avoid the work, but I'll bet I know where my younger siblings did. I would always make a production of these jobs. I was sure I was finding new, easier ways to conquer the obstacles in front of me, and though it usually proved untrue, that didn't slow my attempts at such endeavors.

School was approached with the same vigor and recklessness. Why in the world would I do as I was told when I hadn't even tried it my way? That failure to keep the teachers from noticing me, combined with my wandering mind, opened plenty of doors to the principal's office. The next few years here would be under the charge of lay teachers, including Miss Kraukmann in the third grade. She looked a lot like her name sounded. She spoke in a heavy Dutch accent, and many times compared the streets here to those in her homeland, which, by her telling, were so clean that one could eat from them. I wondered if any other student was imagining her on her hands and knees eating from the sidewalk.

As the years passed, the teachers seemed to go from so-so to worse. I just tried to keep as curious as I was at home. Out of our four classroom walls, one was nothing but windows with a fine view of the great outdoors. The other walls were covered with interesting posters and pictures. The many books we were given took me to many foreign and exotic places. There was always a pencil in my hand and an empty canvas in the form of tablets or pads of paper. Doodles seemed to pour from my pencils and pens. Every year or so was a new ink system as pen tech went from cartridge-filled to ballpoint. Even the new ballpoint pens could produce an inky mess if you sucked on them long enough.

Needless to say, I had a hard time paying attention to the stranger at the head of the class no matter what she had put up on the chalkboard. This was one sure way to get behind in my studies, especially in the more difficult classes. Arithmetic (and soon mathematics) was my Waterloo. I found ways to ask questions that would provoke a teacher. Much to my dismay, the exchange was viewed as curt or smart-alecky. It was in Mrs. Martin's fifth-grade class that we had the California version of duck-and-cover, where the danger was not a red missile but an earthquake. The exercise was kind of fun yet silly, and I couldn't help but wonder what would happen if the earth opened up directly where we were huddled. My mistake was in the asking, and as the reddening face loomed down at me I couldn't help but smile. I was not smiling as I stood in the corner, a quizzical look crossing my face. I wished the teacher could see the sincerity written there, but it was not to be. She may have seen me as an example in the making, while I tried to figure out how to deal with her and her ilk in the appropriate fashion. Would trying my best be good enough? Would the burden be too much for my sturdy little shoulders? Time sped by and I really didn't spend too much time on that moment as new ones were always surfacing. I guess with every new day comes new challenges. At home, my parents scratched their heads.

It could have been the acceptance of my parents, a general goodness of society, or maybe some dynamic of Catholicism, but no matter what trouble I got in, it was always soon forgiven. Saturday afternoon confessions always led to another squeaky-clean Sunday. Before I knew it, I was studying Latin in preparation for my days as an altar boy. I had been given my first communion years ago and now I was going to be given the honor of serving the priest during Mass. We would enter through the back door of the church and don the wardrobe that fascinated me so. Watching the churchgoers say 'ah' and stick out their tongues in anticipation of the host never got old. I also enjoyed filling the chalice with water and wine from the bottles on the nearby tray. While I poured the wine the priest motioned with the chalice to add more. Having worked the bar at many of my parents' parties, I knew just what he meant.

There were also a lot of little good times to enjoy, like Tuesday lunches. Tuesdays were "Hotdog days", and in our school where everyone packed their own lunches, and especially for hotdog lovers, this was a special day.

On First Fridays, we (the entire student body) would walk the couple of miles or so to our church and celebrate mass. Both ways we would pass right in front of Pomolita Junior High, laughing and moving noisily along in groups of various sizes. Gauged by the way they looked and hollered at us, St. Mary's must have seemed very different and perhaps a little strange to those public school students, of whom many were friends. Upon return to our school, we would go to the auditorium where hot chocolate and glazed donuts awaited us. Pure bliss.

Recess was another activity that helped avoid the structure of the classroom. There was a huge grass field, and when the mower had just done its job there would be an equally huge amount of grass cuttings piled up here and there. Jumping or running through them was a lot of fun. A creek ran along one border of the field and when the rains were heavy the creek was terrifying to watch. It was completely accessible and the fact that no one was ever swept downstream is a tribute to dumb luck. There were swings and monkey bars and a fast merry-go-round to play on, and one summer the school installed three tractor tires half buried upright. We could climb on them or get inside the rubber cocoons and feel a million miles away.

As I blended in with the chaotic free-for-all, I began to understand the dynamics of recess I had misinterpreted years before. Was it simply a release of energy, or perhaps the spilling of youthful exuberance onto the pavements and grasses of the schoolyard? What's gotten into us?

What I can make no sense of is how all those rowdy youngsters become so docile upon reentering the school buildings. As if in a trance, we all just become like so many ... adults. Actually, this class of mine has quite a few misfits and characters, myself among them. It was this pool from which I found my closest friends. The standouts were usually defined as the teacher's ruler came down on the palms of their upturned hands. We knew to count out the dose as we were made examples of in front of the rest of the class. Sometimes the teacher would not call us to the front but instead hurry right over to mete out her business at our desk. I guess she couldn't wait for us to rise and hustle to her side for what was coming. Tony and I were constantly in the running for leader of the whack. That's how friendships are born. This whole unhappy exercise did nothing to further my fondness for the institution.

My shot at the honor roll was greatly jeopardized one morning while the teacher was mistreating one of our classmates. This grown woman had the poor girl at a terrible disadvantage, shaking the rubber-tipped pointer in her face and backing her down the aisle. I had had enough, and you can blame it on chivalry if you like, but I sprang into action. Grabbing the yardstick from the eraser tray, I charged the duo and stepped between them. I then turned on the old bat and positioned myself for battle. Our wooden weapons threw off splinters as we engaged. I had my opponent on the defensive now, and as she turned her back I reached for the girl's hand and lit for the door. We were down the hall and out the school doors in no time flat. I stopped to think of our options, then we ran for the tires. We climbed inside and sat facing each other. She smiled at me as we heard the school doors rattle open. My finger went to my lips. We sat in silence and a moment later the doors shut again. We were safe for now.

We answered for our mistakes with restrictions and after-school punishments. There is one time I remember with fondness when a half a dozen or so boys and girls were held after school and given assignments. After a few remarks and some snickering, the teacher stormed out in disgust. Once in the hallway she locked the classroom door from the outside. As the silence turned to hushed remarks of glee someone said, "Well, I'm out of here" and proceeded to climb out of a window. Now, these windows were unscreened and only a yard or so off of the floor which made for an easy exit. As I pulled my bicycle from the bike-rack, I looked back to see that the whole bunch of us had escaped. I don't know if the teacher forgot about us or returned later and thought she had gone crazy, but we all returned the next morning for class as if nothing out of the ordinary had happened. Apparently nothing had.

Finally Christmas vacation would arrive. The most exciting time of year would start with a huge tree delivered by Father's friend who worked in the forest. We would drag it inside, leaving a pile of needles in its wake. Setting it up and decorating it was a big part of the holiday. Balancing it in a pail of stones was no small task. Then the big box would come out of the basement, and up would go the ladder and on would go the lights. A precious angel would adorn the very top. Mother would carefully extract a variety of shiny ornaments and assign us the job of hanging each, one at a time. Tinsel and a little snow finished it off. Christmas time just shines.

The regular items around the living room would be replaced by Christmas-related ones. The wreath would hang on the front door and the spirit of the season would be upon us. Carolers would show up in our front yard and entertain us with their reveling.

Soon it would be Christmas morning, and after breakfast we would all line up by age (youngest first) at the living room door, waiting for the go-ahead. The door would slide open and we would rush in, looking first for those presents too big to wrap—bicycles and the like. There would usually be a few of those for one or all of us. Father would be calling out names and handing out presents to each of us as we established a place in the room to call our own. That's the place we would unwrap and pile the gifts we received. The adrenaline would last all day.

By the time dinner was underway we would be about worn out. Mother was a fine chef and Christmas dinner was the pinnacle of our meals. The year I received a unicycle I spent all day moving along the length of our station wagon to get the hang of it. It took weeks before I felt comfortable enough to ride it to school, but eventually I did just that. I must have looked like I was a lost performer trying to find my circus as I wobbled down the street toward school. Well, I made it without any mishaps but I didn't make a habit of it.

School seemed to permeate all aspects of my life. All my friends I knew from school. Most parents (including my own) wanted to know all about how it was going and so forth. Then there was homework. Of course, that was to be done posthaste. Though I seldom asked, there was never a shortage of help with my home studies no matter what the subject. We were allowed to sit at the dining room table for this job. Homework was one of the few reasons we could be in the living room. We had a decent library there including a fine set of World Book Encyclopedias (and later a new set of Encyclopedia Britannica.) Once I opened them I was off to the races. I would start in one place with one thing or subject in mind, but before you could say 'mint julep' I was a thousand miles or a thousand years away. I'm sure I learned plenty from those tomes but it didn't seem to impress the teacher. Occasionally I would put together a report or project that impressed or confused them enough to put a proper grade on the front page. Soon I would squeak through another grade level.

Summer school became necessary during the latter years of elementary school. That was but a small part of the vacation months as there was so much to do. In some ways it was no more than a very long weekend, doing artsy-crafts projects in the house, or playing around the yard, the neighborhood, or the town. Summer Wednesdays meant matinee films at the Ukiah Theater, which were a treat. Those afternoon movies would pass the scrutiny of the Vatican critic, which meant Mother's keen eye would give it the okay as well. More than once she came into the theater and hauled away one of her kids who was there against her wishes.

Some nights we would take our bedrolls to the side yard and sleep out under the stars. There were nights when friends could stay over and sometimes I would stay at their houses. The most fun was staying with the friends who lived on ranches. There were always so many adventurous things to do while getting dirty and hollering at the top of our lungs. We would play in the barns and climb up on old equipment as if it still worked or was something more than just a rusty old machine. The very first piece of equipment I ever operated was a tractor out on the Kircher ranch, and it was quite a thrill lumbering along trying desperately to negotiate the dusty, narrow aisles of the pear orchard. I just wish they gave a Boy Scout merit badge for the experience.

One summer some of us kids joined our father to gather river rocks for a new office building he was having built catty-corner from the St. Mary's school field. These stones would make up the fascia above the flower bed on the front of the building. It was a small part of the project but it was fun helping to sort through the rocks and watching them being placed. This new office still smelled like the old one, especially the closet at the end of the hallway where the medicine was kept. That is one smell I will never forget.

We took an annual summer week when Father could afford to get away from his practice for a family vacation. Other than one week in a houseboat on the Sacramento River Delta, we usually spent the week in a cabin over on the coast. Friends of the parents would loan us their small house on the Mendocino County coast. It sat upon a bluff and had its own beach, accessible only by a path through a dense thicket of coastal plants and trees. This dark overgrown forest included a thick canopy and came to be known by us as "The Tarzan Trail". We never tired of beachcombing for interesting-looking driftwood or dying things like jellyfish or kelp, and exploring the tide pools for starfish, sea anemones, and sea urchins. Some nights we built bonfires and roasted marshmallows.

In the summer of '67 the folks rented a U-Haul trailer and loaded it for a road trip. Mom pulled it behind the wagon and we headed for Denver and points east. When we weren't visiting family we would stay in cheap motels, renting rooms with kitchenettes so as to save money. We sure watched a lot of TV. This would be our last summer together, as my eldest sister would be off to college in the fall. The parents, nine kids, and our dog were on the road, and I'm sure there were times when the dog looked at us as if we were crazy. Dad brought his car also and went as far as Nebraska for a reunion of his side of the family. We stopped in Denver for a visit with his mother, Carrie. Then Becky and I joined Grandma for the next leg of the journey. We traveled by train. For some reason, I was less than welcome in the cars. Was it something I said? The train ride was an adventure in itself, as anyone who has ever ridden the iron horse knows, and a welcome change from the claustrophobic environment inside the Ford. Grandma allowed us to explore the cars on our own and that freedom was most refreshing. It was a nice change from the ever-present vigil Mother kept over us.

Too soon we were joining the family in Omaha. In California we were without extended family so everyone here was a stranger to me. I was left to the familiarity of my siblings. Before we knew it, Father was ready to return to Ukiah, and the rest of us were eastbound. I had turned down the offer to accompany Dad westward with my promise of good behavior. Whenever we loaded into the car we were required to sound off with our number so the mother hen knew all her chicks were aboard. Deb would start the count with "one", then Pam said "two", etc all the way down to Paul who finished it off with "nine". It worked well and was actually kind of fun. I think it acted to bond us in some unseen way.

We headed for Chicago and a visit with Mother's father, Livingston Cullen, in Evanston, Illinois. He had visited our home a few times and loved to act up with us kids. He was ancient by this time and lived in a large, old house with many strange rooms into which we peeked. On one exciting morning we went to Chicago's Hotel Allerton on Michigan Avenue for the Don McNeill Breakfast Club Show where our adventure was mentioned by the host himself. As this was a lengthy trip, we didn't stay in any one place for long. Mother always said, "Guests are like fish—after three days they begin to smell."

Next stop Jackson, Michigan, for a visit with Dad's brother, Ted, and Ted's wife, Aunt Beverly. Getting to know our cousins, Chris and Scott, was easy. Scott is my age and a pleasant chap.

From there, we went north to the Detroit area where we visited the Henry Ford Museum, among others. Once inside that immense collection of machinery, I immediately struck out on my own with no regard for anything familial. Eventually, I was reunited with my genetic group and I'm sure I paid no attention to any scolds coming my way as the overwhelming data continued to swirl around in my mind.

We traveled northeast into Canada and then into New England, bound for the Big Apple. Mother had attended Manhattanville College for Women there so she had old friends with whom to reminisce. We stayed with some of them and they had a far-out enclosed swimming pool in their backyard. In the city we did all the touristy things including seeing the Von Trapp Family Singers on Broadway.

We continued down the East Coast with a stop in Washington, DC, among other cities, on our way to Macon, Georgia. Mother had spent much of her childhood on a farm there, and again we were to visit kin and old family spots. New Orleans was a must-see and crossing Texas was a hot and long journey in itself. I had never seen bugs like that before. Painted deserts mesmerized us all while rolling through the Southwest, and soon we were capping off the adventure with a visit to the most exciting childhood adventure of all, Disneyland. Actually, Disneyland is second only to the Nevada Northern Railway Museum, or Chicago's Museum Of Natural History, or The Henry Ford Museum, or New York's Met, or Guggenheim, or The New York City Fire Department Museum, or The Smithsonian, or... well, you get the point.

We arrived home with no shortage of "What I did this summer" material. In eight years I was never asked to write a "What I did this summer" paper. It wasn't usually a shame, but that fall it certainly was. Soon we would be back to school.

My birthday falls in the same month as the start of school. You learn to take the good with the bad. On our birthdays Mother allowed us to choose our favorite dinner, and mine was always either stuffed peppers or kidney beans, rice, and ham. Dessert was always Mother's knockout chocolate layer cake. She had a way with desserts and generally all things sweet. According to her, sugar was its own food group, which we were served on a daily basis. After dessert it was time to tear into the wrapping paper that stood in the way of the annual gifts. I most enjoyed the plastic model kits. I received mostly cars though at times boats or airplanes were given. I enjoyed building the car models the most and assembled quite a collection over the years.

Back in school there was the advancing subject materials and the occasional new opportunity that one finds throughout life. I joined the crossing guards and could now wear the badge, parade belt and cap, and carry a hand-held stop sign along with the other guys pulling that duty. Stopping cars was surprisingly easy and occasionally some old-timer would try and stare me down, but I he they couldn't see my eyes through my black-rimmed glasses. Nonetheless, I would encourage the crossers to make like the chicken and get to the other side quickly. Power such as this could go to one's head, but I believe I managed to keep fair in all things street-wise.

I did occasionally stray from the basic rules of the institution and, during one such episode, desiring to be the first to get outside for recess, I went tearing ass through the hallway. My over-exuberance was over-extended and my footing suffered completely. I sailed headlong through one of the vertical plate glass windows that bordered the double doors. I don't know how long I lay there before I awoke. I'm sure it was a morbid sight to behold, my limp body draped across that transparent guillotine, a growing puddle of red darkening the concrete. As I came to, I noticed that I was spitting a stream of blood. There was a dull throbbing in my face, and lifting my head, I focused in on Father's office in the distance. Now, that really made me feel better. I was assisted to my feet and soon found my lip being administered to by my favorite doctor. He actually made it fun. I think his magic was in the joking during the situation no matter how hard it seemed, though I don't remember the joke. A pat on the head and I was back on top of the world.

We got a new kid in school that year and he was a real tough. He came down from Willits to attend our school. He smoked cigarettes and carried a knife. Once, lying in the grassy field during recess, Nick dared himself to throw the rock he was palming. Now the whole side of the building was nothing but glass windows so all he had to do was hit the broadside of the thing, but it wasn't the throw that impressed me but the idea and then the execution. Well, he let loose the stone and we immediately turned back to our business. As I heard the distant crash my heart was pounding, and I felt as guilty as I knew he was. The culprit was never discovered, and Mr. Mondine had another cleanup to do.

I wasn't always an angel, and if I became too much for my mother she would threaten to hand me over to Father. More than once she lived up to her promise and put me under Dad's already busy care. Many an evening I waited in the waiting-room of Ukiah General Hospital, sitting in a wheelchair, looking through *National Geographic* magazines or making trails through the sand of the ashtray with a leftover cigarette butt, always under the watchful eye of the shift nurse. Sometimes I would accompany him as he made his rounds or on house calls, which often included fast rides to and from.

Father loved to go fast and never seemed to mind the smile on my face. I always felt more welcomed than in trouble. I could even tune in the radio to find music of my liking, which was rare in Mother's car. Her dislike of rock 'n' roll was no secret. The only fun when she was driving was the never-ending driving lessons, the speed at which she drove, and lighting her Camel cigarettes for her. Then, of course, there was the time we gave Miss Kraukmann a ride home after church and Mother mistakenly put the car in neutral when the old lady got out, accidentally knocking her down and breaking her leg. Mom felt pretty bad about it.

The final couple of years of elementary school found me somewhat disconnected from my studies. In band class I studied trombone and enjoyed blowing that horn, and of course, practicing at home was encouraged. It hardly seemed like homework.

I was now mostly interested in playing and visiting with friends. There were so many adventures to be had. The importance of dressing up for Halloween was replaced with collecting and stashing eggs and plotting out strategies for their use on the night of the dead.

When our pool filled up from the stormy winter rains, we laid some long boards crossways from side to side and one of us played Friar Tuck preventing the others from crossing. With makeshift wooden weapons, we did battle till someone fell into the cold, murky waters. Then we played rescuers, throwing a rope to the victims in need. With used nails and old wood, we threw together a one-room shack in the back corner of the yard. We used it as every imaginable type of abode, encampment or fortress.

Mother began to work at father's office some hours a day and that meant we were left to manage ourselves after school—and that suited us just fine. There was always a project underway, whether building a coaster in the garage, building models, or just drawing in my room.

If, when "It's dinner time" was called out, I was in the middle of a critical step in the building process, I would eventually pull myself away and head downstairs. If late, I would often receive a scowl as I took my seat. Missing grace was frowned upon. If I was in a T-shirt I would have to go put on a button-down shirt. T-shirts were underwear and were not allowed at the dinner table. At that time T-shirts were white only and were indeed underwear. No shirt at all was strictly verboten anywhere inside. Father was often late but would always receive a chorus of "Three Cheers" as he came to sit in his seat at the head of the table.

The last day of school was coming soon and I focused on hollowing out a book to hold the celebratory Black-Cat firecrackers I had acquired. Fireworks and anything that went boom had become of interest to me and I was going to be prepared for graduation. High school was becoming more and more of a reality. Not only because of its impending nearness, but also I had begun to watch my sisters complete their four-year commitments and head off to college. I knew my time was approaching fast.

How very different high school was from St. Mary's. It was about the same walking distance but in the opposite direction. There was a huge three-story building known as "The Main" with a full auditorium attached and a couple of other buildings full of classrooms as well. There would be no more homeroom but different classrooms for all the different classes, each with its own teacher, and all these new students.

We had free dress every day and it should have been called "freaky dress," with all the stripes and paisley garments. The full cafeteria with sticky buns for breakfast and super tasty burgers for lunch and personal lockers was completely new to me. This full-blown Phys. Ed. was new and the boys' locker room had showers. Weird. No more nuns. Not weird.

In band I was taken off trombone and given a sousaphone instead. In the doing, my left shoulder gradually became impervious to karate chops. Art class was a nice respite from the rigor of all the serious courses. I notice no one played during recess. We just hung out in the groups of our choosing. At the parking lot across the street was a smoking section for the harder cases, and hideaways for young lovers were here and there. Occasionally, when in the right place at the right time, you would see some outlandish displays of behavior. In the back of the school there was a hill leading down to the school bus shop, and one day we stood around all lunch break watching some of the boys riding motorcycle wheelies up the hill in contests of bravado. If the stench of weed was in the air, someone would be keeping an eye out for the dean who was a known lurker.

While you're keeping an eye out you learn to keep your ear to the ground, as you never know where the get-togethers might be. "Where are the parties this weekend? At my house? Are you sure? Yeah my parents are out of town this weekend. Huh, okay. Meet you there, I guess". We had more than a few parties over the years when the folks were away, though certainly fewer than the folks threw. At one of those parties someone made off with this far-out whisky tumbler of Father's. He had received it free, from a pharmaceutical company. They send doctors tons of stuff plastered with their logos, from pens and pads to ashtrays and pocket protectors. This particular glass had "LSD" in bold red letters emblazoned on it, along with the chemical formula for lysergic acid diethyl-amide. It was quite a loss. Overall, our ill-advised parties proved quite civil.

It was during my freshman year that Di returned home with her new baby boy, our nephew, Josh. It was like a new little brother had joined the family and, of course, he fit right in. His healthy, hearty cheer was a welcome addition to the brotherhood. The home dynamic changed little and we all adapted naturally, as we always had.

The most notable shine fell on Father who loved to spend his time with his first grandson. At one jam session, I watched Josh enjoying himself when Uncle Ben, Dad's dearest friend and a horn player, offered the toddler his trumpet. Josh eagerly put the instrument to his lips and blew. The note was perfect, and every witness laughed enthusiastically. The parties of our parents were very much like that episode—just plain fun. A lot of friends and families nicely dressed, listening to good stories told well and good music played well, some dancing and a lot of eating and drinking and laughing, and if you want to smoke a cigar, take it outside. When it was over, everyone pitched in to clean up before turning in.

While contemplating the stars one night, probably after having shared a cigar with one of Dad's friends, I was lying back in my sack in the side yard and sighted the most remarkable shooting star. It wasn't life changing or anything like that, but it did see me realize the biggest difference between grade school and high school. More than anything, it was the newness of it all. So many new chances and opportunities were arising. These new places and things and these new people all busy with their own devices left me to mine. It wasn't likely anyone was going to tell me what to do or how to do it. As we all know, this is the time when the guardians become extra cautious about sending the kids in the right direction. I was listening, to be sure, but the sounds were muffled by the ideas and hopes I was trying to sort out on my own. Conflict. Drama. Life. I surely received plenty of support. Not that I wanted any, but I couldn't keep it from coming my way, and every one of them was determined to give it. Of course, they would have to catch me first.

Hanging out on my friend's couch one afternoon, we were passing back and forth his father's Colt 45 revolver. Big and heavy it was, with wooden grips and a long barrel. I'd handled it before but this day I had a couple of bullets. I loaded them across from one another leaving four empty chambers, two on either side. I could pull the trigger twice before it was live. If I then half-cocked the hammer, I could rotate the cylinder one place, release the hammer, and click the trigger twice more before it was ready to fire again.

Actually, I could keep doing this—and did—in a rhythmic fashion until I lost my place. Luck? Divine intervention? Random happenstance? *BOOM!* You tell me. We looked at one another with faces like two idiots (which we were), then we slowly looked up. The slow-moving cloud of smoke couldn't mask the half-inch hole in the ceiling. Tony unloaded the gun and returned it to its rightful place. I had the big door open, airing out the room, when my best friend returned with spackle and a putty knife. We did a good job restoring the ceiling, then climbed up onto the roof to search for the errant hole and survey the neighborhood for signs of the Man. He wasn't to be found, but we tracked down the slug lodged in one of the shake shingles and dug out the keepsake. Then we left. Fast.

We went to hang out downtown. Ukiah really has only one main street. Before they cut a four-lane through the Ukiah valley,

State Street was the Redwood Highway, and now it is just the main street through town. On a Friday or Saturday night we liked to cruise it, looking for friends and parties and watching the hot-rodders make noise. They would take off from one of the three stoplights or pull next to one another, and before you knew it they would spontaneously erupt into an ear-splitting drag race. Many weekend nights you could hear the stock cars racing legally down at the Mendocino County Fairgrounds' paved oval. We always found something to do and somewhere to spend the evening. And we always managed to stay out of trouble—or at least out of jail.

In my sophomore year the main objective was to get a driver's license. I sat through dozens of lessons given by Mother to an older sister. The school class was simple and nothing new. I soon had a learner's permit, and in no time I was riding with a teacher to show that I could turn a corner and knew what a yield sign meant.

Staring down at my name on the envelope from the DMV about made my knees weak. It took a while to solo in one of the parents' Fords, but I knew it was only a matter of time. I started with my sister Di. She had a used Volvo sedan she lent me for sitting Josh or just as a favor to me. I began to get some wheel time. I found that if you turn the key in gear, the starter would move the car and then fire up the engine. There are so many neat things to learn about cars and I'm willing to learn them all.

I soon learned a valuable lesson about driving big-engine vehicles when Father let me get my hands on his 429-powered Ford XL. When you get in trouble, do not leave your foot buried in the gas pedal. A couple of my buddies were with me that evening when I turned onto Gobbi Street. Halfway through the turn I punched it and the ride began. As I overcorrected and headed for a schoolmate's house, my lesson started. I managed the front yard pretty well, but leaving his driveway I wasn't as successful. Just to the left of it was a power pole, which I hit dead center. I don't know how fast I was going when I hit that pole, but I believe my foot was still to the floor. The engine, however, was no longer running. We all jumped from the smoking car and ran. I didn't get but a few yards when the realization hit me. I'm busted.

After taking a good, long look at the destruction, Father admitted he needed a new car. When he went shopping at the Ford dealership, to his amazement, the car he almost bought four years ago was in the used-car section. Mother had helped convince him that the sedate XL was a more appropriate choice for a doctor, but now the '69 Fairlane he had wanted back then would be his. The fact that it had the Cobra package (428 CJ engine, four-speed transmission) thrilled me no end. Naturally, I received plenty of advice and warnings before I was allowed to drive it unattended. I never kept my foot buried in the gas again, although I won't forget what Jackie Stewart said about the subject (when applied to racing): "Don't step on the gas until you know you can leave your foot in it."

Cutting classes had become a bad habit of mine and our garage had become a haven to me. Upon the rafters we had pulled up many planks and secured them with nails. There I placed carpet remnants and old blankets. In this place I would sleep my mornings away until schoolmates showed up to call me down for play and that day's remaining adventures. Churchgoing, or my lack thereof, had become a bone of contention between Mother and me. When I did go I didn't participate. I preferred the balcony where you could kick back, relax, and smile at someone if you wanted. My studies remained difficult to care about.

That didn't mean I wasn't learning things. Do you know that if you open the business end of a shotgun shell, empty *all* the pellets, and tape a steelie marble to the primer end, you can throw it in the air and the weight of the steelie will bring it down, steelie-end first, every time? That will ignite the primer and make one hell of a ka-boom. Also, I found out that between all the local hunters who load their own ammo, and the sporting goods stores, there is an abundance of black powder, and you could find it just about anywhere. I'm learning so much.

Still, there was plenty of light at home to keep hope alive. As letters from sisters traveling in far-away places were read, Father would take our little globe and spin it to the locations under discussion. Dinnertime meals, chores, and the parents' stories and lessons of encouragement continued to keep the homestead interesting. Mother helped keep the household civil quoting jewels like, "If you can't say something nice about someone, say nothing at all," or heading off an excuse with, "The road to hell is paved with good intentions."

With several of my sisters gone, the bedroom arrangements changed in my favor. My new room faces west and the big sliding window on that wall and the balcony built as a fire escape make my comings and goings much easier.

My junior year of school has started and I have no idea how I finished last year. I dropped band and French was a complete disaster. I don't remember the last math class I attended, let alone the subject matter. I don't know how long I can keep up with this regimen.

I soon forgot that trouble. I had Di's new Toyota Landcruiser up in the hills yesterday and Zack was the only one who would ride along as I took it across this hairy washout at the corner of a collapsed dirt road. There was hardly enough room at the bottom to start the climb up the other side. Later we would have to do it again as that was the only road back. Those things climb like mountain goats. I really like these getaways.

It's a beautiful afternoon for a bomb. I think I'll make one. I had a few syringes I had taken from Dad's kitbag. I sent Zack downstairs for an old extension cord. My buddy brought the gunpowder. It was in a Coke bottle. I took the cord and cut off the female end and peeled the rubber insulation back to expose the wire strands. Then I took about two of those small strands from each side and twisted them together. Now these live ends I stuck into the end of the syringe where the needle would normally go. The next step was to add the powder and cap it with the plunger. I squeezed it in real good and tight and taped it securely. Then we lowered the device over the edge of the balcony and plugged it in. *BOOM!*

Man, that worked great. The small strands heated up immediately and ignited the powder. How simple. I pull the cord back into the room and inspect its frayed ends. Nothing left but a fresh start. I rig up syringe number two. *BOOM!*

Same result. It just never gets old. We went through all the syringes but not all the gunpowder. I took another drag off my cig and studied the bottle of powder for a few seconds. Not nearly long enough. I poured out some of the contents. Again I studied the amount. I poured out a bit more. How little material would I need to watch a cool flame shoot out the opening? I watched my cigarette butt get closer as my outstretched arm neared its physical limit. It was as if the hot coal hovered over the opening of that bottle for a long time as I steadied my aim. I released the smoking smoke and thought I saw it falling gently into the waiting charge, but that was strictly an illusion. Things went all white-hot and ugly and numb.

I was thinking of my classmates, so far away, as I slipped a bucks' worth of quarters into the coin slot of the vending machine. They've started their final school year about now. The barracks hallway is quiet and it's a cold evening outside. It's snowing early for this part of Germany. I made my selection and the can fell with a clunk to the outlet at the bottom of the machine, and I reached down and retrieved my treat. I popped the top on the frosty American beer and raised the can to my waiting lips. Mmmmm, I believe I deserve that. My first day at Stuttgart American High School went well and next week I'll be celebrating my eighteenth birthday during a field exercise to the demolition range. You know what? Sometimes the wisdom of the US Army can be kind of spooky.

Santa with Prissy
Zack and Pam

Santa with David
Becky and Diana

Santa with Valli,
Paul and Debbie

Dad and Boys

Mom and Girls

Becky and Zack kneeling
Valli Prissy and Debbie on couch.

Roommates Valli and Becky
have a great Christmas.

Becky shows off her hematoma.

Paul riding the porch railing.

Becky and Grandma Carrie ham for the camera during our trip around the USA.

Wilson reunion in Omaha NE 1967.

Mom with Paul and Debbie

Pam holds onto Paul and Zack, but David is on his own.

Hanging out in the living room with Becky, Pam and friend, Prissy and Debbie. Di covers Robbie's eyes.

Debbie makes David a S'more on Mendocino beach.

Diana thinks about life and Paul skips a rock.

Dad entertains Mom with a little soft shoe on the Mendocino coast.

Di with a Beatles cut 1966.

Zack gives Paul some advice during weekend chores.

Pam during a songleading number.

Grandma Carrie and Zack deep in conversation.

Josh hangs the Christmas stockings.

Paul and Prissy are teenagers.

Paul shows off his lithe body and celebrates his cool demeanor.

Mom's ready for work: a quick smoke and a glance at the paper in front of her Country Squire

Mom always drinks coffee

The famous Zebra car.

David and Paul are growing up.

Becky graduates from high school.

Audrey Gerber - The 10th Voice

Margie enjoys the festivities.

The 7ᵗʰ Voice ～ Rebecca Jo

One winter evening through the cold and heavy mist lit vaguely by the street lamps, a five-year-old walks down the alley hand in hand with her father, traversing the short distance from the house where they live to the house they call home.

I AM THE SEVENTH CHILD. I AM ONE OF "THE LITTLE KIDS," ONE of "the boys," and my mother's "baby girl." I don't have my sisters' beautiful red hair. I can't sing like my sisters, I have a "tin ear." I am not pretty or athletic; I am smart and stubborn. I don't like to be told what to do, but if I am asked I will do most anything. I am quiet because when I try to speak I feel drowned out by the eight or ten others; they don't have the patience to wait and listen to the whole story.

I grew up in a house filled with music and games and laughter and fighting, chores on Saturdays and church on Sundays, hats and gloves on our shopping trips to San Francisco, counting off in the car to be sure no one was missing, and "Three Cheers for Daddy" at dinner.

I don't really remember my early years, but I have been told that my very early formative years were guided by my sweet older sister Pam who adored feeding me and caring for me. I was beautiful even though I wasn't big on smiling. Behind my baby eyes, my voice would have said to all those who might have thought they could touch me or play with me, "Come near me and you're dead meat!" Grownups seem to miss that babies are people too and may not want strangers trying to ingratiate themselves.

SUMMERTIME

Our summers were spent outside; I went to summer school in the morning every year. That was mom's way of having us socialize with kids who didn't go to St. Mary's or to just get us out of the house. In the afternoons we went to Nokomis School for arts and crafts or gymnastics. On Wednesday afternoons we went to the free matinee. We played all the time. We played baseball in the street, and at night we played shadow tag under the streetlamp. We slept outside and awoke to the sprinklers around us.

Most of our relatives lived far away and we didn't see much of them. Zack's godparents, the Fosters, became Uncle Ben and Aunt Margaret—not biologically related but our aunt and uncle nonetheless. Margaret would come to visit. There would be a tap on the door, the door would slowly open, and we would hear, "Yoo-hoo! It's Maaarrrgret." Some of us still mimic that high-pitched intro today. Uncle Ben was the best. He called me "bakery" and made me laugh. He always had great jokes, ones that you could tell kids and adults and everybody cracked up. Uncle Ben taught me to play "Mumbley Peg" when I was about nine years old. We would sit outside on the front lawn and he would take out his pocketknife. I would hold the knife with the tip of the blade on my index finger and flip the knife so that it landed between my feet. Maybe the idea was to flip it off the tip of each finger. I don't remember the rules, I just know I had a blast out there with Uncle Ben and him letting me play this game with him and using his pocketknife.

Every year we would spend a week or two at Rita's cabin on the coast. We played in the sand, built sand castles, dug tunnels, and the big girls—the redheads—got sunburned. One time the boys were digging a tunnel along the berm where the weeds meld into beach. Each from opposite ends, they were hoping to meet in the middle. Paul was about a foot inside the tunnel when it suddenly collapsed on him. Everyone had to help dig him out before he suffocated.

The other great story of our summer visits to the coast is the "kidnapping." One year when we took our usual trip to the cabin a couple of friends came along. Di brought Audrey, and Prissy brought Kathy. When it was time for a quick run to the grocery store in town, Debbie drove and Prissy, Kathy, and I went with her. We got back to the cabin and it was strangely quiet; no one was around. But there on the couch I saw Mom. I thought she was taking a nap. Suddenly, Kathy started screaming and I saw that Mom was lying on the couch bound and gagged. Her hands and feet were tied and a washrag was stuffed in her mouth. We quickly discovered that all the other kids were hiding to see our surprise when we found her. I am certain that it was Pam's idea and that Mom went right along with it, just for a little fun.

Another summer, we took a houseboat trip down the San Joaquin River. We were all on that trip and probably Audrey too. We just floated down the river and slept on the boat at night. Most days we swam, and one morning as we tried to take off, the anchor was stuck in the soft river bottom. I was only about eleven but I could hold my breath longer than anyone else, so I got to swim down and pull out the anchor. It took about three tries but it finally came loose. On that trip, Prissy got appendicitis and had to go to the hospital in Tracy. And one day, Daddy was letting one of the big girls steer the boat and they came too close to the shore. A mop that was on the side of the deck got caught in some branches, went flying off the deck, and broke the windshield in the process.

The big summer was the trip cross-country in the station wagon pulling a U-Haul with all our stuff. The station wagon was one of those old ones with seats in the "way back" that faced each other. Mom drove most of the time, and I can picture her with our little poodle, Cocoa, lying along the back of the seat behind Mom's head. Daddy was with us as far as Omaha, and then he went back to work and joined us again when we got to Los Angeles. At night we always got a motel room with a kitchenette. We each had a sleeping bag, and we mostly just piled ourselves wherever we would fit. Somewhere in Nevada, Daddy and the boys and I slept out on a golf course. We stopped in Denver to visit Gramma Carrie, and then she came with us to a reunion in Omaha with all the relatives on her side of the family. I will always remember riding the train from Denver to Omaha with Gramma and one of the boys; I think it was David. I had never been on a train before and we had a blast. It was scary at first, going from car to car while the train was moving, but once I got used to it I had the run of the whole train. Gramma enjoyed just letting us play all over the train.

We got to Omaha, to Uncle Lyle and Aunt Dova's house, and I got to sleep in the basement with all the boys—my brothers, my cousin Scott from Michigan, and my cousin Dennis' three boys. After Omaha, we went to Chicago to see my mom's family—Papapa, Aunt Jane, Cousin Peter, and Uncle Buddy and his family. Papapa's house seemed so huge; it had tennis courts in the backyard and a pool table in the basement. Mom got really mad at my sisters for going across the alley to hang out with some guys who had a band in their garage, and for the first time I saw the "Good Humor man" selling ice cream right out of his truck.

From Chicago, we went up to Jackson, Michigan, to see Uncle Ted and Aunt Bev and their kids, Chris and Scott. We went north, visited the Henry Ford Museum and then into Canada, and came back into the States through Niagara Falls. In New York City, I stepped off the curb in front of a speeding ambulance and somebody grabbed me by the collar to pull me out of harm's way; sirens have always freaked me out since then. We saw the Rockettes at Radio City Music Hall, went to the gigantic F. A. O. Schwartz toy store, and saw South Pacific on stage.

We went down the East Coast and met up with Aunt Mary and Uncle Morley in Florida. I walked along the beach filling Uncle Morley's pockets with seashells. We went to Macon, Georgia, to see Uncle Tom and Aunt Jane, and then we went through Texas. I didn't know cockroaches could be so huge until I saw them in a diner in Texas. In Texas, they also had signs on the drinking fountains that said, "whites only."

When we got older our summers were spent floating down the river from the dam at Lake Mendocino to Perkins Street, drinking while our bodies broiled in baby oil. Or we went out to Cold Creek to just hang out. The summer of my sixteenth year, my friends Elaine, Janet, and Leslie and I spent what seems like the entire summer at Blue Lakes, camping at Le Trianon. The first night out there we drank ourselves to bed. We awoke the next morning and realized we had only brought beer, cigarettes and pot with us for sustenance. So beer for breakfast it was. Later we went back into town to do some real grocery shopping. At the end of that summer we invited our parents out for a barbeque as a 'thank-you' for letting us go camping so much. Daddy came out for the barbeque but got a call from the hospital just as he was heading out, so he ate quickly and went back to town. Mom stayed with us and drank so much I had to help her to the bathroom—well, it was dark out. After all the parents except Mom left, we all went up to the bar so Mom and Elaine could play pool. Later that night, Mom went home and we enjoyed our last night in our campsite.

School Time

During the school year we pretty much stayed home except for our two trips to San Francisco each year. We would go down at Christmastime and again just before Easter—those were the two times each year we needed new dress clothes, mostly for church. Sometimes during our winter trips, we would stop and have dinner at a restaurant that had a pond in front with ducks and it was all decorated like it was Santa Claus land or something. One year we had my birthday dinner there. Other trips we would stop at Catelli's, The Rex in Geyserville for dinner. Just south of Geyserville, Mom would always point out the pond west of the highway and say just how pretty it was. I still see it and call it "Mom's pond."

We would play games in the car, like the alphabet game where you had to find all the letters of the alphabet on billboards, and the first one to reach Z won; and in San Francisco, Mom would test us to see who knew all the street names on 19th Avenue that were alphabetical from Irving to Wawona; I still remember them all. We would also sing to the radio and Mom would try to get us to name the singer.

Mom would take all the kids, and when we got to the stores, especially the shoe store, she would line us up and the clerk would wait on us like she was working on an assembly line. In the clothing stores, there was always a clerk ready to wait on us and bring clothes to us to try on in the fitting rooms. Before we went to the "city" we would go through all the clothes at home to see what still fit or what hand-me-downs fit someone new each year. When we got to I. Magnin or Macy's, we only got new clothes if we didn't get hand-me-down clothes. What are the chances the sixth girl didn't get hand-me-downs? Okay, sometimes I did get something new—like pajamas, socks and underwear.

We wore uniforms to school so having lots of clothes wasn't really that important. It was much more important to keep your uniform clean, because it was wool, and it only went to the dry cleaners twice a year.

However, I do remember having to buy back my uniform from Mom with my allowance occasionally. Saturday morning was set aside for chores. The rule was: you couldn't leave the house or have friends over until your chores were done. If a friend came over, they could either pitch in or leave. Paul's friend Bobby McCoey probably did as many chores at our house as any of us ever did. The important thing about doing chores was that when you said you were done you could leave. But Mom would go into our rooms to see if we had actually put things away or just hidden them under the bed or in the closet. If she found our belongings under the bed or in the closet, she would pick them up and take them. If we wanted them back, like to wear our uniform to school Monday morning, we had to buy them back. So we would get an allowance and then turn right around and give it back to her to get back our belongings.

In kindergarten I didn't go to St. Mary's, and I didn't go in third grade either. St. Mary's didn't have kindergarten so I went to Yokayo Elementary. Yokayo was only about two and a half blocks from the house so I could walk to school, even in kindergarten, all by myself. I don't remember much about that, just walking on the rocks at the edge of the grass along the homes on Clay Street—and John Heise.

John's grandmother owned General Hospital, and his dad used to go fishing a lot. His dad would always bring a salmon to my dad and when they delivered it to our house I would see John coming up to the front porch, and I would beat down anyone who tried to get to the door before me. I'm sure I had a crush on John my entire life.

Marjorie, my personal nanny, was always there getting me dressed and sending me out the door for school. I went to the afternoon session of kindergarten, so Marjorie always made sure I had had my lunch and was clean when I took off for school. The only reason I remember the day President Kennedy was assassinated is because Margie wouldn't help me get ready for school that day; she couldn't stop crying.

In third grade I went to Yokayo again because mom didn't want me to be subjected to the same teacher she felt had ruined school for Val and Dave. John Heise was in my third grade class too. I gave him a valentine with a little key, like one from a diary, and I told him it was the key to my heart. One time I called him at home in the evening, when his mom answered the phone she told me he was in the bathtub. I was so embarrassed I quickly hung up the phone and ran to my room to hide. I gave him lots of valentines over the years, and when I was about twenty-five I ran into his mom who told me she had saved them all.

At St. Mary's we had small classes and close friends. We played dodge ball during recess, and in junior high we were hellions. We would hang on the cyclone fence along Dora Street and call out to the kids across the street at Pomolita Junior High School to come save us or set us free. In seventh grade, during religion class, Anita got into trouble with Father Tom. He called her to the front of the room and was going to smack her hands with a ruler. She kept pulling her hands back when he tried to hit her, and I started laughing. Then he got mad at me and called me up to the front of the room too. He tried again to smack her hands and, when she pulled them back, he hit his own hand. We were kneeling on the floor as our punishment, and we started laughing so hard we both fell over.

Anita and I were friends all through school. We even played

together before we started going to St. Mary's. Our mothers would go to school every first Friday of the month to serve hot chocolate and doughnuts to all the students after Mass. Anita and I were always there waiting for our moms to finish up. I also had a group of friends that included three doctors' daughters, the ambulance driver's daughter, and the mortician's daughter. I still have friends from childhood that I see and spend time with—Anita, Dawn, Jessica, and every now and then, John Heise!

I guess we were a tough class; in seventh grade we made Sister Gloria cry. In eighth grade, Guinness McFadden was our first teacher. Halfway through the year Guinness decided to quit teaching and start growing grapes. Mack Ford was our teacher for the last half of the year. One day we plugged up the sink in the classroom with paper towels and left the water running, flooding the whole room. Mack left at the end of the year, got a job with the county, and neither he nor Guinness ever taught again.

On winter mornings Mom would make us hot soup for breakfast, tomato soup with Quip (canned whipped cream) on top. When we came home from school on cleaning days, if the kitchen floor had been waxed, we couldn't go into the kitchen to get a snack. Instead, Marjorie would leave a huge bag of Oreos and a gallon of milk on the dining room table for us to eat.

When I was in seventh or eighth grade, or both, I would come home from school some days to find Zack and his friends stripped down to their skivvies, racing through Mop'N Glo on the kitchen floor. Our house had a long hallway that ran from the living room to the family room. The kitchen was to the north of the hall and had a door into the hall at either end. In the kitchen, there were counters on the north and south but nothing in the middle. The kitchen and hall served as a perfect racetrack, and Zack and his friends made the most of it. I am not sure if Mom ever knew how the floors got so clean those days.

It must have been during junior high when the movie Bonnie and Clyde was released. The boys and I decided we wanted to go see it and we knew there was no way Mom would let us go. So one weekend while Margie was babysitting, we used some string to create a spider web upstairs in the hall, connecting all the doorknobs. It was a huge web that we just left up there. Then we all snuck out and went to the movies – we may have snuck into the theater as well. At some point, Margie went upstairs to check on us but couldn't get past the top step because of the web. Needless to say, she was not happy. We got caught at the theater, and we all got in trouble.

I went to Ukiah High School and graduated after my third year. We were on double sessions when I started high school, which meant freshmen and sophomores went to school in the afternoons, and juniors and seniors went in the mornings. I took extra classes each year, so I had at least one class in the morning my freshman and sophomore years. I tried to get into a P. E. class in the morning session, but the teachers told me that they wouldn't allow me to take P. E. as my first class of the day because I was a "Wilson" and my sisters always cut P.E. I loved P.E.! I ran track freshman year and played softball my sophomore year. One year I played basketball too. I loved playing sports, but my parents didn't go to a single one of my games or track meets—not ever.

Music was a very important part of my family. My sisters sat first chair and were in the "Honor Band." Mom dragged us to all their concerts, whether we wanted to go or not. I played saxophone in the band and I had a great time. I loved being in the marching band and tolerated being in the concert band. Sometimes I would walk or ride my bike to school, so Mom would bring my sax to school for me. Half the time I would get to the band room for class, and Mom would have forgotten to bring my instrument to school. I would call Daddy's office, and the receptionist would tell Mom I was on the phone. I could hear her in the background saying, "Oh damn. Tell her I'll be right there." Then she would bring my instrument to me, and I would be late. (But I'm not bitter.)

Sometime between eighth grade and my freshman year of high school, I started having stomach cramps in the evenings. My sisters always complained that I was being a big baby because I didn't want to help with the dishes. Some days I would stay to help and other days I had to lie down to make the pain stop. Mom would say that if I didn't eat so much my stomach wouldn't hurt. I quit complaining about it, and instead I would take Darvon out of Mom's medicine cabinet, go upstairs, get into a steaming hot bath, and go to sleep. Sometimes I would wake up in the tub in freezing cold water in the middle of the night. Finally, toward the end of my sophomore year, I went with Prissy, Elaine and Janet to the high school talent show. Shortly after the show started I began feeling the cramps. I asked Prissy if she would ask Elaine to take me home. She refused but gave me a quarter to call Mom. I stood in line at the pay phone for what seemed like an eternity, until someone finally asked if any of the ten or fifteen of us who were waiting had an emergency. I groaned, "Yes," so they let me use the phone. I called Mom to come get me, and by the time she got there I was lying on the lawn, writhing in pain. She managed to get me in the car and drove me to Daddy's office where he was still working. It took two shots of Demerol for me to relax enough for Daddy to examine me. He sent me home to bed and scheduled some tests for the next week. When I got home I started a pot of coffee and went upstairs for a bath. After my bath I went back downstairs to get a cup of coffee. As I picked the pot up about two inches off the counter, it slid through my fingers and went crashing to the floor, spraying coffee everywhere. The Demerol had finally fully kicked in and I couldn't even feel the coffeepot in my hands.

The following week I had blood tests, an upper GI, and x-rays. Two days later, I was scheduled for surgery to have my gallbladder removed. I had nothing to eat starting the night before my surgery, waited until 4:00 p.m. to be told my surgery was being postponed a day, then finally had it the following day. Dr. Curtis later told me he stopped counting the stones at one hundred gravel-sized stones. After my surgery, Daddy would come visit me when he was done with his rounds. He would get me out of bed, put his arm under one of mine, and hold me up as straight as he could get me while we walked up and down the halls of that hospital, every day until they sent me home.

My lab tests also showed that I had hyperparathyroidism. So for about a year after my surgery I had to go see a specialist in San Francisco every month. Mom went with me the first time or two, and then, as soon as I had my driver's license, she sent me by myself. I hated those trips. I didn't like going down there alone. San Francisco was overwhelming, and I would just drive straight to the doctor and then turn around and go right back home. On one of my trips to the doctor with Mom, we did a little shopping. First, I wanted a bike, and I had my own money to buy the one I wanted. I found a Zeus, a ten-speed Spanish bike that isn't made anymore. It was beautiful. Little did I know at the time how important this bike would prove to be in my adulthood. The second item on my list was a pair of thirteen-button wool Navy pants, which we found at an Army/Navy store. Mom sent me in by myself to get my pants, and while I was trying them on, one of the store clerks was watching me. I didn't know what to do and I didn't dare say anything to him. So I got my pants and got out just as quickly as I could.

I did like going down with my friends for concerts "On the Green" in Oakland. We would stay with Pam at her apartment before the concert, and as long as I got to stay with Pam I didn't mind going down. Debbie was in San Francisco at the time too, but it seems she wasn't around as much. I know I visited her, but she was married and busy, so we just stayed with Pam.

I always had long hair. One day when I was a teenager, my mother got upset at the way my hair looked hanging down, thick and wavy, kind of all over the place like a "wild woman." She decided she wanted to cut it, but I didn't want it cut, so she started chasing me all over the house with a pair of scissors. I ran into the living room and hid behind Daddy who was playing drums. Mom came running in with those scissors at the ready. Daddy just looked at her and said, "Oh, Josephine, leave her alone."

I really didn't get in too much trouble when I was in high school. As long as I went to school and got good grades, Mom pretty much let me alone. I think she was just worn out already from all my older sisters and brother. She was different after Di and Julie ran away to the Haight-Ashbury. Mom and Dad called the Markovitzes (my godparents) to go to San Francisco from Aptos to try to find them. And after she became a grandmother, Mom worried more about Di and Josh than she did about the rest of us who were still at home.

I always cooked dinner because Mom was at work, and then after dinner, she would fall asleep with her glass of wine and a cigarette. I would quietly ask her if I could go to Janet's house; she wouldn't answer, so I would take the car and go. She would get really mad if she was awake when I got home, or if she found out I had gotten a speeding ticket. One night when I got home, she started yelling at me and called me a whore. I was mortified because I had never even had sex, and I couldn't believe she could think such a thing.

During high school Mom would take me with her driving around town at night, looking for Daddy. We would drive from bar to bar—only the ones that had live music—looking in the parking lots for his car. Sometimes, if we found his car, I would sit outside while she went in to talk to him. He never came out with her and we would just go home. When I was younger, she would always say that he worked all the time. He wasn't at home in the evenings because he was putting food on the table and clothes on our backs. But I know sometimes, on the weekends, he would go hang out at the fire department to watch football because we never had a TV.

I got arrested when I was seventeen for possession of marijuana. My punishment was to attend drug-awareness classes every week for twelve weeks on Wednesday nights at the courthouse. Daddy always went with me. Mom would remind me that this was such an embarrassment for him, a prominent doctor having to spend his only day off going to classes with me. But I loved having the time with him. I also loved being up late, trying to get my homework done, and he would come in to help me. He always had a great way of explaining things and was so patient that it was easy to learn from him. One night after getting in a fight with Mom, I took a beer out of the fridge and was sitting outside on the hood of the car daydreaming and looking at the night sky. Daddy drove up and I tried to hide the beer between my legs with my hands on top. He walked over and just started talking about the sky and the planets and all kinds of interesting stuff. I'm sure he saw the beer, but he never said anything except that sometimes I should be more patient with my mother.

I started getting into a little trouble in junior high and high school—little things like car wrecks and doing drugs. When I was twelve, Mom and Dad were out of town. Di was going out with her friends and I asked if I could come along. She said, "Sure, but you have to do whatever we do." I readily agreed, knowing that once I was in the car with them they couldn't really make me do anything. So we cruised around and found a place to park so they could light up a joint. As soon as I smelled it I decided I would go ahead and smoke it too. When we got back to the house, Margie told Di and me to do the dishes. We started doing the dishes and laughing, and then throwing the dishes to each other. Di washed then I dried, and then I would toss what I had dried to Di, who would put it in the cupboard. We were laughing and playing, and Marjorie was so mad at us she was steaming, but we were having fun.

I worked with my dad at his office for a couple of years when I was in junior high school; that was great fun. I did clerical stuff, but sometimes Daddy would have me help him with things like reading results of urine tests and culture samples. We used to clean my dad's office too. All the girls would go over and start cleaning. One by one, we would sneak into the little closet that held all the drug samples. Each of us had our favorites, mostly I think we took diet pills; I know I did. That was my introduction to pills. A cop once told me he could tell I liked speed and my sister liked pot because I would run the red lights and she would stop at the green ones.

I liked driving, too. Prissy introduced me to driving when I was twelve. We were coming back from the grocery store one day and she was driving Mom's station wagon. Suddenly, she turned to me and said, "It's time you learn how to drive!" I got into the driver's seat and very slowly drove down Oak Park Avenue. When I got to the corner of the alley and started to turn, the car was barely moving. Prissy said to give it some gas so I did, and the car lurched forward—right into a brand-new fence at the Koch's house. The

Kochs were a new family in the neighborhood and I was supposed to start babysitting for them soon. I was terrified. Prissy told me to go tell Mrs. Koch what had happened and then walk home, and she would drive the car back home. I went to the door with great trepidation and knocked. No one was at home, so I walked back to my house. A little later, I called the Kochs and told Mrs. Koch what had happened and offered to pay for the damage. She told me she had already reported a hit-and-run to the police. She called back a short time later and told me a cop was coming down to my house to see me and I should just tell him that we had made an arrangement that I would pay for the damages.

I was sitting at the dining room table, playing cards with Di, waiting for the cop to get there. When the doorbell rang I asked Di to just say that she was me. She answered the door and said, "Yeah, Becky's right here." Then she made me go talk to the cop who took one look at me and asked how old I was. I told him I was twelve and that Mrs. Koch and I had already made an arrangement to pay for the fence. He said he would just leave my date of birth and driver's license blank on his report. That was the beginning of my juvenile career with cars and cops.

As soon as we had our licenses, the boys and I were always taking the car and racing around town. I learned to drive a stick in my driver's education class, but it was a Volkswagen Beetle. Mom made me take the class over in a bigger car because she had a station wagon. Daddy's car was a Cobra Shelby with a stick and a great big engine; it was so much fun to drive! One night, my friend Jeanette and I were out driving around in it when my parents were out of town. We decided to see if I could drive the length of Dora Street, probably three miles through the middle of town, without stopping at any of the stop signs. I did it all the way from the south end to the north end, but when I got to the hill two blocks from the end, I was going a little fast at the bottom of the hill and hit the dip at a cross street too fast. The front end scraped the ground but I didn't stop. I went to get gas and noticed the oil light was on, so we put a little oil in too. Later, after Mom and Dad got back, we found out there was a hole in the oil pan. Fortunately, we hadn't done much more damage than that.

We had keys to our parents' cars made for ourselves, and when they went out of town, we would take the cars whether we had permission or not. One time, Mom left her car at the Ford dealer for some work while she and Dad were out of town, and Zack went down and took the car from the garage to use while they were gone. He then returned it before anyone knew he had used it. That was when Mom figured out we had extra keys. She tried to collect the keys from us, but we didn't give her all of them—some we threw out the window and picked up later.

Another time when Mom and Dad were in San Francisco, I took Daddy's Cobra and Zack and I went out cruising. We had just dropped off Zack's friend Alan and were going north on State Street, when somebody challenged me to a race. We were flying down the street neck and neck, past the truck stop where the two lanes merged into one. There wasn't room for both cars, so I hit the brakes and the car went into a spin. I think the car spun 360 degrees and ended up slamming into the base of the Mendo Mill and Lumber Company sign. This base was a four-foot cube of bricks, and I hit it so hard it moved, but it didn't move quite as far as my shoulder. The driver's door was smashed in and my shoulder was halfway across my chest. My collar bone was broken again. I had to go to the hospital in the ambulance, and Zack didn't have a scratch on him. Officer McCoey came to the hospital to take a report and asked me if I had been drinking, and I said, "No!" He told me he would just get the rest of the information later, because I was going into shock.

I had nightmares and "daymares" about that accident; I could still smell the flying dirt and burning rubber. Daddy never acted mad about the fact that I had totaled his precious car, but a few days later, he came home for lunch and told me he wanted me to see the new car he was thinking about buying. We went outside and he asked if I liked the car. I said, sure, it was a nice looking car. He told me to jump in so we could go for a ride. I was still nervous from the accident, but I wasn't in any position to argue with him. I got in the car. We took a nice, gentle ride through town—and then he hit the freeway. He started accelerating on the on ramp and just kept going faster and faster on the freeway. I was hanging onto the door, white knuckles and all, and he just kept going faster. I thought I would be sick. He was scaring the crap out of me, and he knew it, but I didn't dare say a word. He didn't slow down until we had gone from one end of town to the other. Then we got off the freeway, and he calmly drove home. He bought the car and not another word was said, or needed, about me wrecking his great car.

The only thing I ever remember hearing about our wrecking or damaging cars after that (no, I was not the only one who damaged one of Mom's or Dad's cars) was a story Mom told us. One evening, when Daddy was at the hospital getting ready to go to a conference for the weekend, Dr. Werra asked him if he was driving to the convention or if he was buying a new car when he got back.

DINNERTIME

Dinnertime was when we knew we would see Daddy. It was the one time we had to be home, and we all had to be at the table. Some evenings he would be there before dinner, and some evenings he would walk in as we were sitting down. We used to wait to watch him coming up the walk and then we would all start singing "Three cheers for Daddy!"

We had a table in the breakfast room that was custom-made to fit the room. It had one end cut at an angle so the dining room door could open without hitting it. If you sat at the back of the table against the wall you were stuck until dinner was over, or you would have to crawl under the table to get out. There wasn't enough room at the table for all of us, so there were always three kids sitting at the counter in the kitchen, close enough to feel like we were all at the same table.

We had metal cups with rims that we could hook on our teeth while we leaned back, holding the cup up to get the last drop of milk without using our hands. If we were sitting near Daddy and tried this trick, he would pick up his knife by the blade and rap the bottom of the cup. He chipped the front tooth of each of the boys by rapping on the metal cups while they were holding the cups in their mouths. We liked the metal cups because we could spit our peas or lima beans into them so we didn't have to eat them if we didn't like them. In our house, we had to clear our plates, or we didn't leave the table, so having someplace to hide the yucky veggies was a plus. Later, the metal cups were replaced by empty olive jars, which weren't as good because they were glass and Mom and Dad could see if we tried to hide our vegetables in them.

One time when I was trying to hide my lima beans, Daddy saw me and took me and my beans into the family room. He proceeded to shovel the beans into my mouth and hold my mouth shut until I swallowed. I kept gagging, because I hated lima beans, but he wouldn't let up until I had finished them.

In high school, Daddy brought some kind of new diet product home that he wanted Prissy and me to try. It was some kind of pill that you take with a glass of water just before you eat. The water made the pill expand and fill up your stomach so you are too full before you even start eating.

Also, when I was in high school, I decided to give up food for Lent. I started fasting and had nothing but water for two weeks. Daddy looked at me one day when I was refusing dinner because of my fast, and he told me I had to start eating again the very next day. It took almost two weeks for me to work my way back to eating a regular diet.

My favorite dinner memory was the time that Mom and Dad were gone and we decided to have a no-utensil dinner so we wouldn't have dishes to clean. We took the food and put it on the table, still in the pots and pans. We didn't have plates or silverware; instead, we just dished out the food onto the table and ate with our hands. Every kid should do this once in his life.

Our famous dinner story is the one Mom used to tell when she was teaching a babysitting course for kids who wanted to be babysitters. I'm sure this was her version of a mother's day in hell. Some of my friends remember this story from taking her class.

It all started with one of the big girls cleaning out the fireplace, I think it was Diana. Instead of shoveling the ashes into a bag and taking the bag outside to the trash, she decided to take each shovelful of ashes straight out the door. In this process, she was dropping ashes across the head of whoever was sitting on the couch, making a terrible mess. While this was going on in one room, Debbie was in the kitchen helping with dinner. Her chore was making mashed potatoes from those old, dried potato-flake packages. She had opened the packets on one side of the room and was taking them to the stove to put them in the pot of boiling water. Unfortunately, she carried them from the counter to the stove upside down making the second terrible mess.

When we finally sat down to eat, one of the little boys was in the bathroom. Mom went in to check on him, only to find that he had taken his poop out of the toilet to do some finger painting. While Mom was cleaning up the kid and the third terrible mess, we had started a food fight with the mashed potatoes.

The potato throwing morphed into the worst terrible mess. Our kitchen and breakfast room floors were linoleum, but the dining and living room floors were hardwood. Our living room was a large room with French doors leading into the dining room, which was connected on the other side to the breakfast room. There was a long open area from the dining room to the piano on the opposite end of the living room. Those of us left at the dinner table had removed our shoes, taken a bottle of catsup, poured it on the floor just inside the living room from the dining room, and were sliding in our stocking feet through the catsup into the living room to see who could slide the farthest. That was definitely the worst terrible mess, and the last—at least for that day.

After dinner, we took turns doing the dishes and cleaning the kitchen. After the kitchen was cleaned up we had to do our homework. If we didn't have homework, or when we were done, we had a choice: "Read a book, write a letter, or say a rosary." I think it was a way for Mom to get us to fall asleep. We read the Hardy Boys and Nancy Drew mysteries. Val and I used to read the Reader's

Digest Drama in Real Life. My last choice was always saying a rosary; it always made me fall asleep really fast. To this day, I can't say a rosary without falling asleep in the first decade.

IMAGINATION

We never had a television, but we had great imaginations. We orchestrated bike wrecks. Paul was the youngest and was a skinny little kid. We would maneuver Paul in odd positions with the bike on the street, pour catsup all over him and then hide to see what the next car would do when they saw him. We had a swimming pool we were told was the first in-ground pool in Ukiah. It seemed so huge to me, with a big ramp from the shallow end to the deep end. The only water it ever had in it was rainwater, and then it was filled with leaves as well. We had to clean it out, and when we did, we would roller skate and ride bikes down the ramp. We always had bikes. Sometimes they would get stolen by the kids at the Albertinum, the orphanage at the end of our block, but we always got them back. On at least one occasion, we poured lighter fluid on our bikes, lighting and then riding our cool, flaming bikes until the fluid burned out. I rode my bike with David up around "Moore's Hill." It was the biggest hill in the neighborhood. Sometimes we had to walk our bikes up to the top, and once we got to the top, it was a terrifyingly fun ride down Clay Street to home. The day David and I took on "Moore's Hill" I stayed behind him coming down the hill, riding my brakes in terror. David was much braver than I and went barreling down the hill. I saw him crash in front of me. I don't know how or why it happened. I rode home for help, but before I got anyone to go back to him someone else had come along and brought him home. I am not certain now, but I think he had a broken arm.

David got hurt a lot, mostly of his own doing. One day at school, I must have been in the fourth grade, my friends came running to tell me that David had gone through a window and his face was missing. As it turned out, he had run into a plate-glass window next to a door and had split his upper lip completely open. Luckily, my father's office was right across the street, so he was taken over there and was stitched up. My dad was a great seamstress, and today you can't even see a scar where the three layers of stitches held his lip together. Another time, David, Zack and a friend decided to make some bombs upstairs. They were using gunpowder and had it in a Coke bottle—one of those old bottles of thick green glass. I was sitting downstairs with Mom after dinner when, all of a sudden, there was a blast that shocked us to the core. At first, it felt like an earthquake, and then I thought the radiator in the basement had exploded. As I headed toward the basement door, I heard some yelling upstairs. As I passed the stairwell, I looked up to see David standing at the top of the stairs with his head in his hands and blood pouring through his fingers, over his hands and down his arms. Mom grabbed a cold wet rag to put on his face, and off they went to the hospital to find Daddy. David ended up in surgery in Santa Rosa to repair his cornea; his friend Tony had little nicks on his arms and hands; and Zack had just one little chard of glass in his belly near his navel—as usual, no medical attention required for him. For David, however, this was the beginning of my trip through hell. But more about that later.

David wasn't the only one who had injuries growing up; I had some too. I must have been in third grade when Zack and I decided we really didn't want to go to bed while it was still light out. So we snuck downstairs, got one of Daddy's long coats, and decided to play a trick on everyone. I put Zack on my shoulders and he put the coat on, then we walked around the house to get to the front door. Zack was guiding me along. As we neared the concrete porch in front, he told me to step up. Our timing was off just enough for me to trip on the first step, which sent me crashing head first into the next cement step, which I hit just at my left eyebrow. We got so scared that we would be caught, we went running back into the house and up to our bedrooms. A short while later, my mother called me downstairs and said she thought I might need some ice on my eye. I still don't know who told her, but I was thankful for the ice. I ended up with a black eye that covered half my face and permanently discolored my lower eyelids. About ten days later, while we were all outside playing baseball, Daddy came out and asked Pam to go to his office with him and asked me to go as well. When we got there, he put me up on an examining table and had Pam help keep me calm as he numbed my left eye at the brow. Then he took a scalpel to slice open my eyebrow and remove a blood clot as big around as a quarter. He put a butterfly bandage on my eye and took us back home.

When I was about seven years old, we were all over at the Winslow's playing standing statues. For those of you who don't know standing statues, it is a kind of tag game where one person is "it." That person spins the other players and when they are released, they must stay in whatever positions they landed in until another player comes to tag them so they can move. It was Val's turn to be "it" and she was spinning me. I was younger but bigger than Val, and our weight shifted, so I was spinning her rather than her spinning me. When she let go of me, I went flying and landed on my left side and shoulder. I played a little longer but my shoulder hurt, so I went home (while my siblings jeered at the "little baby that had to go crying to Mommy") and told Mom that I hurt my shoulder. She took me to my dad at the hospital. I got my shoulder x-rayed, my broken clavicle taped, and then my dad put me in the car with Dr. Kraft to get a ride home. Try to imagine your average seven/eight year old with a broken collarbone being sent home with a relative stranger who is at least six foot four inches tall, gangly, big black glasses, wild hair and a moustache, smoking a pipe. I knew the guy was okay or my dad wouldn't have sent me with him, but it was frightening just the same.

In second grade, or maybe the fourth (I know I was wearing a St. Mary's uniform), I was in the boys' room after school one day. We had rope ladders to use for a fire escape from the second-floor bedroom and decided to use them to climb out the window. The old windows had weights and pulleys, and my job was to hold the window open while the boys lowered the ladder and climbed down. I was wearing a short-sleeved, button-front blouse and holding the window open. Suddenly, bees came swarming out of the hole in the wall where the weight on the pulley was housed, and flew directly into the sleeve of my blouse. I had thick hair down to my waist, and the bees were all over me—inside my blouse and all through my hair. I started screaming and Debbie came running in, ripped off my shirt and started swatting the bees. They had to use pliers to pull about a dozen of the stingers out of my back and scalp.

Here's the big one. For those of you who think you know the story, pay close attention. One day when I was in sixth grade, I got home from school and David was outside playing with all his friends—all the best guys who were a year or two older than I. They were playing Batman out in the yard, and I wanted to play. I got an umbrella and went up on the roof. I stood at the edge of the twenty-foot roof and called down to them that I wanted to be the Penguin. I told them they all had to come up on the roof and then I would jump off, just like the Penguin. The next thing I knew, they were all there behind me, so I opened the umbrella and jumped. I didn't realize the umbrella was broken, so when I jumped it just turned inside out, and down I went. I landed on my feet then fell immediately onto my face with the wind knocked out of me. Carl had stayed down in the yard and came running over to help me. He pounded on my back to get me to breathe and it worked. I remember sitting in the dining room with Daddy later that evening, while he drew pictures for me to show all the different ways I might have landed and all the different injuries I would have suffered, had I landed in any of those positions. Apparently, I landed in the best possible position and only suffered fractures of three vertebrae in my lower back.

PUNISHMENT

We got into all kinds of trouble growing up, just like most kids I suppose, and like most kids we got punished. The boys and I took brand-new shingles off the neighbor's garage to put on the fort we were building in our backyard. When Daddy found out he spanked us. He told us to go out to the garage and get a stick and to be sure it was big enough to last through the four of us. Another time when he was spanking us, we were all lined up outside his bedroom door waiting our turns. Zack put on about six pairs of underpants so it wouldn't hurt when he got spanked. Daddy made him take them off and Zack started crying. I was standing outside in the hallway even though I had already gotten my spanking. When Daddy came out and saw me laughing at Zack, he took me back in for another round—the second time around was not as gentle as the first.

I was in junior high, and Val must have been in high school when we got into an argument. Daddy called us downstairs to explain what was going on. Val got to tell her side of the story first, and I got mad. I said to Daddy, "She's lying," and then said to Val, "You bitch!" Daddy stopped dead in his tracks, took me by the ear, and dragged me, staying about three steps ahead of me the whole way, all the way upstairs to my room. And that was the end of that.

In high school, I got into an argument with Mom over something I can't remember. She was really mad, and I went flying upstairs to my room with her close on my heels. My bedroom was right at the top of the stairs. As soon as I got to it, I ran inside and slammed the door in her face! She came in behind me, madder than ever, screaming at me as I lay on my bed. She looked around the room and found a dictionary on the desk—an old huge dictionary, the kind you need two hands to hold. She picked it up, walked over to me, held it over her head ready to slam it into my face, and suddenly, in her practical fury, she said, "Take off your glasses. I am going to hit you!"

I looked her straight in the eye and said, "You bought them. You can break them, and then you can buy me some new ones."

And it was over.

When we were little she would send four or five of us to bed at a time. For a long time six of us shared a room. The three big girls had one room and the six little kids had the other. There were two sets of bunk beds and a single bed in the little kids' room. I think Paul and Zack shared a bed because they were the littlest. In the winter our beds always had quilts on them. If we were noisy at bedtime, she would move us out of the room, one at a time, and spread us out through the house—one in bed, one at the top of the stairs, one at the bottom of the stairs, one in the living room and so on. Sometimes, we would still talk and send messages back and forth from one kid to the next and back again. If we were really noisy, she would get really frustrated and send us out to wait on the front porch "until your father gets home," which could sometimes be the middle of the night. We had to remember to grab our quilts when we got called downstairs, because if we ended up outside without our quilt, we would think we were freezing to death. When Daddy finally got home, nothing ever happened he would just send us up to bed.

After the house was remodeled, there were four bedrooms, so the three boys shared a room, Deb and Pam shared a room, Di and Pris shared a room, and Val and I shared a room. My room was over the family room, which had a nice big light fixture in the center. One night, Val and I were jumping rope when we were supposed to be going to sleep. As we jumped rope, the light in the family room swayed back and forth. Mom quickly figured out that we were not in bed where we belonged, so she called us downstairs. She told us if we wanted to jump rope we could go in the living room and jump rope until our father got home. Seems like we jumped rope for hours that night, but I think we must have gotten too tired and went back to bed before he actually got home.

My mom had nine dishwashers (her children) and at least four babysitters (the big girls). When she and Daddy would go out at night, one of the big girls was usually in charge. One night Prissy was in charge, and Val and I were in bed arguing. Val and I shared a double bed for many years until we broke it, and Mom bought twin beds for us. This particular night, we were still in the double bed and we were arguing about something. I got mad at Val and told her not to go to sleep or I would kill her. Priscilla heard some muffled cries and came running in to find my hands wrapped around Val's neck. Val had decided to go to sleep, so I had reached over to strangle her as I had promised.

Another time, when Di was babysitting and Audrey was helping, I got mad at Audrey. I think I was in seventh grade or so. I don't remember what started the whole thing, but I clearly remember that Audrey was not the boss of me. She must have been telling me to do something. We were standing in the dining room at either end of the large table. I reached over and, picking up a very heavy eight-inch-round glass ashtray, said, "Why are you here? You don't live here. You aren't my sister. You aren't my boss. You can't tell me what to do. I hate you!" And with that, I threw the ashtray right at her, just as hard as I possibly could. Fortunately for me, it didn't hit her, and it didn't break.

Being Terrorized

It is hard to grow up in a family with eight siblings and not get terrorized, especially if you are one of the youngest. When we were really little and the six youngest shared a bedroom, we would sometimes go to bed in groups. I remember Pam putting Zack, Paul and me to bed. She helped us create a kind of fort by hanging blankets down from the top bunk so that it created walls around the bottom bunk. She made it sound like this was going to be really cool and fun if we all went in the bottom bunk to go to sleep. Once we were in there, she tucked the blankets around so that it was very cozy and dark. Then she started making scary noises and stuff and scared us silly.

Later, I was terrorized by my brothers. I had psoriasis on my elbows and sometimes it was so bad that if I bent my arm, the elbows would crack and bleed. The boys called me the "Psoriasis Kid, able to wipe out brick buildings with one swipe of her elbow." They thought it was funny, but for me it was awful, because I already had to go through all the stuff medically trying to get it under control. The psoriasis was painful physically, but the boys making fun of me hurt more. (I am over that now.)

Then there was David. When he got into high school, he went off the deep end. He would get out of bed in the morning and hide between his bed and the wall so Mom would think he was gone. Then he would skip school and do who-knows-what. He would come home while I was supposed to be cooking dinner and start a fight, or just bully me until I would leave. I would go next door to the Cooks' house to hide from him. It got to the point where David would walk in one door and I would walk out the other. Mrs. Cook would see me come into her house and ask if David was home. Whenever I said, yes, she would ask if I wanted to call Mom or if I just wanted to wait until she got home. When I called Mom, I would simply tell her that David was home and that if she wanted dinner to be ready when she got home, she needed to talk to David. Sometimes David would leave and I could go back. Other times, I would just wait at the Cooks' for her to get home.

Then there was Zack, the big man of the house. One night I cooked dinner for everyone while Zack was working at McDonald's. When he got home, he didn't like the dinner I had cooked, so he told me to make something he liked. I refused, so he went to Daddy who proceeded to cook whatever it was he wanted.

Zack and I used to fight a lot. We were pretty close to the same size, so I guess it seemed like an even fight, and God knows I was not about to back down when something started. One day I was arguing with Paul and I called him a "fucking baby." Zack got mad and told me to apologize to Paul. Of course my reply was, "Fuck you too." Then Zack wanted an apology for Paul and him. I said, "I guess you didn't hear me. Fuck you!" So Zack said, "Either apologize, or I am going to hit you." I left the room. Zack followed me into the family room and said, "Apologize right now or I am going to hit you in the face!" I looked him dead in the eye and said, "FUCK YOU!" Then bam! He socked me so hard in the eye that he broke my glasses. I screamed and he ran. I reached up to wipe the tears out of my eyes and came back with a hand covered in blood—and I screamed again. Prissy was sitting in the kitchen, listening to the whole thing, and decided if I screamed once he hit me, twice I was hurt. So as I walked into the kitchen, she met me with a wet washrag and the car keys to take me to the hospital. I got twenty-seven stitches in my eyelid, and Zack got a long conversation with a priest. Apparently, when he saw the blood, he took off running and found himself at the rectory. When Mom got home, I told her, "The next time he comes after me, I am going to head for the stairs. And if he chases me, I am going to turn around halfway up the stairs and kick him as hard as I can. Don't blame me if he breaks his leg falling back down the stairs." She just said, "Okay, dear." And every time after that when we would get in a fight, he would catch me halfway up the stairs and sock the crap out of me.

And last is the dream that terrorized me. I had a recurring dream, and I think all of my siblings had the same dream, but in each version the person having the dream was the last one still in the house. Here it is:

We are home on a nice weekend day when a truck pulls up in front of the house. A man comes to the door and tells us he has our bicycles. One by one, each person goes out to the truck. And one by one, they disappear. The dreamer quickly realizes that the man does not have our bikes, but instead, in the truck is a huge meat grinder and he is throwing the others into it. The person having the dream knows the man is lying and tries to convince the rest of the family that it is not safe, but one by one, they go out to the truck. In my dream, Prissy is the last one left in the house and I am desperately trying to keep her with me, but she goes out to the truck. I wake up.

MUSIC AND PARTIES AND GAMES

Even with all the fights and punishment and sibling terror, we had so much fun. There was always music in the house—the radio, records, someone practicing an instrument or singing or, best of all, a party with Dad's band playing. We had great parties—all the local doctors and other jazz fans and friends would be there. I loved to sit and just watch all the people. Mom would ask me why I wasn't out mingling and having fun, but for me, the best fun was watching, not mingling.

My sisters all sang, but Mom wouldn't let me because she said I had a tin ear and couldn't carry a tune. (It's okay, I got her back. I sang as loud as I could at her funeral.) She would make me and the boys do little things on stage with the girls when they were singing. They did recitals for the state hospital and convalescent homes around Christmas and Easter. And they were always singing at the house, practicing. I knew all the songs by heart, but I wouldn't dare sing loud enough for any of them to hear. When no one was home, I would go to the piano and play and sing to my heart's content.

Some days, when we weren't listening to music, we would listen to comedy albums like Bill Cosby, Bob Newhart, Stan Freberg and Copp and Brown. I think we still say things to each other that no one else understands because it is a line from Copp and Brown. My favorites are still "You don't suppose this is a highway, do ya?" and "I skip, I skip … and so do I." Or we sing Stan Freberg songs, especially "Green Christmas."

We played games, too, and cards (always according to Hoyle), Parcheesi, Scrabble, Yahtzee and dominoes. And we worked jigsaw puzzles—those big wooden ones with thousands of pieces. So often, our dining room table had a puzzle in progress and we would go in and work on it when we felt like it. I think we learned to strategize; I know we learned to be competitive.

I will never forget playing the dictionary game with Gramma Carrie at the table one Thanksgiving after dinner. She had such a great sense of humor she would stun me with some of her answers, and I would just laugh forever. Someone pulled out the word "yerk" and we all had to write what we thought the definition was. So Gramma Carrie wrote: "What a hair-lipped dog says." We had to stop the game until we could all stop laughing. Gramma's favorite game was dominoes; I remember spending hours playing with her. I think I was really lucky to be one of the little kids as far as Gramma Carrie goes, because I got to spend more time with her when she moved to Ukiah. I got a chance to know her, and she really was a great person.

We played lots of games during the holidays because the holidays were special. Mom and Dad always made sure that birthdays and Christmas were special. On our birthdays we got to pick what we wanted for dinner. On Christmas, we usually got one big family gift in addition to our individual gifts and stocking goodies. One year it was a trampoline (Diana jumped right through the living room window); another year it was a unicycle. The best year was the surrey with the fringe on top.

SONGS AND SUCH THAT I REMEMBER

We had songs and little sayings that I can't help but remember. At various times during the year, Mom would drive around town pointing out her favorite trees or beautiful yards. She knew what was blooming in whose yard and when, so she would take different routes to get places to show us the dogwood in bloom in the springtime or the colors changing in the fall. She loved the beauty of nature and would often say, just out of the blue, "Thank you, God, for a beautiful day!" While Mom was driving us around town in the car, she would see a guy, and in her very Southern drawl, she would say, "Hey, handsome, you spoke for?" Or she would tap the brake as she sang, "Hip! Hip! I had a good job but I quit! First they hired me, then they fired me, then by golly I quit!" She would always tell us, "It's nice to be nice," until I thought I would puke. Now I feel differently about that one. We had songs we sang as little kids—catchy little ditties that I still hum to myself now and then, like:

Good morning, good morning, my face is shining bright.
Good morning, good morning, my teeth are clean and white.
I combed my hair, I brushed my teeth, my hands are nice and clean.
I'm ready for my breakfast, my cereal and cream.

Another was:

My fork goes on my left; my knife goes on my right.
I eat with my fork, I cut with my knife.
I pick my napkin up from off my little knees,
I wipe my face, I wipe my hands,
I say excuse me please. "Excuse me please!"

And the most famous Wilson tune of all:

Three cheers for Daddy
Three cheers for Daddy

Someone in the crowd is yelling
Three cheers for Daddy
One, two, three, four, who ya gonna yell for?
Daddy, that's who!

We learned so many things growing up. We are kind and caring, we understand and accept disappointment, and we expect fairness. We are polite and gracious and intelligent, and we still have active imaginations and a healthy respect for and awe of nature. Although we have similarities, we are distinct individuals. I am proud to be a member of this family. I love each and every one of my siblings dearly and thank them for contributing to who I am today. I love my parents as well; I wish I had gotten to know them better. Even still, they and my siblings are a part of me. I know because sometimes I hear their voices when I speak. Thank you (all) ever so much.

THE 8TH VOICE — ZACHARY CULLEN

I REMEMBER WHERE I WAS WHEN PRESIDENT KENNEDY WAS KILLED. I was sitting at our odd but fashionably shaped dining room table at 416 Oak Park Avenue. I think Margie was there with me. Funny thing, though, we weren't living at 416 at that time. We were living down the street at the house ever after occupied by the Swans. I was four years old in the fall of 1963, and anytime anyone asks, "Where were you when Kennedy was killed?" I tell the same story, just as I remembered it. To this day, I don't know which is true. That is how I recall all my childhood memories.

It wasn't really our dining room either. It was a smaller, less formal dining area adjacent to the dining room. Our dining room was for more proper occasions: Thanksgiving, Christmas, and Easter dinners or when special guests graced us with their presence. Now that I think of it, nothing bad ever happened in there. It was always full of laughter and food. Someone brought a tape recorder to dinner one night to capture the frivolity. The most prominent sounds were those of silverware scraping plates. One of my most favorite memories included one of my best childhood and now lifetime friends, George Ginochio. A friend of David's was also there, Danny Thomas. Danny brought to dinner with him a visitor from a faraway land. He was Asian and in his culture, people only said hello the first time they met each day. So if you saw him in the morning, you would greet him with "hello" and then never say it again for the rest of the day, even if you didn't see him again until dinnertime. Of course, we all kept saying hello every time we saw him anew, even just moments later. He didn't think it was as funny as the rest of us did.

George was as much of a clown around us as the siblings were. He had long hair, as most boys did back then. George came to the table with his hair pulled high into a ponytail, just like John Belushi's Samurai character on *Saturday Night Live*. He wouldn't take it out, and we couldn't stop laughing. The best thing about that formal dining room was that Dad was usually there with us, while he was most often absent from or limited by time in our regular eating room.

Many of my memories are of photographs. I have no idea where it is now, but the most memorable of photos is one of me in my Masonite Little League uniform, white with green trim, and my bat pulled back, ready to hit—although I don't remember too many hits. The uniform pants were old-school, called knickerbockers. One day I dumped a full box of Fudgsicles down them and walked out of Westside Grocery without paying. Of course, I shared them with my teammates.

I wasn't very athletic. I swear I was only allowed on the CYO basketball team for the fights afterwards. I do remember many of those fights. I don't think any of us were very athletic. Becky excelled at softball, and Valli always seemed to be in shape. I hope I'm not missing any important part of a sibling's athletic career. Mom and Dad weren't athletic either. I guess you can't do everything.

Music is where this family devoted most of its time. Today, there are some excellent musicians among us. Some just need a little dusting off. I will always remember all the girls singing "Kiss Beneath the Mistletoe," and I remember Di winning awards in band.

I have a few of my own favorite music memories. I started as a trumpet player. After sitting center stage at our seventh-grade concert, playing trumpet at St. Mary of the Angels school, Mom commented about the hole I had in the knee of my brown corduroys. She was good like that.

In high school, freshmen started in the Cub Band and unless they were really good and were promoted sooner, they moved into the concert/marching band at the start of sophomore year. Instead, I was switched to French horn. My band career was over by midyear. No harm done—brass instruments were hard for smokers, which I was. I also had a singing career (although my wife and kids wouldn't believe it). Mom told me I had the same singing teacher (Mrs. Cox) as Johnny Mathis. Anyway, that's the story I tell.

I sang "Bald-Headed Lena" with my best friends, Joel Corippo and George Ginochio, in seventh grade, and I sang "On Broadway" on my own in my eighth grade talent show. That was the peak of my singing career, and we probably ought to leave it that way. My final and favorite music memory is of Roland Neilson, our high school band teacher. Roland was a great bandleader, a good teacher, and a sweetheart of a guy. I was still in grade school and went to a high school football game one Friday night. Di was playing in the band. I was hanging out with her, trying to open a bag of potato chips by ripping the top off. Mr. Neilson saw me struggling. He took the bag from me, held it by the top middle of the front and back, and pulled it apart at the top. Every time I open a bag of chips like that, I think of him. I always wanted to name a son Roland, just because I like the name.

I had wonderful parents. I miss Mom the most now, because I don't know how to do anything without being told. She always told us we could be anything we wanted to be, and I think she believed it. She put a high premium on education and held doctors and lawyers in the highest regard. We all remember driving around town or anywhere with her as she pointed out the beauty in nature.

Two things I remember Mom telling me: "you can't do twice what you don't do once," and "don't get yourself in a position where things can go bad." Sometimes I wish I had been paying attention.

Mom also stated often, "a wise man learns from others' mistakes, a smart man learns from his own mistakes, and a fool never learns." I don't know if that little saying was reserved for just me. I assume she told that to my siblings as well.

Mom had a great singing voice and I was so impressed with her recordings that I played them for anyone who would listen. I vaguely remember Mom leading us in prayer in the living room by candlelight or very dim light. I was really young at that time, and I remember it almost like a dream; maybe it was. From birth to age eighteen, I don't have a single negative memory of Mom. That's pretty cool!

One of my favorite memories of my mom occurred during an annual trip to the Coast. We rented a little house in or near Fort Bragg, California, a coastal town where the ocean spanned the horizon, and the Pacific was wild and cold. There are pictures of us walking along the shore, wearing long pants and sweaters—not the typical vision of California surfers or beach bums.

Audrey and Kathy Tracy were with us on that trip and having just arrived, half of us went to the local grocery store for supplies, while the remainder stayed with Mom to ready the house. I don't know whose idea it was at the time, probably Mom's, but those of us who stayed behind decided to play a practical joke on the others when they returned. Instead of getting the house in shape, we tipped over furniture, made the place a mess, and tied Mom up on the couch. The rest of us hid, and when the others came home to find the family in distress (you should have seen the look on Audrey's face), we jumped out and yelled, "Surprise!" Mom let us have our fun and even joined in, but she didn't let it get out of control. Others may disagree, but I think that typifies how she treated us.

Mother was also the strict disciplinarian of the household but always looked out for her children. On my first day of first grade at St. Mary's, Mom took me to school and sat me down next to another little boy. She then told the teacher, "The first time Zack gets out of control, just slap the kid next to him. Zack will get the message."

My parents threw a lot of parties when we were growing up. Dad's band would play, and they were terrific. Dad was the drummer and he was fantastic. Barbara Curtis was the pianist and also the sister of Ralph Sutton, the piano player for The World's Greatest Jazz Band. Vince Angel, the local pharmacist, played the upright bass, and he was no bigger around than the neck of the bass. Rod Pacini was the saxophonist, and he wore a Van Dyke before they were fashionable. Back in the day, he was very groovy. My godfather, "Uncle Ben" Foster, played trumpet and valve trombone. He was a great guy and probably my inspiration for choosing trumpet. It was either that or that Mom realized when I came of age our family didn't have a trumpet player, and she just assigned it to me. Dad's band was awesome. They occasionally invited other musicians to sit in. When Dad died, one of the more recent contributors played trumpet at the burial. With tears streaming down his cheeks, he played Dad's favorite song, and everyone could hear the sorrow in the notes as he blew. I will never forget that.

The parties were always a blast, and when guests arrived, Mom would answer the door, with all of us lined up as a welcoming party. She would introduce us to our guests and them to us. We would always shake their hands and say something gentlemanly or ladylike. That was a fantastic ritual that has served us well throughout life. Mom taught us to respect our elders and to be just as respectful of others.

During those parties the alcohol was plentiful, but I never remember my parents or their friends being drunk. The dining room table was always spread with great food. My mom was a wonderful baker. Desserts were plentiful. Lincoln Log and Icebox Cake were my favorites. I found out later in life that the reason Mom always brought dessert to a function was because she never arrived anywhere on time.

Birthdays were also very special, not because we were inundated with gifts but because Mom would always make us whatever we wanted for our birthday dinners. My regular birthday dinner was lamb shanks, rice, and some vegetable. I chose Lincoln Log for dessert. That is still my favorite meal. The way my mom made those lamb shanks was absolutely heavenly.

My dad was great too. He wasn't home much—maybe that was part of his greatness. He rarely, if ever, came to my ball games, he never took me fishing, and he never encouraged me to do or be anything. And I had to learn how to play drums without his help. But still I sense that he was a great guy. He was honest and caring and a pillar of our community. Whenever we went out to dinner or just out anywhere, people would always approach him with a warm smile and a welcome voice. He would always respond in kind. It seemed people would do anything for him. Anytime he went with us to see a movie, it never failed that halfway through the movie, a ticker-tape would come across the bottom of the screen: *"Dr. Wilson, you have a telephone call in the lobby."* I don't know if he ever saw an entire showing.

I have only one negative memory of my father. I was seventeen years old and in the spring of my senior year in high school. Dad and I got in a fight for some reason (let me guess: I was probably acting like an asshole). It was about to get physical and ugly. My mother literally stepped in to break it up. As she did so, she announced that Dad had recently been diagnosed with cancer and was very sick. He died six months later.

On a positive note, my parents never did anything illegal. They wouldn't dare think of stealing—you know, grown-up rationalized stealing, like not paying taxes or inflating an insurance claim. Mother always made us repay any clerk who accidentally gave us too much change and often she imparted lectures of honesty as the best policy. If she caught us stealing, she would make us take it back and apologize to the clerk or owner. While I was not dishonest as a child, I stole anything I could get my hands on. My escapades as a childhood thief could fill a chapter by itself. One day, some of my friends and/or brothers went to Cal's Variety on a shoplifting spree. As I was leaving, I was stopped and accused of stealing a hammer. Apparently, my greed got the better of me, because the clerks didn't know that the hammer was about the tenth item I'd shoved down my pants. The first nine went undetected until then. I should have played the odds.

Shoplifting was quite the ironic conundrum because we never needed to steal anything. We weren't rich growing up, but we never wanted for any necessities. Mom had charge accounts all over town and we could use them without restriction. Often on our birthdays, she would just send us somewhere to pick out some clothes and tell us, "Charge it. Happy birthday."

Let me make one thing perfectly clear: excluding my time behind the wheel of any automobile, as a man, I live a law-abiding life, and honesty is a cornerstone of my existence. I'm definitely honest as a husband and father. At work and in my professional relationships, I am *honest to a fault*. This is now; that was then.

I think my favorite times with my dad were when I would accompany him on a medical house call. He was an old country doctor, and when he visited patients in their homes out in the boonies, he occasionally took me with him. He drove an old green Ford Fairlane. It had a bench seat in front, and I would lie across the top of the full-length seat back as we drove and talked. I don't have a clue as to the content of our conversations or where we went or who we saw, but I always remember being happy when I went with him on those house calls.

I think our collective favorite memory is the following:

Dad came home for dinner every night around seven o'clock or a little after. We were already all seated and usually eating when he walked in. As he did so, we sang out:

> Three cheers for Daddy,
> Three cheers for Daddy,
> Someone in the crowd is yelling, "Three cheers for Daddy!"
> One, two, three, four, who ya gonna yell for?
> Daddy, that's who!

Then Dad did a little soft shoe and danced to the dinner table with a great big smile on his face. That was great! He was great!

I have a great story about Grandma Carrie, Dad's mom. Dad bought a house for his aging mother just across the alley behind our house. He also bought her a television, although we never had one when we were growing up. One of us would always go check on her in the evening but usually only as a precursor to watching TV. One night at about eight o'clock, I went to Grandma's. As I walked in, she was in her nightgown and doing her dinner dishes. We talked for a little bit, and then I asked her if I could watch TV. "What is on at this time of morning?" she asked. "Grandma, it is eight o'clock at night!" said I. "Oh my," she said. "I just finished my breakfast dishes."

Apparently, she had fallen asleep, and when she awoke just an hour later, she thought she had been asleep all night. What a hoot.

I love all my siblings very much. I find it fascinating that we all get along so well. I think we always have. I think we always will. I think the casual calmness, the love, and the humor are the ties that bind us, and I believe those came from our parents.

Debbie is ten years older than I and therefore, I have few memories of her. I do remember her listening to Wolfman Jack on the radio as she was getting ready for school in the morning. When harkening back to the good old days, I equate Debbie with Loelia Bell and their Ladybug Club. I also remember her first wedding. It was a really big deal and a lot of fun. What was Debbie's most significant contribution to my life? Easy—it was one of her Silva Thin cigarettes that my best friend, Joel Corippo, and I shared when we were in first grade. I finally quit (almost for good) twenty-seven years later.

Pam was next, and while I don't remember her being particularly mean or violent, I do remember the day when I thought I could finally take her. While I don't specifically recall the following, I do remember Pam's bragging about it: Every night Debbie went across the street to Loelia's. Every night Pam waited in hiding near the hedge gate. Debbie would come running home and Pam would jump out and scare her. Every night Debbie would run to Mom and complain. Debbie would always be scared and Pam always seemed to find some joy in that. I also remember all of Pam's friends—they were cheerleaders; let's just leave it at that. And I remember her boyfriend, Jim Hotell. Pam was very social and because I was also, I think we had a special connection that continues today.

I have many positive memories of Diana. She was in eighth grade when I was in first. She was in charge of getting me to St. Mary's every morning, and we always made it. I guess I have her to thank for my academic success. Di always had interesting friends. Of course there was Audrey, but I also think of Rob Gilley, Fred Near, and the Grover boys. I've never forgotten that Henry Grover used to put me on his shoulders and ride me around on his unicycle. As youngsters, we often went tubing down Cold Creek while Di and her friends lay out on the rocks. I think Di and her friends unwittingly introduced me to many things, for which I am eternally grateful.

Prissy has always had a great sense of humor. I knew I could always get a laugh from Prissy just for my simple commentary on some of life's oddities. I know I can still get a laugh from her. Prissy seems to understand me. I think she understands the lot of us, and I'm not sure she is given enough credit for that. She also had some totally hot friends. I wish I hadn't been so lame with the ladies back then. Prissy was also the driving instructor for all our under-aged friends. Unfortunately, she wasn't very good at that.

One quick story of Prissy that comes to mind is when she babysat Paul and me. It was a school night, but we wouldn't go to bed, so Prissy offered us ice-cream sundaes. We didn't know they were doctored with Seconal. She must not have known that we'd be knocked out until noon the next day and couldn't wake for school. Mom was furious.

Along with Pam and me, Valli was one of Dad's favorites. Valerie was always the athletic one; at least, she has always been in great shape. She seemed more adventurous than all the rest of us, more willing to take chances, but it wasn't always that way. One vacation at Konocti Harbor, a resort in northern California, Valli stood fearful at the end of the high dive. "Jump, you chicken!" we all yelled. "I'd rather be a live chicken than a dead duck!" she yelled back. I don't think she ever jumped.

I don't have many memories of Valli, but I'll always remember this one: as a young boy, I always asked for a BB gun rifle. Every Christmas and every birthday, I begged my dad to buy me a BB gun. After six or seven years of not getting one and maybe thinking I never would, to my surprise, I did. It was the same Christmas that we had hung some ornaments on the small trees outside in the front yard. David and I went outside and began popping off those little glass balls. Valli must have said something, because to my chagrin, David took the gun and shot Valli in the ass with it. Dad took it away, and I've never seen it since.

I assume it was also David who attached a fishhook to our

light switch one night before bed. Maybe he was anticipating an unwelcome intruder into our bedroom, possibly Valli. Nonetheless, it was Valli who came in, switched on the light, and let out a yell. Watching Dad remove the hook from her finger was very cool.

One "Valli moment" that has stayed with me through the years is when she was in high school, and she found out her boyfriend, Tom Burke, had been killed in a boating accident. Her reaction was painful to watch. That was probably the first time I encountered real tragedy in my life.

My big brother David wasn't a typical older brother. He was very artistic, while I was not. He was always building model cars and working on real ones. Those weren't my interests. The model cars were just for wrecking when I got mad at David, and when it came to auto mechanics, I didn't like the oil or getting greasy and dirty. My mother said I was the cleanest boy she'd ever known. David wasn't athletic, he wasn't a gambler, and he wasn't a fighter, which is what interested me. Unfortunately, I wasn't really any of those three either; I guess I just wanted to be. David didn't teach me how to deal with women or show me the ways of the world. He did, however, stop me from ever using drugs. I give David total credit for that. As young boys learning of our older sisters' experiences or experiments with drugs, the three of us brothers swore we would never, ever try drugs. A few years later, Paul and I caught David smoking pot or possessing some sort of controlled substance, which got us saying, "Hey, you said you weren't going to do that" or something to that effect. David said, "Wait until you get to be my age, and you will start. Everybody does." I bet him fifteen dollars that I wouldn't ever do drugs. I wouldn't ever smoke pot. And I didn't. So ... thank you, David!

Becky was Mom's favorite. I know she'll hate me for that remark and would deny it, and I don't even know if it is true, but it sure seemed like it at the time. However, Becky is the youngest girl and is separated from the other five girls by David. She got along well with all my friends, and I don't ever remember excluding her because she was a girl. I wouldn't describe her as tomboyish; she just happened to join in when we three boys and/or our friends were up to something, good or bad.

Maybe I thought Becky was Mom's favorite because of Mom's never-ending mantra: "Quit hitting your sister. Quit hitting your sister." Boy, that got old! I did finally stop. One night when Prissy was babysitting Becky, Paul, and me, I thought Becky owed Paul an apology. I pinned her down and threatened to hit her unless she apologized. (Did I tell you that Becky was really stubborn?) I hit her pretty hard. I broke her glasses and cut her eye open. She let out a yell like a banshee. I jumped up and ran all the way to the rectory. I needed forgiveness in a big way, and I needed protection from my mother. Apparently, Mom was pretty understanding and maybe just very happy that I didn't kill Becky. I know I was. When I got home, Becky had a big patch of gauze covering her eye. We all made up, and then whenever she said something stupid, I said, "That's pretty bold talk for a one-eyed fat girl."

I think Paul and I were most connected when we were kids, probably because we were brothers so close in age and we shared many mutual friends. John and Bob McCoey lived just around the corner. John was my age, and Bob was Paul's, and we'd more often than not hang out together and share mischievous experiences. I think I looked out for Paul and didn't want anyone but me to pummel him. I also took advantage of him, which I am now attempting to rectify. I had a morning paper route when I was young, and Paul helped out. He did virtually the same job I did. I may have rolled or bagged a few more papers and carried the heavier bag, but he pulled his weight. Herein lies the rub; I made about twenty-five dollars a month. I kept twenty and paid him five dollars. He never complained.

To this day, I have different relationships with all of my siblings. Again, I love 'em all equally, and they have all played significant parts throughout my life. If we were back in my childhood, we would be scraping the ice off the freezer shelves with a little metal cup. Then we would fill it with grape juice, just like a slushy. Boy, was that delicious.

Here's my story:

As a young'un, I always had stuff in my pockets—miscellaneous stuff like a bottle cap, a slingshot, odd coins, or a pocketknife. Mom always said, "A man without a knife is like a day without a kiss." That doesn't sound like Mom; maybe that quote is attributable to the attendant at the Chevron station on Perkins Street where Mom always gassed up. As I got older, too often that stuff in my pockets was unpaid-for merchandise from one of many local merchants. It seemed I would steal anything I could get my hands on—anything, anytime. I don't know what that was all about, but I had a penchant for stealing. While I thought I was pretty good at it, I did get caught occasionally. Fortunately, that bad habit has not followed me into adulthood.

While my siblings were great, I think I lived more for my friends. And it seems like I had a million. I don't remember ever not liking anybody, and as a general rule no one ever treated me badly, with few exceptions. On the other hand, I was a first-class punk and said too many mean things to too many people, probably just trying to get a laugh.

Joel and George were two of my very best friends back then. Marty Swan made three. He lived three houses away from me, but he didn't go to St. Mary's Elementary School, so Marty spent more of his younger years with other friends. Joel used to work for our neighbor across the street, Mrs. Catherine Golden. He did landscaping in her yard and along the sidewalk that stretched the length of her property, from our house past the Swans, three doors down. When Joel would be on the outside of Mrs. Golden's fence and across from the Swans, Marty would pump up his pellet gun and take potshots at Joel. Joel would hide behind the trees, and from my house, I could hear Joel yell, "Marty, knock it off, you asshole." I know Marty would laugh about it, as would I. Joel never saw the humor in it. Marty and I laugh about it still today. I don't think Joel does.

Marty wasn't always the aggressor. Brother David liked to make nooses. He also liked to hang people. I did it once, but only when David assured me he would cut me down when I said "now." I didn't realize at the time that I would have a hard time yelling "now" with my airway cut off. Marty also took a turn, but I remember it was against his will. Home he went with rope burns on his neck, and his mother restricted him from ever coming back to our house.

My family didn't have a television growing up. Who ever thought that was a good idea? My mother always said, "An idle mind is the devil's workshop." We boys kept pretty busy. We didn't much care for reading, and we were very, very adventurous.

We spent some of our days hiking to the "U," a big letter atop a nearby hilltop standing for our hometown, Ukiah (much like HOLLYWOOD in Los Angeles). On one occasion we attempted to hike to the coast, about forty miles away. I think we were in eighth grade; that would never be allowed today. There were six of us: Marty, Matt, Dean Vance, Joel, Paul, and me. It was like the *Stand By Me* trek to see the dead body. We went pretty far the first day and then got rained out that night. Walking the next day in soaking clothes was a bitch. We ended up in some little country store, right out of *Deliverance*. We entertained and were entertained by the natives, and then we called Joel's mom for a ride home, never reaching our destination, but we had a blast nonetheless.

It was on another hike, but other than Paul, Tom Jarrod, and me, I'm not sure who was there. Paul had an air rifle and occasionally used it as a crutch or walking stick, never knowing he was packing dirt particles in the muzzle. Paul lifted what he thought was an empty rifle and leveled it at Tom's face. I think they both were surprised when Paul pulled the trigger and unloaded a hunk of dirt in Tom Jarrod's mouth. Unfortunately, I know we didn't learn anything about gun safety from that episode.

John McCoey and his brother Bob, Marty, and my brothers and I were the original Oak Park Commandos. We were infamous, at least on Oak Park Avenue. Our favorite foil must have been Catherine Golden—the same Mrs. Golden for whom Joel worked when he doubled as a target for Marty. She had a little pond in front of her house that was filled with goldfish. I'm sure all the Oak Park Commandos spent some time in that pond. Mrs. Golden's front porch was the first place we ever tried the "burning bag of shit" trick. I don't remember the result. I do know that Paul and Bob threw rock-laden dirt clods through her bedroom window, and Marty might have taken part. That is when we were given the name Oak Park Commandos. I'm sure we gave Mrs. Golden a scare on occasion, but we really were just simple pranksters by today's standards.

I personally never did anything specific against the Goldens, and my favorite Golden story has my dear brother David outside in our side-yard, swinging a golf club. At one point, with a full-swing follow-through, the driver slipped out of David's hands and sailed over our hedge, across the street, and slammed into the driver's side car door of one of Mrs. Golden's visitors. I remember a sizeable dent, but I don't recall it ever being reported. Often, our tomfoolery went undetected.

I have to tell you my favorite golfing story: my parents bought me my first set of clubs for my fourteenth birthday. They were a fine set of Patty Bergs. I was short; maybe Dad thought they would be a better fit. Anyway, Matt Goodacre came over, and I was showing him my clubs in our family room, the room with the really nice chandelier. Matt took an iron, and at the top of his backswing, the chandelier shattered. At least Dad didn't take those away.

Living on Oak Park Avenue was fun. It was only a block long, and it was a quiet street. We always played touch football in the street, rode our bikes, and rarely encountered any cars. There was the time a bunch of us were playing outside. It wasn't too late, but it was dark. We were running around, playing ditch the cars or something like that. One car, a blue fastback Volkswagen, came screaming around the corner. We all ran and hid behind the trees that lined the sidewalks. The car pulled right up to the tree behind which I was hiding. The driver looked like a drug-crazed maniac— bulging eyes, frizzed-out hippie hair, and a scraggly beard. I got scared. I jumped up and ran toward my house. He put it in reverse and chased after me down the street. I stopped and ran the other way down the sidewalk. He pulled onto the sidewalk and raced after me. I just made it to Dorothea Fraga's house and ran up onto her porch.

The maniac blew his horn, moved off the sidewalk to avoid the trees, and raced on down the road. That was a scary childhood moment.

Here's another scary story, albeit self-inflicted. The Oak Park Commandos decided to have a flaming arrow fight. We had a fort in the backyard that was about six feet by eight, with an open door and a small window in front. The roof shingles were courtesy of Ms. Cox, next door. We ripped them off the backside of her garage roof. She simply had it fixed and sent Mom the bill.

We divvied up into cowboys and Indians. David and Paul were cowboys for sure. I think Bob McCoey was also a cowboy. They controlled the fort and were armed with BB guns. I was an Indian, along with Matt Goodacre and a few others. We had bows and arrows and a picnic table adorned with bowls of lighter fluid and candles. We put little kitchen sponges on the working ends of the arrows, dipped them in lighter fluid, ignited them with a candle, and then fired them at the fort. Why the cowboys had a small Tupperware container of lighter fluid in the fort, I will never know, but the inside of the fort went up in flames when one of our arrows flew through the door and knocked over the container. We put that out soon enough, but of course, that didn't stop us. The cowboys just boarded up the door, leaving a small gap at the top, and play resumed. I shot a flaming arrow through the small opening atop the door and into the fort. An insider threw it back out. I snuck up, picked it up, still afire, and threw it back in. As I turned to sneak away, some cowboy inside grabbed it and threw it back out. The arrow, still ablaze, struck me in the back of my head. My hair went up in flames as I did the wildest Indian rain dance you might ever witness. I was waving my hands back and forth through my hair as others came to my rescue. I was on the ground at the bottom of a dog-pile of saviors and my hair was singed, but the fire was extinguished.

The real problem was what to tell Mom. It was off to the showers. My brothers were as quick to make an adventure out of this next step as they were with each of life's situations. Scissors and barber shears, shampoo and cologne—Mom knew something was up, but I don't think anyone ever gave her the real story.

It often seemed when David and I were up to no good, our friend Tony Grams was with us. Tony's dad owned a restaurant, so we had the egg advantage on Halloween. We had a tree fort in our walnut tree, nearly twenty feet up. In the late afternoon, in preparation for that night's combat, Tom Jarrod and I were in the fort, and David and Tony were on the ground. Tom and I had the eggs up top, just as our enemies came by. We engaged and because I was in a better offensive position than Tom, I was firing, and Tom was keeping me loaded. I reached my hand back for another egg and none came. I turned around, and Tom was nowhere in sight. I looked over the back edge of the fort, and Tom was lying on the ground below. He had fallen and landed flat on his back. We declared a cease-fire to deal with Tom. He survived. That was an occasion when someone was looking out for us.

We weren't always that lucky. David, Tony, and I were in David's bedroom one day. We had everything kids needed to have a good time: cigarettes, matches, a Coke bottle, some plastic bowls, a syringe, some electrical wire, a 12-volt battery, and a big old bag of gunpowder. The Coke bottle was filled about halfway with gunpowder, and it was on the floor beside the bed, where I was lying, just a few feet from Tony and David. Tony would pour a little gunpowder in a bowl and light it. *Poof*—a big flame and big puff of smoke; it was awesome.

David, meanwhile, had filled a syringe with gunpowder and inserted wires where the needle would be. He attached one wire to one prong on the battery and then one on the other. *Bang!* That was cool. All the while I was thinking about dropping my cigarette butt into the powder-filled Coke bottle. To this day, I don't know what stopped me. I thought a flame would shoot out the top. Instead, I suggested David do it. Fortunately, he first emptied all but about an inch of powder from the bottle, and then we all stepped back. David dropped a cigarette butt into the bottle and tried to get out of the way. *Boom!* The bottle exploded, and glass went flying. A small piece hit me in the stomach, and Tony's legs got cut up, but David almost lost an eye. A piece of the glass hit David in the eye and cut his cornea. That was bad, but it could have been worse. Tony was a good friend, but not an Oak Park Commando.

Along with the Oak Park Commandos, I had a lot of childhood friends, many of whom are still my friends today, including Joel and Marty Swan. Most of the others I met in grade school, St. Mary of the Angels: Chuck Anderson, Mark Christiansen, Manuel Mendez, Tom Gulyas, Trinidad Salgado, and Steve Thatcher, just to name a few. George Ginochio joined us in second grade. And then there were the girls: Lisa Ghiringhelli, Lynne Wilson, Molly Oswald, Mary Thomas, Ann Johnson, Jennifer Thatcher, Liz Angel, and Mary King. With Lisa, Lynne, and Molly, I shared a desk grouping in the later elementary years. Every day before class, Molly would retrieve her Bible from her desk and read us stories of Mary "Hairy-Legs" Thomas. I swear Molly was reading word for word. Although Mary was killed in an automobile accident years later, and we haven't seen hide or hair of Molly, Lisa and I still laugh about it when we reminisce at high school reunions.

I used to fight a lot when I was a kid—too much. I was pretty good at it for a while. I was always the last one chosen for my skills on the basketball court, but I was picked first for the after-game fight. Win or lose, I was tough—still am. If you judge the toughness of a man by the way he can survive an ass-kicking, then I'm your man. Maybe it was that training I went through as a child. David, Paul, and I would hang each other from the rafters in the garage, our wrists wrapped with rope, arms stretched above our heads. Then we would put a leather belt or strap around our waist and slide a piece of wood the size of a hatchet handle in between the belt and skin. Then, we'd twist the wood, tightening the belt around the waist of whoever was hanging. It just seemed like an advanced game of "Uncle." The belt would have to be cinched pretty darn tight before anyone would get a peep out of any of us.

I was pretty good at fighting, for a while. I would take all comers ... and then I met Fory Brown. I like to say he sucker-punched me, but I think he probably just punched a sucker—me—over and over again. It was the first time I really took a beating. We've been friends ever since. Fory went to public school, as did Steve Stout, Matt Goodacre, Wes Weigle, and Marty Swan. Most of my St. Mary's classmates and friends left after seven years and went to Pomolita, the public junior high school, for eighth grade.

I started meeting others from Pomolita through my St. Mary's friends, and we all reunited at Ukiah High School. It was that connection that got me elected as Ukiah High School's freshman class president. Students from St. Mary's just didn't get elected to high school offices.

My reputation as a tough little punk must have preceded me into high school. I also started meeting upper classmen, apparently with something to prove. One day, late in the afternoon, I entered the gym locker-room. Two varsity athletes grabbed me and submerged me in one of those stainless steel Jacuzzis and held me there. To this day, I don't know who they were, but I know they had every intention of scaring the crap out of me, if they weren't intent on drowning me. Coach Al Snarski's arrival saved me from an untimely demise. I don't remember being scared. Maybe in hindsight I should have been. I can only surmise that getting scared didn't happen too often, growing up a Wilson.

High school was pretty much a blur for me. They were the hardest years of my life, with infrequent relief. Although David kept me away from pot, I drank way too much and way too often. I'm sure we were having kegger parties almost monthly, and I remember getting drunk twenty-four Friday and Saturday nights in a row, most often with Alan Graybeal. We would all meet in the woods by Yokayo Swim and Tennis Club. We'd play drinking games, get smashed, and throw up all over the place. I guess I got it out of my system, because I drink very little as an adult and really never have since early adulthood.

Fory, Chuck, Marty, and I once drove out to a keg party in the country. We followed an old winding country road through the hills to someone's farm or ranch or whatever. When we came to a gate, an attendant charged us three bucks apiece for party cups. We paid and continued on up the road to the party. Once there, we tried to use our previously purchased cups, but the host didn't accept it. We had been ripped off and had to pay again. A couple of hours and a few beers later, we headed for home. We did stop at the gate, however, and sold our cups to the next group of unsuspecting party animals.

One of my favorite drinking memories was Thanksgiving break of my sophomore year. It must have been Friday evening when I stole a quart bottle of Early Times whiskey from a local liquor store and met Randy Smith at school. We drank the whole bottle straight and in equal shares. Quite honestly, I don't remember what happened to me that night, but Randy ended up vomiting in his bed, and although he rolled around in it, he never woke up. He told me later that his dad had him out pulling weeds at six thirty the next morning.

While I probably have a million high school drinking stories, I have to regurgitate one more: another great high school friend was Brian Carter. He came to Ukiah in our sophomore year from the East Coast. He was a big Redskins fan. He was more preppy than Ukiah was used to and always wore a Stetson fedora, one like Al Capone would wear. He had a brand new one the night he went drinking with Marty and me. Brian was in the backseat of Marty's new Celica. Brian had had way too much to drink, so he stayed in the backseat while Marty and I went into a store to buy some more liquor. Marty turned to Brian and said, *"Don't puke in my car."* We went inside and upon our return, we found Brian still sitting in the backseat but with hat in hand. His hat was turned upside down on his lap and filled almost to the brim with vomit. Brian is still a classy guy.

Looking back over my high school life, I think one of my greatest regrets was during my freshman year. As the class president, I was required to partake in most of the extracurricular activities, one of which was an auction of freshmen to be slave-for-a-day to the highest bidder. I probably seemed like the best bargain, because I think I went for about seventy-five cents. The only bidder was Debbie Schwank. She was an upperclassman and an absolute babe. I was so scared and intimidated by her that I called in sick the day I was to report for slave duty. In my mind, I now imagine that could have been an excellent experience. She never got her money's worth.

I probably didn't show up because boy/girl relationships weren't easy for me. Although I thought I was extremely charming, I wasn't the cutest guy around, and I was, probably like most kids, very self-conscious. I would just like to say thanks to Rhonda, Cheryl, and Carol for making my formative years quite delightful. Enough said.

Back in the mid-1970s, it seemed that drinking went hand in hand with driving. It was a great time to love cars—the era of the muscle cars. David had a Dodge Charger and a Javelin. My favorite car of all times was the Dodge Polara, which I purchased at a police auction for about four hundred bucks. It was fast and handled very well, especially when I attached a suicide knob to the steering wheel. It still had the police spotlight mounted just outside the driver's door. I used to play policeman and pull over my friends. David wrecked it, and he probably still owes me for that.

Dad had a Ford with a 428 Cobra jet engine. It was fast. At fifteen, I would sneak out at night with David, push it down the street, and start it up when we were out of earshot. We would drive around for an hour or so and then coast it back to its parking spot. I don't ever remember getting caught. One night, John McCoey was driving—fast. He lost control and spun out. We ended up in a pear orchard. That was a close call, but we managed to get it home that night.

On another occasion, I had a car full of people. I burned out the clutch about five miles north of town. My parents were out of town, and this happened at one in the morning. The county sheriff's deputy arrived on the scene, and all my friends scattered; only Joel stayed by my side to face the music with me. The sheriff had the car towed and never checked my license. Instead, he gave Joel and me a ride home. En route, we scanned the countryside for our fleet-footed friends. They arrived home about three hours after we did.

Becky ended up wrecking that car, with me in the passenger side. We were racing a Road Runner, and we were clearly in the lead when Becky lost control and smashed sideways into a brick wall. Becky broke her collarbone; I came out unscathed. I was fifteen and without a license, but I should have been driving.

My parents wouldn't let me have a motorcycle, so I bought one anyway. It was my first mode of transportation, a Honda Elsinor 250cc. I hid it from them for about two weeks before I got ratted out. They took it away but eventually caved in. Even considering my license was temporarily suspended three times in my first year of driving, I was pretty safe. Most of the dangerous stuff was off-road, and many of my friends had bikes. I used to jump my bike with Joel, and on one occasion, I was racing George on a dirt trail. While in the lead, I came around a turn and laid it down. George didn't skip a beat; he just ran over my head. It was the one time I wore a helmet.

Along with drinking and fast cars, all my friends loved to gamble. Poker games were as regular in high school as Monday Night Football at the Swans' house, a tradition that exists today whenever we're in town on an autumn Monday night. Those Monday nights with Marty's parents (Bob and AC) and a small group of friends at the Swans' were probably some of the best nights of my life. Bob and AC Swan have always been two of my very favorite people and like second parents to me.

Most of my friends' parents were good people. Steve's dad, Bob Stout, was at a high school awards ceremony one night. I asked him to buy me some beer. He said, "Zack, you must think I'm a pretty good Joe." I do, but he didn't buy me the beer. I was always welcome at his house, and I think that was true of the homes of all my friends, in spite of me.

Although we rarely communicate any more, Joel Corippo was my best friend during the years covered in this chapter. We really grew up together. I always thought of Joel first whenever making any plans. He was as much a brother to me as David and Paul during my formative years and through high school. We had our first cigarette together and probably our first drink. He inspired me to play Little League baseball, even though he was twice the player I was. We started Pop Warner football together, and neither of us made the weight minimum. He was always there for me, especially whenever I had to face the music after starting trouble. We shared a box of macaroni and cheese almost every day before school (high school started at noon for our first two years) while we watched *$10,000*

Pyramid. He was there with me when our dog, Coco, died. While circumstances beyond our control put us together, I think I was very fortunate to have started my life with Joel.

All in all, I had a pretty darn good childhood. I have many friends whom I love dearly, and they will always be friends. Geography keeps us apart, but I see them when I can, and I think of them often. They make up who I am, deep down in my soul. To all of them I want to say thank you and I love you.

I would like to finish my chapter with two comments:

1. If I had to live my life over again and could only change one thing, I would leave earlier. Nothing good ever happened late.
2. To the parents of all my friends and to those kids and the parents of those kids who suffered physically or emotionally because of my misdeeds or who were the butts of my many jokes, "I'm sorry!"

THE 9TH VOICE ~ PAUL SHANNON

I remember I remember
1961
In February out the oven
popped another bun
and finally the wilson clan
had a little fun

I AM TOLD THAT AT THE AGE OF FOUR OR FIVE, I CRUSHED A KITTEN to death with my bare hands. I was apparently hugging the tiny beast and didn't realize my own strength. I say I was told, because I don't really remember it as much as I remember hearing that I had done such a thing. How I must have loved that kitty. No matter, there were hundreds more to follow. Hello, kitty! Good-bye kitty!

Battling for first place in my earliest memories, both from the time I was five or six years old, are the following:

I went out with my mom to a shoe store on the corner of School and Perkins. What a great place. There must have been a million shoes in this store, as well as shoe polish in at least four colors. There was a scale for measuring feet, not just length but width as well, thus giving the most comfortable fit to be found. My feet were rather small in relation to all those crazy shoe sizes represented on that scale. There were many other accessories for one's feet—socks and slippers, shoelaces in stripes and solids, shoe shine kits or brushes. But most important, there was a magic stick. This stick was about three feet long and made of a beautifully crafted wood-like plastic, with a silver knob handle on one end and a widening, plastic tortoise shell, slightly scoop-like attachment on the other. Now get this, the bearer of this device had the ability to put on his shoes without bending over or squatting down or sitting on the floor. Yes, my friends, step right up and cast your eyes upon the shoehorn—not the typical three-inch one-piece plastic shoehorn, no, sir! No bending on one knee or putting your foot up on the sofa (a real no-no, as I recall) but a handcrafted, three-foot-long shoehorn. Well, by God, that shoehorn was going to be mine. Nothin' was gonna stop me.

I'm not sure exactly how I did it. I either slipped it down my pants or up my shirt (maybe both), but I got it out of that shoe store with no one the wiser. I clamored up into the station wagon and plopped my skinny self into the passenger seat. (Early photographs of me look like stick-figure drawings. Instead of a comforter, I just used a pipe cleaner.) Anyway, once in the car with the door closed, I knew that I was home free. I pulled out my newfound treasure and began admiring it and imagining the jealousy of my friends and siblings when they saw what I had acquired. Within seconds, my mother, always the killjoy, asked me where I had gotten it. I looked up at her and stared blankly. What was she—some kind of a moron? In the shoe store, duh! I didn't say anything; I just stared back at her. I thought maybe it was a trick question. I got the uneasy feeling that somebody was about to get a slap or a spanking, and I knew it wouldn't be her. "You stole that. didn't you?" Oh, how I wished I'd studied law in kindergarten. I think I just said yes. My mom said very sternly, "You can't just take things that don't belong to you. Now you are going to go back into that store and give back the shoehorn and apologize for stealing." I considered jumping out of the car and hiding in the bushes until I was old enough to come out of the bushes and … well, maybe I didn't think it through that hard. I got out of the car with that cursed stick and strode humbly back into the shoe store. I handed it to the store owner and said, "I'm sorry. My mom stole this from you. She's a kleptomaniac." Okay, I didn't really. That would have been great. I actually began to cry as I handed over the stolen item and said I was sorry for taking it without asking. That sounded slightly better than "stealing." I don't know if he responded, but I turned away and slunk back to the car, sobbing. I got in the car doing that little kid shaky-inhale thing, and we drove away. But I learned a very valuable lesson that day. Don't ever show your mom the stuff you've stolen.

This next story isn't quite as exciting or dramatic. I pulled an elephant out of a deep pit by its tail—that's what I tried telling people was the reason for my hernia. I don't think anyone really believed me. I remember being in the hospital for a double-hernia operation at age six. I can remember thinking what fantastic food was served to patients in the hospital, in little plastic trays with separate compartments for each kind of food. Wow! The nurses would bring it in and set it before me, and I would gobble it up. I had with me a giant Bugs Bunny doll that could talk when I pulled the string in his back: "What's up, doc?" and "Mmyeah, could be!" How I loved that crazy Bugs. I remember staring sadly into the trash can where Bugs lay in state some years later. In my mind I'm two years old, in reality I was probably fourteen.

Other than the aforementioned stories, most of my pre-first-grade years are a blank—except for the picture in my mind of a true goddess, Mrs. Gulyas, my kindergarten teacher. Hubba, Hubba! What a fox! She taught me how to make butter. And we'd sing and laugh. I thought the good times would never end. If I'd had my druthers, we would have run off together and lived happily ever after just like Mary Kay Letourneau and Villy Foulau. Oh the missed opportunities of a wild misspent youth. *C'est la vie, mi amore!*

I slept on the bottom of our bunk beds for many years. I was beneath my sometimes protector and sometimes archenemy and torturer, Zack the Crack. Sometimes, just for fun, I would kick out all the slats holding up the top bunk. Zack came crashing down on top of me. I found this to be rather humorous. Being crushed under the weight of the slats and the box springs and the mattress and my brother Zack was a small price to pay for the joy of knowing that I had upset Zack. More often than not, he wasn't upset, so I had to do it a lot to really get his goat. Then we'd just get started laughing or fighting, and a wretched sound would emanate from the heater vent at the foot of our bed, followed by Mother's angry voice: "You boys be quiet and go to sleep. Don't make me come up there." Oh, Mother, you're so cliché. The heater vent led to the furnace via our parents' bathroom. I think she would spend most evenings there, just waiting for us to get too loud or to fight so that she could drag her hairbrush across the vent, making that awful noise. More often than not, she would have to come up there. And more often than not, the punishment would be that I would have to go to sleep in their bed or at the bottom of the stairs. Just where the stairs curved before they ended was one wide step. It was just big enough for an angry little boy to curl up and go to sleep. That was also where I would be sent for crying. "You go sit on the stairs until you're done crying." I'm not sure of the value of that little lesson, but I sure got to like the bottom of the stairs. Sometimes if I sat there crying, Coco, our toy poodle, would come over and sit there too. I just assumed she'd been crying, and Mom made her come join me.

The fights that occurred in our house during my formative years are too numerous to be recounted in a single book that the average reader might be able to lift. Perhaps the Donnybrook Encyclopedia would do the trick. I'll just touch on a few of the more memorable brouhahas—and these are in no particular order, as my mind doesn't work that way.

I was, one day in my teenage years, being bothered by Becky for some menial nonsense that I'm sure I was taking way too seriously and had probably started. I fear I was often the cause of my own torture. She wouldn't leave me alone, and I kept getting madder and madder and telling her to shut up. I got so mad that I bent a spoon (not with my mind unfortunately). Zack stepped in to protect me, and a heated debate ensued. I don't recall the exact exchange but it was something like "Fuck you, bitch" "Make me" etc. Vocabularians are a dime a dozen in my family. Eventually, this all turned into a bit of a shoving match and finally, a rousing race about the house, with Becky just slightly in the lead. Her lead, however, was short lived, as Zack quickly caught up with her and threw her to the floor. He was sitting atop her chest, with one hand holding down her head or neck and the other hand cocked back in a fist awaiting its command to strike the deathblow. He was shouting directly into her face, "Take off your glasses. I'm going to hit you." She was yelling back, "Get off me, you asshole!" For a short while, Zack continued with his demands, and Becky continued her refusal. She was no dummy. If he was waiting for her to remove the glasses before he hit her (ever the gentleman), she would be spared the pain by simply retaining control of her spectacles. But, as is the way with anger, gallantry soon lost out, and Zack's heavy fist grew weary and fell full force into Becky's face, thus ending the melee. Needless to say, her glasses were ruined—shattered and covered in blood. Becky's face was also covered in blood but not entirely ruined. I don't know if it was directed at me or mom or no one in particular but I distinctly remember Zack saying as he got off her, "I told her to take off her glasses."

On another occasion, when I was in my early teens, I was sitting on the kitchen counter, happily nibbling away at a delicious cheese sandwich that I had made not three minutes prior—two slices of Kraft American singles between two slices of the whitest white bread I could get my hands on and slathered with more mayonnaise than the French or even Paul Prudhomme could stomach. To this day, I'll sometimes slink off by myself and slap together and enjoy this very same sandwich in the privacy of my dining closet. But I digress. As I sat snacking on my suburban delight, I was well aware of the incessant sounds of a volcanic shouting match coming from another room. Mother was at home at the time, so I had little worry that I might be in imminent danger. Therefore, I simply smacked my lips to the beat of the curses flowing rhythmically into the kitchen. The anger-filled epithets grew louder and ever near, but I continued in my cheesy pursuits. Suddenly, I saw Valerie fly into the kitchen, followed by David. She was screaming, "Don't call Mom a bitch!" I'm sure he parried with some fantastical retort like, "You fucking cunt." I cautiously continued in my enjoyment of processed foodstuffs. Valerie wasted no time in her response. She went straight for the knife drawer, where we kept all the perfectly sharpened silvery knives—chef's knives, carving knives, butcher knives, steak knives, paring knives, a meat cleaver and a melon-baller. I wondered which instrument of death she would choose. As the drawer slid open, I froze, with my gourmand's nightmare clenched in my fists and pressed to my lips, my eyes wide with enjoyment. David was very quick and had borne the brunt of the business end of stainless steel many times before. As Valerie reached into the drawer, David placed one hand on her back and the other against the flat front of the knife drawer. He slammed it shut with such ferocity that I jolted and jumped, and my handsome comestibles flew up and hit the ceiling. After catching Valerie's hand hard and knowing a little something about the volatile mixture of rage and pain, David turned quickly and bolted from the room. Valerie pulled her hand from the drawer, clutching a large knife. As my sandwich hit the floor with a splat, I was on my feet and following Valerie out of the kitchen and into the living room, in pursuit of her prey. She dashed out the front door and across the porch, down the steps, and through the gate. I stopped at the porch railing with a view of the gate and a little distance down the street. To my astonishment, Valerie had grabbed two knives while bracing through the pain of a semi-crushed hand. Now, she stood, one knife in midair hurtling toward David, and one more clenched in her fist, cocked back and ready to fly. David was well down the block at this point and in no danger from the first knife, so certainly throwing a second would be fruitless. Valerie came back through the gate with angry tears welling behind stoic eyes. As she passed me, she was shaking her hand and saying, "Ow, fuck." David came back eventually and, as with all the fights that I can remember, all was soon forgotten. Or at least ignored. Maybe hidden away to fuel a future anger that needed more heat.

When I was very young, I walked into the backyard, just past the pool, and saw two groups of kids, a mixture of siblings and friends whose names all escape me now. They were standing twenty to thirty feet apart, throwing rocks at each other. Large rocks. Thrown, it appeared to me, with the intention of doing great bodily harm. I missed the beginnings of this hurling battle, so I can't say if there was anger involved or just stupidity, but I was about to show them all just who was the stupidest child in this family—I walked into the middle of this rock fest. I like to agree with the few of my siblings who say I was trying to be a peacemaker, but more likely, I was being just plain dumb. As I started to speak, a boulder struck me square in the forehead. I paused for a moment, thinking, *Wow, that musta hurt.* As the blood began to cascade down my face and into my eyes and mouth, I turned around and ran, sobbing uncontrollably, toward the house and the comfort of my sweet mother's arms. It's interesting how Mom could be so sweet and necessary at times like these and such an evil bitch when it came to things like my showing her my prized possession that I had just stolen right under her nose. Mom made everything better, not so much because she mopped up the blood and bandaged my head and kissed me and told me that she loved me, but because she went right outside and yelled at those uncaring bastards who had dared mar this beautiful countenance. Eventually, my entire person became a virtual scar museum, but this was the first unintentional scar I can recall—my double-hernia scar being intentional and the two on my wrists arriving apparently without my knowledge. None of my siblings have an answer for how they got there, so I can only assume that one or more of my loving yet curious and pioneering siblings were experimenting on me as a baby.

When I was fourteen, Zack and I took self-defense classes together in summer school. They were really karate classes, but I guess they had to call it self-defense so no one would get the idea that they were teaching us how to fight better. I was pretty good. I became expert at doing a roundhouse kick while wearing my steel-toed boots. I did not receive any belts of any color. I now am not sure that I ever learned any actual form of karate at all, as today I'd be hard-pressed to defend myself against a horde of insults. One day, several months after these lessons in mayhem, Zack and I were in our room—we now had a room to ourselves, as David had been given his own room. David then went on to paint his room light blue, with a rainbow stripe going up one wall across the ceiling down another wall and then back up to connect with itself and having a loop somewhere in the middle. David was incredibly cool. Again digression has gotten the better of me.

Zack and I fought like cats and dogs. I was the cat. More like a kitten really. A declawed toothless kitten. On this day, we were arguing about something stupid. My guess is that I was probably trying to prove that I was, in fact, the alpha male in the room, and he had better shut his festering gob. Or something to that effect. As the argument heated up, I picked up something to throw. I knew I couldn't take him hand to hand, as fisticuffs was certainly not my forte but if I could knock him out from a distance, I would smell at least a temporary victory. So I picked up the nearest thing of his (why would I chance damaging something of my own when there was plenty to grab with his name on it?), and I threw it at him. I missed but did manage to break the item I had hurled so wildly. While I didn't really regret breaking something of his, the look on his face told me that there was an urgent need to leave the state. I began by leaving the room. I ran through the hall and careened down the stairs. All the way down the stairs and through the kitchen, I could feel his hot, angry breath on the nape of my neck. I passed through the laundry room and put my hand on the back doorknob, but something inside me said, "Uh oh." I was way too slow to get out the door before a fist or a foot was going to take me down from behind. I turned and took the stance that I had learned not six months earlier. Now was the chance to test my skills as a master of the martial arts. I became Kuang Chai Kane. Had I paid a little more attention, I would have seen that Zack had taken that stance before I ever turned around. And he looked like he belonged there. I pictured him, shirtless and Asian, and me as the silly cowpoke who just finished saying, "Whatchyoo doin' in our town, Chinaman?" However, I began a barrage of roundhouse kicks to that motherfucker's ribs that would have impressed Bruce Lee. I was wearing my steel-toed boots, no shirt, jeans, and an angry grimace that should have made Zack at least a little nervous. Zack was built a tad more solid and stocky than I was. I was no longer the skinny, gawky child of yesteryear (not three years earlier I had moved from pipe cleaner to standard twin blanket) but I was no Zack Wilson. He was stronger, tougher, and—most important—older than I, so part of me knew I couldn't win. But oh, those kicks were sweet. For that brief moment, I was kickin' his ass. Then he punched me. He punched me right in the face. He punched me so freakin' hard that that one punch was all it took. I crumbled to the floor, holding my bleeding face and fighting back tears with every ounce of fortitude I could muster. He may have won, but he couldn't make me cry. Never again would I let that bastard produce a tear from my eyes. By God, I was just as tough as he was. Then Dad walked in the room. He had probably heard all the commotion, finished reading the paper, and then come to see what all the fuss was about. The moment he entered the room, I began to wail like a widow at an Italian funeral. Zack was in big trouble now. I was on the floor, bleeding profusely from one eye and crying as loudly as I could. My dad's response to Zack's defense ("He started it; he kicked and bruised me") was, "Well, he looks worse than you." I think Dad wasn't so worried about our fights as long as no one ended up in the hospital. Oh just wait till we get our driver's licenses, Dad.

The following might not count as a fight, but it did to me. We used to make weapons, just for fun. One day we made whips—I should say one month, we made whips. These weapon-making sessions would go on until we perfected each item. The whips we made were from long pieces of electrical wire, cut into six- or eight-foot lengths and then attached to a wooden handle, usually a piece of old furniture leg or a cut twig, if it was sturdy enough. The wire was attached to the handle by a bent nail and then covered with electrical or duct tape, and then the whole handle would be taped up to make it easier to hold and hang onto. We were quite adept at really hurting each other with our whips. I would practice in the backyard on trees and fences and even making it crack in thin air. That was a beautiful sound. I would sometimes stroll around the backyard, whipping imaginary assholes and laughing like a villain.

One day in our whip phase, I was sitting on the couch in the family room, minding my own business, when David came in with his whip and pronounced that I was not allowed to get off the couch. If I were to leave the couch or make a serious attempt to leave the couch, I would feel the harsh sting of his newly mastered whip. Let me make one thing perfectly clear: nobody—but *nobody*—could tell me what to do. So rather than ask any questions or pry into his motives, I immediately stood up. *Crack!* That whip hit my thigh just above the knee so fast that I didn't even notice David's arm move. I was back on that couch, trying to rub a welted goose egg back into smooth skin. I was also begging to be let up and asking why he wouldn't let me off the couch. The weird thing is, looking back I had no intention of getting off that couch until he told me I couldn't. I was mad as hell and I wasn't gonna take it anymore. A part of me, perhaps a perverse part of me, loved the challenge. And I was up for it. I knew I could get off that couch and out of harm's way with a minimum of pain. I just needed to figure out how much pain it was worth. As I would move from end to end, never leaving the safety of the couch, David would crack the whip very near whichever end I went for. I tried going quickly from end to end to test his prowess, and I discovered, to my dismay, that I'd "accidentally" get a sharp pain in one of my legs if he had to switch directions too fast. I don't know if he was that good, but I assumed every strike was intentional. I started for one end of the couch and flipped myself over the back and off it in one move. As I crawled and ran out of the room, I heard the whip's crack, and I felt one last time that sharp pain right down the center of my back. I headed for the back door and realized by the sound of his footsteps that he was about to head me off at the proverbial pass. Okay, the laundry room, just before the back door. I changed course and headed through the kitchen toward the front door. This gave me a number of options if he came after me. I could backtrack through the hall next to the kitchen. I could cut left into the dining room and maybe get out the French doors. That was a last resort because those could jam, and then I'd be trapped. Or I could continue straight into the living room and out the front door. The one thing I hadn't thought about was that David, with his brilliant military mind, might just continue out the back door and run around the house, where he'd be waiting for me on the front porch. Not hearing approaching footsteps, I continued on my direct route out of the house. In the living room, I sensed danger but thinking it was from inside the house, I grabbed the doorknob and took half a step out—and screamed like an old horror-movie negro. There he was, that pincer-moving bastard. I spun on my heels and heard the whip slap against the front door as I slammed it behind me. But now, where could I go? Just then, Mom honked her horn, signaling that we had to go out back and help bring in the groceries. Never before had I wanted so badly to carry in groceries. I would have gladly lugged each and every bag into the house for my mom and savior. I don't think I mentioned the whippings to Mom, and nothing more came of it. But I felt I had won this one. Make me stay on a couch? Puh-lease.

In one of several staged fights between David and Zack, they drew knives on each other to test their respective mettle. Zack had a utility knife, and David had a switchblade. This really was a friendly fight between brothers, a simple battle of halfwits. They squared off and began circling face-to-face, very much like the Sharks and Jets from *West Side Story*. Bob McCoey and I sat ringside. They talked a good game. ("Come on." "No, you come on. What? Are you scared?") They were all smiles. When Zack lunged, David sidestepped and made a fake lunge, causing Zack to step back. They both laughed. When they lunged in unison, they both leapt back, not quite frightened but surely cautious. They both laughed a nervous laugh. When Zack lunged again, David sidestepped and swung down, cutting Zack's arm. Zack quickly lunged again, plunging the fully extended utility knife into the center of David's chest. Zack, Bob, and I ran inside. Zack grabbed hydrogen peroxide and bandages. Bob and I grabbed fedoras and cameras. We all ran back outside together, and as Zack and David helped bandage each other up, Bob and I pretended to be reporters, covering the bout. I think Bob McCoey and I had a lot more fun that day than did either of my brothers.

In another, I think David had just gotten out of the army, and he and Zack were having a very intelligent debate about who could better fend off a kick to the balls. Of course, Zack had some fantastic karate move that couldn't fail, and David laughed, "Of course that can't work." David, oddly, didn't express exactly how his move worked; he simply said Zack couldn't effectively kick him in the balls. Of course, the only way to prove an argument of this sort was through scientific testing. So it was decided that David would attempt to kick Zack in the balls, and Zack would then be allowed to reciprocate, each having but one chance to protect the family jewels (i.e., scrotum and its contents).

So David stood a few feet away from Zack. Zack readied himself, standing with his feet slightly more than shoulder-width apart and his arms straight and not quite at his sides. As David's foot left the ground, Zack crossed his arms in front of him and thrust them downward, attempting to intercept David's approaching foot. This method was immediately proven incorrect. The main problem with this technique is that the thrust of the foot causes the arms to continue crossing to the point that the kickee appears to be hugging himself as he is kicked soundly in the balls. After a few minutes of recovery, the time had come for David to take his medicine or prove himself more adept at testicular protection. He took the same basic stance Zack had and announced his readiness. As Zack's foot left the floor, so did David's, only his simply slid sideways, knee up, the way a coed might pretend to be coy. Thus, David's package was protected by his entire calf, which is precisely where Zack kicked him, causing him and David equal pain. Yet David did not have to endure the pain that we all know as having been kicked in the balls.

One fight that began as a friendly game of handcuff-your-neighbor-to-the-tree ended as a not-so-friendly game of dodge-the-flying-knives. David, Zack, Tony Grams, and I were in the backyard, playing with a few sets of handcuffs—very real handcuffs, metal, with a short connecting chain and a simple metal key. I was handcuffed to the tree at one point, as was David. Tony may or may not have been but Zack definitely did not want to be cuffed to the tree. Unfortunately for him, the rest of us wanted him cuffed to that tree, and the majority ruled. As we began, we got a single cuff on one wrist, and the three of us pushed and pulled, trying to get his arms wrapped around that tree. One realizes just how powerful Zack can be when attempting, even with the assistance of two cohorts, to handcuff him against his will. He was becoming angrier by the second, even as we became more giddy. When he finally broke loose, we discovered what a circus trainer must feel when a rogue elephant turns on him. Zack was swinging and not to any big-band tune. We decided it was time to cut and run, but like the rogue elephant, Zack had just begun seeking his revenge.

He chased David and Tony into the house via the side door. I ran toward the back gate, preferring the expanse of Ukiah over the confines of the house's walled-in rooms. The portions of chase that I missed must have taken a slight detour through the kitchen, for when Zack emerged a few seconds behind Tony, he was armed with several manageable throwing knives, one of which stuck in the fence between Tony and me. I went immediately out into the alley and peered back through the fence. From this vantage point, I saw Zack turn on David. David had been standing in the yard, watching, preferring fun over freedom, when Zack must have smelled him. He prepared a knife for throwing as he turned and then flung it in David's direction. David then turned and headed for the front gate, with Zack in hot pursuit. Two more knives flew before I lost track of the action and strolled down to the corner store for a Coke or candy or whatever I could steal. We all laugh about it now.

Once when David was racing his stingray around the yard, I devised a simple, evil scheme to get the better of him. This was long before the whipping incident, so I'm not sure what brought on my vengeance at this time. Perhaps I just needed a laugh. I took a garden hose and tied it around a fence post at one corner of the house, pulling the other end across a four-foot pathway between the pool and the house. I wrapped the loose end around the faucet for leverage. It was the only narrow spot in his path. And I waited out of sight until I heard him pedaling just as fast as he could toward my trap. As I saw the front wheel of his bike, I pulled as hard as I could on the end of the hose. The hose tightened and rose up to catch the bike just at the front sprocket. To my astonishment and glee, David was projected from the stopped bicycle and landed headfirst on the hard dirt next to a tree. He was out cold, and I was victorious. Then he was still out cold, and I was victorious and very worried. Then Mom came out, and I knew I was dead. She took David to the hospital, where he was treated for a concussion and released. Thankfully, I was only grounded, not killed. Oh yeah, and thankfully, David was okay too.

One other occasion when I harmed my brother David was purely an accident, much less severe, and a lot more fun. We went fishing with my dad and Zack. Personally, I didn't care much for fishing, and I think David felt the same. I spent my time fashioning knives out of sticks until I had something that I thought resembled what the Indians might have used to hunt buffalo. I cut a few leaves with it and then I threw it at David—and it stuck in his shoulder. I was astonished and overjoyed. I felt like an honest-to-God warrior, until Dad got all upset just because I had stabbed my brother in the shoulder.

I didn't see my dad very much, but a lot of the time, he was upset. Once, David devised a rope into a noose that could be worn under the arms, with one piece of the rope tight along the front of his neck, so he could hang safely but look dead. It was so cool. We put it on me and hung me in a doorway from a chin-up bar. About a minute after we got me hanging there and immediately after I had perfected my dead look, Dad walked upstairs and stared at me. I opened my eyes and smiled at him. He walked back downstairs to my mom and said, "Our children are crazy."

We had a spray attachment on our kitchen sink that sat off to the side of the main faucet. To use it, we'd pull it up and press the lever on top. When we were done, we would place it in its cradle facing the front of the sink. I discovered that with the water turned off, I could jam a toothpick into the lever to hold the lever down. Anyone who turned on the water would get sprayed right in the chest. One day Dad came home for lunch, a rather unusual occurrence, and started to make some soup. He didn't think it was funny at all. I wouldn't admit that I had done it, but he probably knew, as I was the only one home. (I still think it was funny.)

One other time when Dad came home for lunch, we were all

jumping off the roof onto a pile of mattresses and couch cushions—
we'd taken the mattresses off all the beds, except for Mom and Dad's,
and we took the couch cushions off three sofas, including all the back
pillows. We piled them all in the side yard under a lower portion of
the roof. And then, whe-e-e-e. We would jump off the roof and land
butt first onto the mattresses. That was real fun. Dad came home for
lunch while we were in the middle of our circus acts for dummies.
He didn't think this was a good way for us to have fun. He thought
someone might get hurt. Becky got hurt—pretty bad, too—but that
was another time. She jumped off with no mattresses; she just had
an umbrella. Anyway, Dad was plenty upset that day.

One other time that Dad was upset occurred when he was dying
of cancer, and I asked to borrow his car. He didn't act very upset but
looking back on it, I think he was. I would have been. And when he
was in the hospital and those "fucking nurses" wouldn't take out his
IV and just let him die, he was really upset then. That's the only time
I can remember him swearing. He was a really decent man. I forgot
to tell him that when he was alive. Oh well, live and learn.

He always test-drove really cool cars. And sometimes he bought
them and brought them home knowing full well that one of his
idiot children was going to wreck it in due course. He bought a Ford
Fairlane with a 429 Cobra jet engine and a manual five-speed. That
car was fast as hell. Zack took me for a ride in it and scared the hell
out of me. I never did get the chance to drive it. Becky drove it into
a cement pillar on the freeway. She's so lucky. And David wrecked
the LTD, or maybe it was the Gran Torino, and one of Zack's friends
wrecked the LTD.

Dad had the best speakers, custom-made, for our living room.
They were about six feet high, with extra speakers on top of them.
The neighbors often called the police on us to turn down the music
when Dad wasn't home. He let us use his amazing stereo, as long as
we took care of it and handled the records, even our own, only by the
edges. To this day, I'm kind of a freak about keeping CDs in their cases
and handling them carefully. I think he'd be proud—proud only of the
way I handle my music collection, not all the other stupid stuff I do.

He let me put two stitches in myself once. That was one of the best experiences of my life. Outdone only by each and every sexual experience I've ever had. One day when I was maybe seven or eight years old, Bob McCoey and I were playing down on Christmas Tree Lane. We were leaping with wild abandon into a field of very, very tall grass. The grass grew up to about two feet above the sidewalk. We would jump in with our hands in the air and fall down, and then get up and jump in again. I never felt any pain, and the only evidence that something was amiss was that my left pant leg, from the newly formed tear at the knee all the way down to the ankle, was soaked in blood. We were no doctors but we knew that wasn't right. So we sat down and did a little investigating. Sure enough, not only were my pants torn but my skin had been torn wide open too. A Good Samaritan happened upon us and drove me home. He was a friend of the family. Everybody in Ukiah was a friend of somebody in the Wilson family. He took me inside, where I sat on the kitchen counter, holding open the wound so that I could have a good look at the muscle and tendons and bones inside. It was fascinating.

He took me to my dad's office, and the first and only pain I ever felt in this whole experience was the sting of a needle piercing my skin as Novocain was injected. I watched every stitch being put in and was allowed to put two in myself, in the second of the three layers of stitches that it took to close up the wound. I was very careful to do them just as I had watched my dad put them in. He smiled and took back the needle, probably so I wouldn't fuck it up any worse. When he finished with the sutures, he put a cast on my leg from my hip to mid-calf. He asked if I wanted crutches or if I thought I could stay off my leg without them. I was a kid, of course I wanted crutches. They weren't the least bit bothersome; they were a cool toy, like stilts.

At about twelve years old, I got another scar, this one on the back of my head near the crown. No, I wasn't wearing an actual crown. I wasn't that kind of a king. I just mean the top of my head. I was standing on the bumper of our station wagon. I wanted desperately to go with the girls wherever they were going. I didn't know where; I didn't care where; I just wanted to go, and they said no. What choice did I have? I jumped onto the back bumper of the car and hung on to the luggage rack. If they thought "No" would get rid of me, they had another think coming. They told me over and over, "Get off the car," they warned me one last time, and then they drove off. I was all smiles. As the car picked up speed, I decided I didn't really want to go with them after all. So I jumped off. Knowing nothing of the laws of physics, (I didn't pay much attention to the laws that I did know so there's a good chance had I studied physics I would have done the same thing) I assumed I would land on my feet and stroll jauntily back home. That's not quite what happened. I did land on my feet—initially. My feet planted on the pavement while the rest of me headed farther down Oak Park Avenue. I had, at the time, cat-like reflexes and sensing my forward motion, I quickly corrected myself and slammed myself backwards to the pavement, splitting my skull wide open. I spent the next few months with a cartoonish bandage wrapped around my entire head and evidence of a massive goose egg protruding from the top rear. More blood loss and another lesson learned. Well, not really. Now that I think about it, I spent much of the next ten years climbing out of, over, and around moving cars. For instance, one of us would be driving, and two or three of us would change seats by climbing out the window over the roof and back in another window.

While we're on the subject of scars, I got one more. We had a "swimming pool" in our yard. At one time it was an actual swimming pool, but for the entirety of my life, it was a cesspool. The only water in it was put in by God or Mother Nature, depending on what you're into. At one time a generous helping of frogs was added, just to make sure this wouldn't be mistaken for a swimming pool. Every summer we had to get in the cement pond and clean out the leaves and muck and whatever trash we had thrown in throughout the year. Sometimes this could be fun, sometimes dangerous, but mostly it was just a pain in the rear. Catching and torturing the frogs was fun, but the cleaning part wasn't. Once we put firecrackers—three tied together with the wicks twisted to make one and then lit—in a metal pipe, quickly followed by a hapless frog, and boom, froggy'd go a courtin'.

One summer I went out to clean the garbage pit and jumped in about midway between the shallow and deep ends. I landed directly on a broken Coke bottle bottom that had a particularly nasty shard sticking straight up. The glass penetrated my tennis shoe, through my sock, and more than halfway through my foot. I climbed gingerly back out of the pool, pulled out the torturous Coca-Cola remnant and hobbled into the house for medical care. I was, as always, deposited at my father's office, where I was sutured and bandaged and sent home, free from pool cleaning for the rest of the year.

My final scar story is rather banal. I was dancing a knife between each of my fingers, faster and faster, to prove how agile and fearless I was. My stupidity had been proven long ago and several times over. Fearless, yes. Agile, I think not. On about my second go-round, with the knife tapping the wooden tabletop between each finger, the knife mistook my finger for a piece of polished oak. I dropped the knife and just concentrated on not bleeding to death. I grabbed a paper towel and wrapped my wound, soon enough realizing that I should have grabbed a bath towel instead. This laceration, however, required only two stitches, and I was back playing with knives within the week.

Like all of the fights, there are many stories involving guns and cars, and each one is more gripping and fascinating than the next. Zack had a .22 pistol that we used to play with. He had gotten blanks for it, and we would fire them off for fun in the house, outside, wherever. Once, when playing some game of cat-and-mouse, or cops-and-robbers, or dumb and dumber with BB guns and such, I stood in the center of the front porch and watched as Zack, with his back against the corner of the house his blank-filled .22 pistol clutched in his hands and pointed at the sky. He waited patiently. When he felt that Bob McCoey was close enough, he made his move. Bob had been sneaking up on Zack with a BB gun. Moving stealthily along the edge of the house toward the porch, Zack moved first and stepped off the porch, leveled his weapon, and fired. He shot Bob McCoey with a .22 (a paper wad projectile flies out of a gun any time you shoot blanks) from approximately three feet away, right between the eyes. Bob came screaming around the corner, holding his face. "I'm blind. I'm fucking blind." To all of our relief, he was not blind, but he did have a welt between his eyes and a red circle around them that was not going to be easy to hide from all the nosy parents. The redness went away by the next afternoon but the welt lasted a little over a week. It was a pretty good shot on Zack's part.

Once, Larry Stewart and I took my Plymouth Fury up Cow Mountain with Zack's .22 rifle to try and shoot some snakes or rabbits or squirrels. Whatever moved, we were gonna shoot it. We pulled off the road at one point and couldn't find anything to shoot. So I shot my car. It was kind of cool. Well, it seemed fun then. We commenced to shooting both the driver's side and the trunk full of holes. Sometime in the middle of our revelry, a state park ranger stopped and asked whose car that was. I told him it was my car, and he drove off. When we had finally killed the wild Plymouth and probably run out of bullets, we started driving home. As we approached the end of the road, a sheriff's patrol car came around the corner, headed toward us with his bubble-gums ablaze. Being the conscientious citizen that I am, I slowed and pulled to the right. As he went past, another patrol car and two unmarked cars came around the corner and pulled over in front of us. I looked in the mirror and saw that the first patrol car had U-turned and was pulling up behind us, followed by the state park ranger we had met earlier. Larry and I looked at each other and shrugged. Then all the police officers, in unison, got out of their vehicles, with their guns drawn and aimed at us. They announced over the PA system that we should put our hands out the window, open the door from the outside, and step out of the car, keeping our hands where they could see them. I was a little scared, but Larry started laughing and that made me laugh. We might have been a little high, but we hadn't done anything wrong. We were in an area where we are allowed to fire guns. It was my car. *You can't regulate stupidity, Officer.* They separated us and questioned us for a few minutes, while other officers searched the car. Then they let us go. All the way home, we could not stop laughing.

Soon thereafter, David and I decided to redecorate my car. David was the artist and while I had commissioned the work, I was also the artist's lackey. We fashioned an odd template out of cardboard that was two wave-shaped pieces that were held apart from each other, always at a slightly different distance and angle, thus creating natural zebra stripes. David, the artistic genius, had pointed out that no two zebras are alike, thus random stripes were truer to nature. Now with its *Hatari* look, the car needed bigger and better wheels. David had an old Dodge pickup that ran, but not well. These huge all-terrain tires looked cool, but they jammed against the fender wells of the Fury. Easily remedied. We cut out the fender wells. Now it looked great. If only it were a convertible. "Convertible," said David. And the very next day, we cut off the roof with an air chisel. An air chisel, however, does not cut a smooth line—not by any stretch of the imagination. The air chisel tears a very jagged line. Easily remedied. Hammer the sharp bits under. This car was becoming more beautiful every moment. We removed the smaller and weaker 318 V-6 engine that the manufacturer had mistakenly felt was powerful enough and replaced it with the big block 383 (V-8) engine out of the aforementioned pickup. The new and much more powerful engine, bolted down on one side, didn't match up with the engine mounts on the other side. Easily remedied. A short yet sturdy piece of chain wrapped around the frame became an adjustable engine mount. Perfect. And because the hood wouldn't fit back on yet, we could watch the engine jump to one side whenever we revved it up. Again, very cool.

I had a friend whose father was head of the chamber of commerce and about to be grand marshal of whatever parade was forthcoming. He told us, maybe even promised, that he would ride in my spectacular car at the head of the parade. By God, this would be the best grand marshal car ever. We took a large, pink leather easy chair and bolted it onto the trunk. On each door, we placed a placard made of thin plywood. In keeping with the times, we painted on one placard "Tehran or bust" and the other "Hostage Rescue Mission." We drove it down to the school, where everyone had gathered for the beginning of the big parade. We told the officer at the gate that we were there for the grand marshal. He looked over the car and told us to get lost. I said, "Call Mr. Fowler. He knows about it." He talked into his radio for a while, paced with his back to us for a bit, and finally came back over to the car. I smiled proudly at the officer, and he said, "Get the hell out of here, or I'm going to have you arrested." Wow. We were really pissed off. Wet hens were using us as examples. We drove home, removed the placards, turned them over, reattached them, and wrote "Pigs Fuck" on both. Then we drove around just as close as allowed to the parade route. I guess we showed them. We removed those within a day or two and continued perfecting the car. Roll cage. Custom-tailored hood. CB with PA system. Antennae decorated temporarily with a real fish head. The last time I drove that car, the windshield had been removed for unknown reasons. I wore a helmet and goggles. I felt I was driving a 130 mph go-cart. I loved it. Then we gave it to an orchard to be placed in the river to help shore up the banks. A fitting funeral.

I remember when Zack first got the previously discussed .22 rifle, and we were playing with it in the bedroom. We shot one of the posters on the wall. Oh, shit. But nothing happened, and we ended up shooting those posters for target practice a lot. When we realized we were putting some serious holes in the wall, we stopped.

I once aimed what I believed to be an empty air rifle, pumped up quite a few times, at my friend Tom Jarred. When I pulled the trigger, I embedded a BB into his lower lip that a doctor had to remove. Before he went to the doctor and immediately after taking in his lower lip's uninvited guest, he turned his own air rifle on me while calling me some of the vilest things I had ever heard. I was on the run long before he could take good aim and only took a few rounds to the back, and those were through a jacket, so while they hurt, they didn't take refuge in my person.

Bow and arrows were another fun pastime in our carefree teenage years. I remember more than once going up Low Gap Road, where about ten of us would stand in a circle. One person would step into the center of the circle and pull back his arrow, aim it up into the air as straight and true as possible, and let loose the perilous projectile. Anyone who moved before the arrow hit the ground was considered to be quite a big pussy. No one ever moved, and no one ever got hit.

If that's not exciting enough, how about this one: I walked through the side yard, and as I approached the house, I happened upon my brother David, standing on the back porch with a bow and arrow in his hand. He had it at the ready, the bowstring pulled back to near the breaking point. He was sort of looking around for a worthy target. He saw me stop and look at him and smile. So he looked at me and smiled back. He aimed the arrow at me, and I said, "You wouldn't shoot me with that arrow, would you?" That was exactly the wrong thing to say. It was almost like a dare. He laughed and began lowering the bow, and then suddenly he aimed it at me again and let loose. I froze. The arrow pierced the fur-like collar of my faux police jacket, rubbing against my flesh, actually touching my neck. Frighteningly surreal, we just stared at each other. "Holy shit!" I think we may have said it in unison. "Are you fuckin' crazy?" That was just me. Then we both started laughing. Perhaps we were both crazy.

David showed us all how to make flaming arrows. We would take a sponge and push it onto the arrow with just a bit of the arrowhead sticking out. Then we soaked the sponge in lighter fluid, pulled the bowstring back to its full capacity, and touched the sponge to the flame on a candle that was placed precariously close to the tub of lighter fluid. Aim and fire. In every sense of the word. We played cowboys and Indians, only now everybody wanted to be the Indians. So David and I capitulated.

I wanted to be just like David (except when he was picking on me or whipping me—then I wanted to kill him). When he was mean to Mom, I didn't want to be like that. She was so easy to ignore that I didn't understand why everybody fought with her. All you had to do was say, "Yeah, okay, Mom," and smile and then do whatever you wanted. Was I the only one who figured this out?

David and I went into our fort. This was a real fort. We'd built it from scrap wood we had stolen ... oops I mean found in the garage and people's yards and stuff. The fort had a small window next to the front door, about four feet up and a little back room. I don't know what that was for but David and Zack were the architects; I just tried not to cut my fingers off with the saw and hammered nails where I was told. We covered the roof with the shingles we had borrowed from Mrs. Cox's garage. We had a table in there, and this particular day we had two Cool Whip containers full of lighter fluid. The first barrage by the Indians sent a flaming arrow through the window and into the lighter fluid. The fluid burst into flames and poured off of the table and onto David's lap. What the hell he was doing sitting down while we were under attack I'll never understand. As he stood up, the flames poured off of him, right along with the fluid. It was pretty cool. He picked up the still-flaming arrow and tossed it back out the window where, unbeknownst to him, Injun Zack had snuck up really close. The arrow coming back out of the window hit Zack right in the head. That head was clad in a fancy-schmancy Indian headdress that he wouldn't let anyone else wear. The flaming arrow caught in the headdress. The feathers, Zack's hair, and everything burst into flame as fast as that fluid did. Time out. All of us jumped on Zack and threw him on the ground, swatting him with whatever we could find. At the same time, we dragged him over to the water spigot and shoved his whole head under there. We got the fire all out –but ... his hair was gone. Not the sixties or bee-bop kind of gone. I mean like not there. I exaggerate only slightly—there were some wisps and strands here and there. We took him upstairs and washed what was left of his hair with shampoo and conditioner to get rid of the smell, so Mom and Dad would never know what really happened. We gave him a horrible little trim job and perfumed it up. They knew.

I've been saying "we," but I just went with the flow. Not because I was some kind of wanna-be goody two shoes. I just happen to be the youngest so what ever I said didn't mean squat anyway. Even as the youngest, I almost always got to share in the punishment. As an example, there was the time we all took turns hanging each other from the apple tree. I never actually hung anyone, nor did I hang myself. There were some awfully funny moments, though, like when David set up the rope and noose so that when he kicked out the bench, his toes just touched the ground and kept him safe from hanging. My friend Tom Jarred, who was a foot shorter than David, watched him do it and called out, "I wanna try." And he got up on the bench, put the noose around his neck, and kicked out the bench. He dangled there for a few seconds as we all watched him clawing at the rope and gasping for air. Then we grabbed his legs and set him free. Then Zack got up on the bench, put the noose around his neck, and said, "When I say now, you guys gotta get me down." Of course, we all enthusiastically agreed. What none of us knew was that he couldn't say "now" while hanging by the neck and choking to death. Fortunately, we could tell by his pained expression and flailing limbs that it was time to get him down. And we did. Marty was restricted from our house for the whole summer that year. He also had a bad rope burn around his neck. Oh, it was hysterically funny. Those madcap days—I remember them fondly.

We used to practice throwing hatchets too, not at each other but into trees and the fence and the telephone pole out back. It was fun, but I never got very good at it. I guess it didn't really seem like a practical weapon. And if you couldn't use it to harm someone in a future battle, what was the sense in learning the thing?

One year we discovered gunpowder. We could go into Western Auto and buy small kegs of gunpowder, which was used, I would later learn, for refilling shotgun shells. I don't think I bought any, but somebody did because there it was in David's bedroom, just looking for a place to explode. We took cardboard tubes from pants hangers, blocked one end with clay and glue, filled the tube with gunpowder, and packed the other end with more clay and glue. We drilled a hole in the middle of the tube and stuck in a wick pulled out of a firecracker. *Voila*—dynamite. We set it out in the backyard, lit the fuse, and ran like hell. Or we'd toss it off the balcony into the pool. It was the loudest freaking explosion you ever heard. And David was the real genius. He devised timing devices, using alarm clocks and batteries. And the simplest of all: he took two electrical wires, twisted one end of each together, and stuck it in the wick hole. Then he took the other ends as far from the bomb as he could and attached one wire to the negative pole of a car battery. As soon as he touched the other end to the positive pole—*kaboom*—so much joy to be found in one fleeting, destructive second. He also created a bomb that we never got around to building. This one would have surely killed someone or, at the very least, landed one of us in a federal penitentiary. Picture in your mind's eye a five-gallon water bottle filled nearly to the top with gunpowder. Duct taped to the outside is an alarm clock and a small 12-volt battery connected by electrical wire. This could be set for up to one hour or, without the proper insulation on the clock hands, less than a second. That would be the someone-being-killed scenario. Fortunately for everyone, a smaller disaster would strike before any one of us had the chance to accomplish our Wile E. Coyote-style destructo device.

One evening we were in David's room, playing with gunpowder and smoking cigarettes, making bombs and experimenting with just lighting bits of black magic in the air or in an ashtray. I got called downstairs to help with the dishes. After only a few minutes in the kitchen, there was a huge explosion from upstairs. Before anyone could react, David came running down the stairs with torrents of blood pouring over and out of him. He seemed to be trying to hold his eye in place, with his hand pressed firmly against his head. Mom and Dad began tending to him and pretty quickly left for the hospital. I went upstairs with whoever else was there and found the room covered with glass and soda and bits of blood. Zack and Tony Grams had been in the room at the time. One of them had little glass bits in his stomach; the other had glass up and down his legs. All the posters had blown off the wall, a bottle of Coke had burst, and the huge window shade had been torn to pieces. Apparently, David had filled an empty Coke bottle one-quarter with gunpowder and dropped in a lit cigarette butt. He surmised from earlier experimentation that the lit powder would shoot flames out of the top of the bottle, which it did for approximately one one-hundredth of a second before exploding, sending shards of glass everywhere, including into David's eye, Zack's stomach, and Tony's legs. And once again, I missed all the excitement. David spent some time in the hospital in Santa Rosa and came back minus his peripheral vision and the will to ever attend school again. Within a year after this incident, David enlisted in the army and was sent to Germany, where he learned to blow up bridges. While in Germany, he also painted one of the most amazing murals I've ever seen. It's of the Golden Gate Bridge, done freehand from a postcard. It was about six feet high and eight to ten feet wide.

One summer when I was eleven or so, David, Zack, and I went on a crime spree. We *planned* greater heists than we ever pulled off, but we did manage to pull off some pretty dumb ones. We broke into the corner store one night. We held a board covered in a pillowcase up to a small back window and bashed it in with a hammer. After clearing out all the glass, I was sent through the opening. I was still the skinny little kid at this point, so I fit perfectly through that window. Not a scratch on me. I then unlocked the door from inside, and we went searching for the thousands of dollars in cash that must surely be lying around such a wealthy establishment. We opened the register. Nothing. We looked behind the counter. Nothing. We checked the back rooms. Hell, we looked everywhere. No dough. So we just began taking what we wanted. Cigarettes, beef jerky, sodas—whatever we liked and could stuff into our thieving little pockets, we took and then we hightailed it out of there. We stashed our booty in the tree fort. This was different from the previously mentioned fort. The tree fort had only one wall but was built as well as the other one, only this one was in a tree. Zack went to bed, and David and I got on our bikes and rode about twenty minutes out to Talmage, maybe even further. David knew of a house on East Side Rd. where there was a shotgun we could steal, presumably to use in our more elaborate future capers. We stashed our bikes on the road and crept up the driveway in the dark. The garage door was open, so we went in and began looking through the cabinets. We found shotgun shells and an axe but no shotgun. We were both a little too nervous, so we took the shells and the axe and headed back to our bikes. We rode home in the beautiful glow of predawn. As we headed up Oak Park Avenue, we saw an unmarked police car parked outside of our house. We rode slowly and tossed our ill-gotten gains in the bushes at the corner of the yard. As we approached the front gate, Mom came flying out in her bathrobe. "David, damn it, get in here. Where were you?" (What was I? Chopped liver?)

We were led into the living room where two detectives sat with Mom and Dad and Zack. Zack looked very guilty of something; I'm not sure what it was. There was a pillowcase lying on the coffee table between Zack and the police. I recognized the pillowcase from the initials embroidered in it. They were JCW. Well, it was Mom's pillowcase; she must have done the crime. This was the reason I knew to shut up and do as I was told. If the thoughts running through my head were released, we would all be executed. The three of us were taken to the police station and booked or something. I just kind of followed everybody around and then took my spanking and restriction like a man—a very small, skinny, stupid man. The very next day, we began hatching bigger plots that included the full-on armed robbery of a Circle K convenience store. We would escape in rafts down the Russian River. None of these later plots came to fruition, which is why we are not writing our respective chapters from a prison cell. Yay God!

Early the next summer, Bob McCoey and I were at the municipal pool, trying to decide if we wanted to stay there and swim or do something else. Either way, we needed a little cash, and the money drawer was often left open or unattended. We stood at the front counter, waiting for an opportunity. When the lifeguard walked away, we reached over the counter and pulled open the drawer, each grabbing a small fortune. We hopped on our bikes and fled. About a half-mile down the road, we were stopped by the police and arrested for petty theft. Bob's dad was a cop, and this wasn't the first time we'd been sitting here waiting for our parents. I felt bad for Bob. My mom was mean, but his dad was scary. He was a wonderful man whom I always liked. I remember wrestling with him and Bob when I was a little kid. But he was a cop, and Officer McCoey was about six foot four and over two hundred pounds of muscle. I was just glad he wasn't my dad whenever we went to jail. Another instance was when Bob and I were in the attic of our garage, where we kept our stolen street signs. I'm not sure Bob and I actually stole any of them; they may have been Zack's stolen street signs. But they were there, and so were we. We had a BB gun and were shooting stuff from the garage window overlooking the alley. We shot at mailboxes. We shot at trashcans. We shot out most of the windows in the cars parked along the alley. We were still up there when the police showed up. They came right up into our stash of stolen government property. Lord, have mercy on my wretched soul. There is no worse crime than taking from the government. We were arrested and taken to jail, where we awaited our parents.

For some reason, until I was sixteen or seventeen, the only official retribution I can remember is sitting in jail, waiting for my parents to come get me. This one, though, would surely bring heavier punishment, because our parents were required to pay for all the broken windows. That meant we were gonna pay. I worked mowing lawns and other odd jobs to pay back my debt, and we all thought surely I had learned my lesson. (Don't be silly. I still haven't learned my lesson. I've just been lucky.)

Each summer when I was very young, the whole family would drive to the coast to spend a week at Drivells' cabin in Fort Bragg. I loved playing on the beach except for the sand in my toes and crack at the end of the day. But there was a path leading from the cabin down to a cove and then the beach. We used to refer to it as the Tarzan Trail. It was covered with bushes and monkey vine that we could climb in and around and swing on. It was fantastical, a veritable jungle just for the few of us to enjoy. One year we found caves in the side of the hill very near the beach. What appeared to be two caves was actually one cave that circled around to a second opening. We climbed the short distance up the hillside to get into the caves. They were like secret sand palaces, with room enough for four of us to crawl around comfortably. There were even some areas where we could almost stand upright. Some of us carried beach shovels and garden trowels into the caves to try and make them even bigger. While we were all digging and shoveling out dirt, I stuck my trowel into the earth above me, and sand and dirt started to fall on my face. Suddenly, the whole ceiling came down on me. The next thing I remember was opening my eyes on the beach with Mom and Dad looking down on me. They told me the ceiling caved in and buried me. Zack and Becky and Valli dug me out and brought me outside. Valli was there on the beach with us. I looked over at the caves, and Becky was halfway inside and Zack was on top of the hill jumping up and down. They both wanted another cave in. Valli was yelling at Zack to stop it. Mom and Dad were enjoying the sun. Now that was an exciting vacation.

On another of our visits to the cabin in Fort Bragg my sisters brought friends with them. Audrey was there and Kathy Tracy. One afternoon while Di and Audrey and some others were out for a walk, someone came up with an idea to scare them. I'm guessing it was Pam. Northern California around that time was well known for its wacky serial killers and disappearances in the woods. So this simple practical joke wouldn't be hard to pull off. Somehow, Mom was talked into participating in this horrible ruse, and we set about overturning chairs and lamps and tables. Then Mother was tied up and gagged and laid on the couch. We made the place look ransacked and left the front door ajar and the back door wide open. Then the rest of us all hid and waited patiently. When the girls finally returned, they were horrified at the sight they found and were quite scared— not nearly as frightened, though, as they became when we all burst from our hiding places and came noisily running down the stairs and through the back door. They had tears rolling down their poor, terrified faces as we burst in on them. The only thing more palpable than the fear was their ensuing anger as the joke was exposed. I don't know how my mother was convinced to participate, but she played the part beautifully. All in all, Mom was a hell of a gal, and with all her flaws, I love her still.

My mother loved me very much and worried constantly about me. She thought that for sure my only crime was hanging out with the wrong people. I wanted to say, "You mean my brothers?" because that would have been funny and poignant. Instead, all I did was agree with her and say okay. Then I'd do just as I pleased. But I knew for sure that it was a mother's blind and unconditional love when she came to get me from the police station one night. I heard her say, with frustrated tears in her voice, "Why are you always picking on my boys?" How could I ever have doubted her love? She was so easy to appease because she just wanted to believe that we were good, honest children.

And to make her believe that, all I had to do was tell her that straight to her face and without cracking a smile. She knew I could never look her in the eye and lie to her. She loved me, and I loved her. So if I could say it looking her in the eye, it must be true. I fear my siblings never learned this simple truth, because they all argued with her all the time, argued over points on which they knew she would never concede. I just wanted my mom to be happy, so I lied right to her face through a charming, heartwarming smile. And by God, she was happy. Once, after my divorce, she said to me, "Paul, are you dating?" I said yes. She then said, "When you take girls out, you don't have to bed them. Go for a walk or read a book together." I was thirty-six, and I liked sex even more than the next guy. So I looked her right in the eye and said, "Mom, that's exactly what I'll do." And she was happy.

You may notice some of my siblings missing from my accounts of my childhood. They were older than I, and since I don't have a great recollection of my preschool years, I just know them as really cool older sisters who, by the way, I do love dearly. I remember my sister Deborah reading to us from *The Mouse and the Motorcycle* and *Five Children and It*, as well as other memorable titles that have slipped my mind. Thank you Deb, for my love of reading and my ability to enthrall a crowd, (well, more often a small group) with my literary interpretations.

I remember my sister Pamela tempting me into the deep end of the pool with the kind and soothing words, "I promise I won't let go of you this time." And sure enough, just like Lucy with the football, she'd abandon me in the deep end of the pool. Terrified, I'd make my way to the edge and climb out, crying. I am today a proficient swimmer and once saved my own life in Lake Mendocino out of sheer determination. Thank you, Pam, for my horrific swimming lessons.

I remember my sister Diana, who took me in when I was a horrible thirteen-year-old and taught me valuable cooking as well as life lessons in Arizona. Thank you, Di, for my love of food and all my liberal thoughts that keep me firmly centered between uncaring asshole and flighty idealistic fruitcake.

I remember my sister Priscilla, who often helped my friends and me out of jams, usually at her own peril, and who gave us rides almost anywhere simply because we wanted them. Thank you Prissy, for my generosity.

And to all my siblings mentioned above and throughout the previous horror stories, thank you for my diversity and my open mind, for my love of music, and for my appreciation of all people, no matter how preposterous their views and opinions, for it was really all of you who raised me and made me who I am. Let it be on your heads! I love my parents dearly, all ten of them.

And then there's more ....

Audrey's Voice

So AFTER IT'S ALL OVER, I HAVE MY SAY. THEY SMELLED DIFFERENT. They had a definite Wilson smell...of Dial soap and Castile shampoo and ironed woolen uniforms. And their "pooh" as they called it, not "poop", as most referred to it (or "hard" as my family so poetically named it...don't get me started) smelled different. And no matter how much I wanted to be just like them, that was one obstacle I couldn't overcome. It was made of tomato soup with canned whipped cream for breakfast, and cream cheese and guava jelly sandwiches (on *raisin* bread, for God's sake) for lunch, and parsley rice ring with crab cream dream or some such name for dinner. They ate so exotically. And even if I ate at their table for a week straight (which I did often), I just didn't have the genetics. But I tried. And they let me.

Growing up the youngest of three where I always felt like there wasn't enough to go around, I somehow found enough at their table, in their home, in their beds (poor Prissy). Every potent memory from my childhood is infused with them, all of them (but mostly Di, of course). Diana, who I met one fateful day, taken by a neighbor to their house in the country, and introduced to her, "She'll be in your class at St. Mary's come September." And there she was. Soon I was spending afternoons playing at their house. I would cry when my mom came to pick me up (sorry, Mom). I couldn't bear to leave. Then came sleepovers, or *no*-sleepovers, as I like to call them. We would fight sleep for hours, don't ask me why, doing who knows what. There was some board game with cherry trees that was so magical—that's all I remember about it, cherry trees, magical—little

279

kids to alternately torture and play with, ("Paul, what rhymes with 'luck'?"), bathroom walls to climb, shoe polish to smear all over our faces so we could be like our babysitter, Marjorie. They literally took me in, thanks to Josephine. I think the kids would have dumped me pronto (not Di, okay, sometimes Di), but Jo saw a need in me and took it upon herself to fill it. And I will be forever thankful.

This truly is a compilation of nine different voices. They grew up in the same house, experienced the same family, remember the same incidents—but so very differently. For instance: at least two or three of them remember a trip to the coast where a group went into town, and when they returned, those left behind had staged a break-in with everyone bound and gagged. Someone described the look on my face, being one of the returnees. But … I *wasn't there!* I think it was during a time when Di was being unfaithful to me with Kathy Elder. I think *Kathy* was there. We kind of looked alike, she was taller and nicer (most people were… nicer, not taller. I was pretty tall). I'm sure I wasn't there; at least I'm *pretty* sure. The more I read about it, the more I can picture it. Maybe I was there. And that's how memories go. I do remember a trip to the coast where we ran through the fields (full of wildflowers) up on a bluff above the Pacific and sang "The hills are alive … with the sound of music," with our arms flung back, doing our best to look like Julie Andrews. I think Zack won.

Here's my short list of Wilson memories:

Debbie and Loelia Bell's shop in the basement of Lo's house—the Coleoptra ("Ladybug" in Latin, as I recall). How many fifteen-year-olds do you know who opened a head shop in their basement—with a Latin name, no less? Over the years, Debbie always seeming to be silently screaming, "Get me out of here! I don't belong with these crazy people!" Having her undivided attention as we shared a cigarette leaning out the window in the boys' room, over the trellis and cherry tree. I was about twelve, I think, the beginning of a long love/hate affair with cigarettes.

Watching Pam pinch the babies to make them cry so that she

could comfort them. What a good idea! Learning how to kiss behind the Christmas tree. Pam was the best kisser. Telling Pam (sort of to shock her) all the naughty things Diana and I were doing, only to have her invariably tell her mother everything. And confiding in her again, and her ratting us out again. I think she probably saved our lives.

Too many memories about Diana, my touchstone, my constant. Riding our bikes down to the Hub Cigar Store to buy Beatle magazines. Fighting over the last one with John Lennon's picture on the cover and ripping it. Diana rode away on her bike; I realized I had pushed her too far. She took a lot, but when she had had enough, she'd had *enough*. Going to the house, knocking on the locked door, Prissy answering and saying, "Di's not here." They closed ranks; they protected each other, even from me—especially from me. She eventually forgave me. Laughing until I cried with her, laughing until Oreo cookies and milk came out my nose with her, crying until I laughed with her.

Quiet, beautiful, blonde Prissy, who gave up her bed for me night after night. Somehow I thought it was okay to kick her out of her own bed. Playing in the marching band in high school. I can picture her with a big furry shako on her head. She even looked beautiful with a shako on her head.

Valli, in between the "big kids" and the "little kids". I was horrible to her. Being the youngest in my family, I needed someone below me and I chose her. No wonder she dropped a brick on my head from the balcony (it missed). She had, and has, the sparkliest blue eyes I have ever seen. They dance. It was just a small character quirk that made her trips to Westside Market (all of one hundred yards from the house) for a loaf of Wonder Bread take an hour and had her returning with a jar of mustard, after a phone call or two to check, "What was it you sent me here for?"

David, sitting out on the front steps, crying because his dad had taken Zack with him on his evening rounds instead of him. Telling me, in his late teens, that he thought it would be less traumatic for him to lose his virginity to someone he knew well and felt comfortable with. Was I up for it? I wasn't, but I've often second-guessed that decision. He is a lovely man, even if he wasn't all that truthful in his late teens.

Becky ... Rebecca Josephine, as her mother called her—often. She had a redhead's temper, even if her hair was deep mahogany. She scared me. She still does, until she smiles. She was brave enough to jump off the roof with an umbrella to break her fall. It didn't. But that bravery has served her well in this life. She is one of the bravest people I know. And I know she wasn't *really* going to throw that massive glass ashtray at me as she chased me around the dining room table. That was just her slightly bent humor ... wasn't it?

Zack, with his raspy, gravelly voice and red red red red red hair and ready smile and laugh. I think his was the first diaper I ever changed. It was impressive. (I won't say what "it" was.) He and Paul slept toe to toe on a bottom bunk. I know Paul was tied in; he tended to wander at night. I used to imagine a fire or some life-threatening disaster in the house. Everyone runs outside ... *but they forget Paul!* Not me. I run through the flames/earthquake-shaken stairway/Nazis/whatever, free Paul from his shackles and carry him to safety. Everyone loves me forever and ever. Zack may have been shackled too, but oh well. We do what we can do. I think I knew even then how strong and capable Zack was. Something about that diaper.

Paul was, is, and always will be just plain charming. He added levity to any situation. He spent many an evening charming my own mother, Caroline, at the kitchen counter after everyone else was asleep. Jo would trot him out just for that purpose. I remember him running inside one Saturday morning in his pajamas (no one knew he had gotten *outside*) with a bicycle tire track right up his backside, up his back, and over one shoulder. He'd been run over by a bike; it was just another exciting event in his day, no big deal, almost like he expected it. Maybe his imaginary companion, The Friendly Bee warned him.

As I said, this is my short list. I have cloudy (literally cloudy, from all the cigarette smoke) memories of the kitchen table and playing Hearts for hour upon hour with Josephine. We got so rummy and laughed so hard. We made Jo wet her pants more than once with laughter. She loved me and I loved her. She didn't always approve of my lifestyle choices, and she let me know that I was probably going to burn in hell, or at least do a good, long stint in purgatory for them. And she loved me. How lucky was I? Dr. Wilson (never Lee—never, never) quietly protected me in his own way. He was my family doctor, my role model as a musician, my son's godfather—a quiet, *good* man who was shocked to discover he had nine children of his own and another who would never go home.

I was so lucky. I still am. They are all still here—healthy, strong, creative, fiercely intelligent, and talented. They color my life. I know their parents are so proud.

EPILOGUE

Dad finally succumbed to the three-pack-a-day habit, and his sixty-fifth year was spent enduring the treatments and regimen previously doled out from behind his diagnostic desk. He managed to hold his drumsticks until a week or two before he left us. In preparation for his finale, Mom hosted a good-bye to beat all good-byes. The crowd was there, and the food and the fun were there, and after about five minutes into the music, Dad stood his thinning and pale body up, placed his drumsticks on top of the bass drum, and turned and walked away from the band. He closed his bedroom door and laid down for a nap.

Our living room had a beautiful bay window and Mom thought it the perfect fit for a casket. For two days we had the honor of waking our dad as he lay in his window. We talked to him and held his hand. We did everything short of climbing in to keep him company. When it was time to send him off with the men in the big black hearse, it felt like the end of an era.

Josephine carried on with dignity, never showing angst to the public but endured alone her private heartache—losing Lee, our dad, her dreamboat. Her bookkeeping job at our dad's office provided purpose as she followed through with the mundane and the routine, until one day she was no longer needed there. She wanted, above all, to be relevant and to be appreciated by all of us. Instead, she was relegated to secondary. As our nine lives took us in a thousand different directions, she began tending a new generation. With her dog, Lily, by her side, she nurtured her garden and her grandchildren. And she read. The books she devoured in her spare time piled up on kitchen counter corners, and the little *Reader's Digests* rested in every bathroom.

When the time came to sell her castle, the harsh reality of parting with thirty years of memories was overwhelming. She managed to rescue some of her favorite roses for the beginning of a new garden, but her new house had no high ceilings—it hardly even had a pantry. And it certainly did not have any memories. Perhaps she picked it to begin her wind down. Her waiting was almost planned. As her physical health deteriorated, a melancholy consumed her and contemplating really old and really alone was no longer acceptable. She had now only to put her faith in God and he would show her the way.

It was the bad back that led to the drop foot that led to the walker. And then the walker led to the wheelchair and nearly total immobility. As she put her things in order, dropping hints as to who should inherit what, her plans became a reality.

We all took turns keeping watch that last week. Our mother's tiny frame, encased in the loveliest translucent tight skin, belied the behemoth bed left for her by hospice as they attempted to make her final moments more comfortable. As her consciousness waned, we knew it was our presence that brought her the greatest comfort.

As we closed the final chapter after Mom was laid to rest, we discovered, in settling her things, a tape recording she had made for us only months before. We all sat listening to our mother's own personal farewell to all of us. As she apologized for not being with us on Christmas, just a few weeks away, and in her eighty-year-old voice, she sang *Somewhere over the Rainbow* and added a happy birthday serenade to Baby Jesus. And finally, she read to us for the last time, *The Pagan Fawn*, just as she had done each year on Christmas day at our family's dining table.

END NOTES

CHAPTER 4 ⌢

I'm So Sorry for Old Adam – Anonymous

That's All – Bob Haymes and Alan Brandt; Serendipity Recordings, Inc, 1952

Carol of the Bagpipers (Quanno nascete ninno a Bettelemme, trans Baker 1904) – de Ligouri and Zampognari, ed "Songs of Italy," G. Schirmer, New York 1904

San Francisco – John Phillips, MCA, 1967

Leaving On a Jet Plane – John Denver, prod. Milt Okun, Warner Bros/7 Arts, 1966

CHAPTER 7 ⌢

No information available on lyrics in Chapter 7.

CHAPTER 8 ⌢

No information available on lyrics in Chapter 8.

BIOGRAPHIES

DEBORAH WILSON HECHT ~~ Deborah is a voice, speech, dialect and text coach who teaches at Juilliard and coaches Broadway and Off-Broadway productions and the occasional film. She has taught and/or coached across the U.S, and in Portugal, England, Italy, Croatia, and the West Bank. She lives in upstate New York and New York City.

PAMELA WILSON CULLERTON ~~ At 26 Pamela left San Francisco to find a better climate and a new life - in Chicago. Pam and her husband, John Cullerton, have raised five children and both devote most of their time to Illinois' public life. John is the President of the Illinois Senate and Pam divides her time between civic activities and Board responsibilities and truly loves everything that the most fabulous city - Chicago - has to offer.

DIANA WILSON ~~ Diana has a rich life full of love, laughter and learning. Humanist, feminist, and wannabe philanthropist, Diana has a gazillion amazing children and lives in Santa Cruz, California with her wonderful husband of 30 years, activist attorney Ed Frey.

PRISCILLA WILSON ~~ Priscilla went on to three different colleges and never graduated. She then went to work in the newspaper business, law, real estate, and whatever else struck her fancy. She moved from town to town, then when her kids wanted to stay at the same school, house to house. Among her siblings, she got the first denture, the first hip replacement, and the first RV. Priscilla was among the early group of work online at home parents and has done contract transcription work for the last 16 years. She never married and has two children and two grandchildren.

VALERIE JEAN JACKSON ~~ Valerie decided to follow in her father's footsteps and entered the medical field. After 35 years as a Surgical Technician she still loves her work. She feels lucky to have been able to work with many of the same doctors that worked with and respected her father. She is divorced, but her marriage produced two wonderful sons. She is the only Wilson still residing in Ukiah and enjoys living, walking and cycling around the area in which she grew up. She is happy to say she shares her life with someone special.

DAVID WILSON ~~ David's life has followed a path so varied and interesting that to note all the twists and turns here would be impossible. He currently lives in Los Angeles where he works as a transportation specialist (mostly in the entertainment industry) and car customizer. He is the quintessential uncle to many wonderful nephews and nieces.

REBECCA JO WILSON ~~ Rebecca is retired after 30 years working with children and families. She enjoyed coaching/playing soccer and softball and continues to enjoy cycling. She bicycled across the US alone at age 19; earned her Juris Doctor at 40; completed the Race Across Belize in 2003; and volunteered at RMOF orphanage in Haiti after the earthquake. Best of all she has a wonderful relationship with her daughter and daughter's adoptive family.

ZACHARY WILSON ~~ Zack is a jack of all trades. He served 13 years in the Army and Army Reserves. He was a police officer for 21 years, a village trustee for four, and is now a practicing attorney. He is a drummer in a band and coaches little league baseball. Zack is pleased with all of his accomplishments, but he is most proud of his relationships with his wife of 25 years and three children.

P.S. PAUL WILSON ~~ Paul attempted comedy and acting, but found that real jobs can be more lucrative. He lives in Los Angeles, California where he has succeeded beyond his wildest dreams in the film industry as an award winning location manager. For over 23 years he has worked on several motion pictures large and small, and the world famous TV drama CSI for over 13 years. Oddly, though divorced and childless, he is the happiest of all the siblings.

CPSIA information can be obtained at www.ICGtesting.com
Printed in the USA
BVOW08*0239180214

345198BV00004B/24/P